Silent Warfare

Understanding the World of Intelligence

Silent Warfare

Understanding the World of Intelligence

Abram N. Shulsky
Gary J. Schmitt

Manas Publications
New Delhi - 110 002 (India)

MANAS PUBLICATIONS
(We Convert Fighters into Writers)
(Publishers, Distributors, Importers & Exporters)
4402/5-A, Ansari Road (Opp. HDFC Bank)
Darya Ganj, New Delhi-110 002 (INDIA)
Off. ✆ 23260783, 23265523, Res. 23842660
Fax: 011-23272766
E-mail: manaspublications@gmail.com
manaspublications@yahoo.com

Published in collaboration with: Potomac Books, Inc-USA
(formely Brassey Inc.)

2nd Impression 2014 (FP - 2006)

ISBN: 13 Digits - 978-81-7049-291-2
10 Digits - 81-7049-291-2
₹ 695/-

Designed at : **Manas Publications**

Printed in India at
HS Offsets, Delhi and published by
Mrs Suman Lata for **Manas Publications,**
4402/5-A, Ansari Road, (Opp. HDFC Bank), Darya Ganj,
New Delhi-110 002 (INDIA)

Contents

Preface

Silent Warfare has its origin in a course on intelligence that I taught in 1985 as a visiting professor at the University of Chicago's John M. Olin Center for Inquiry into the Theory and Practice of Democracy. Returning to the academic world and the classroom forced me to impose some order on my thoughts concerning intelligence, a subject with which I had become familiar by virtue of my career in Washington. The book was first published in 1991. Soon after, however, the enactment of new laws on intelligence both in the United States and abroad, the publication of a number of significant new volumes on intelligence, and the demise of the Soviet Union combined to recommend preparation of a revised edition of *Silent Warfare*. But by this time I had already returned to work in the government as an official in the Department of Defense and was unable to devote the time necessary to complete a revision. At this point, I asked Gary Schmitt, my successor as minority staff director of the Senate Select Committee on Intelligence and former executive director of the President's Foreign Intelligence Advisory Board, to take up the task of revising the book. The second edition appeared in 1993.

Since then, the body of literature and resources dedicated to the topic of intelligence has continued to swell. In addition, there has been a slow but steady expansion of laws around the globe designed to regulate intelligence activities and to square those activities in some way with the norms of open and democratic government. But perhaps the greatest change since the publication of the first two editions of *Silent Warfare* has been the advent of the "information revolution," a revolution precipitated by the tremendous progress made in the processing and communication of information. How this change in the availability and distribution of information might affect intelligence—a government activity whose principal function is the collection, protection, and distribution of information—is a question of which this third edition attempts to take account as well.

Although *Silent Warfare* has been revised and updated twice now, the thesis, structure and much of the underlying content of the book remain the same. *Silent Warfare* was never intended to be an account of a particular country's intelligence activities in a particular period in history. While many of the examples found in the book are drawn from the British and American intelligence experiences, they are generally employed to make broader points about basic concepts and issues involved in the practice of intelligence. The passing of the Cold War, the emergence of a new strategic era, and the rise of the "information age" will, of course, change intelligence practices and requirements to some degree. However, a key thesis of *Silent Warfare* is that intelligence is inherently connected to the competition among nations and that absent something akin to Kant's state of "perpetual peace," intelligence will, like diplomacy and military force, remain a regular tool of statecraft. Accordingly, there still is a need for the citizen and serious student alike to understand the basic elements of intelligence, their interactions, and the tensions and relationships between these secret activities and the democratic government and society they are intended to serve.

Work on this and earlier editions has benefited in the past from the assistance, comments, and advice of many students, friends, and colleagues. Eliot A. Cohen, Kenneth E. deGraffenreid, Hillel G. Fradkin, Sam Halperin, Sheila Kerr, Carnes R. Lord, Kenneth G. Robertson, and Diane S. Roark deserve special thanks. The book's first edition was written while I served as a senior fellow at the National Strategy Information Office and was supported by grants from the John M. Olin Foundation and the Lynde and Harry Bradley Foundation. The second edition was revised by Gary, who was also a senior fellow at NSIC. To Roy Godson, NSIC's president, and Jeffrey Berman, NSIC's executive director, our thanks for their support and friendship over the years.

Abram N. Shulsky
Washington, D.C.

Notice to the Reader

No attempt has been made to revise this text in light of the terrorist attacks of September 11, 2001, which occurred as this book was being prepared for press. Indeed, it will be a long time before the full implications of the events of that day become manifest. Nevertheless, it is clear that intense attention will be focused on the problem of bolstering human intelligence-collection capabilities to deal with the very difficult terrorist target; in particular, there will have to be an increased emphasis on "nonofficial" cover for intelligence officers. In addition, one can expect renewed scrutiny of various regulations concerning domestic surveillance; in addition to specific questions concerning wiretapping and other surveillance techniques, a fundamental question will have to be addressed again—whether groups and individuals may be subjected to surveillance on the basis of the political positions and associations, in the absence of a clear connection to a specific criminal act.

Introduction: Writing about Secrets

In the course of the last quarter-century, intelligence—despite the fact that secrecy remains one of its essential characteristics—has been reported on routinely in the news media and has become the subject of a great deal of academic research and writing. Open discussion of intelligence questions is no longer a matter only for titillation or scandal; it is accepted as a normal part of the public debate concerning government activities generally.

Although public discussion of current events in the intelligence world remains to a large extent dependent for its raw material on the vagaries of authorized and unauthorized "leaks" of classified information, the academic literature concerning intelligence has burgeoned. The mere passage of time—augmented by a somewhat more open attitude on the part of many democratic governments—has resulted in the declassification of a great deal of historical material dealing with World War II and the Cold War. In addition, the fall of communism in the former Soviet Union and Eastern Europe has made possible scholarly access to some archives, primarily in the former East Germany and, to a lesser extent, Russia. With respect especially to diplomatic and military history, inclusion of the intelligence "dimension" is becoming standard practice.

Increased public discussion of intelligence matters generally has not, however, necessarily resulted in a better understanding of intelligence. Indeed, the more recent public discussion of intelligence has been characterized by a neglect of fundamental questions about the proper role of intelligence and secrecy in a democracy. More generally, except for a spurt of literature that coincided with the last major attempt by the U.S. Congress to "reform" intelligence (in the early 1990s), much of the public treatment of intelligence issues, when it has not been historical in nature, has dealt with the mechanics of specific espionage cases.

This contrasts with an earlier wave of writing about intelligence dating from the 1970s and early 1980s. At that time, a great deal of the public discussion of intelligence—primarily in the United States, but with echoes in other democracies as well—could be categorized as belonging to one of two camps defined by their approaches to the fundamental issue of the role of intelligence in a democracy and to the associated question of the relation of secrecy to the norms of democratic governance.

According to one camp, intelligence had become, or at least should have become, less of a "cloak and dagger" affair and more like a branch of the social sciences, seeking to analyze and ultimately predict political, economic, social, and military matters. As such, it did not need to be an inherently secretive endeavor. While some secrecy might be necessary to protect the sources of important bits of confidential information, the most important facts, concerning the political, economic, social, technological, and demographic trends that shape a country's behavior in the long run, would not be secret.[1] Thus, not only could intelligence matters be discussed publicly without inherent difficulty but public discussion might, by demystifying intelligence and encouraging the flow of ideas between the intelligence and academic communities, help intelligence progress even farther toward its proper goal of becoming more like a social science (and intelligence agencies more like "think tanks").[2]

According to the other camp, the purpose of public writing about intelligence was to expose alleged misdeeds and incompetence and to help bring about change for the better in the way intelligence agencies operated.[3] From this perspective, the secrecy with which agencies did business was either the cause of misdeeds or a necessary precondition for them; hence, public discussion of intelligence was itself part of the cure. Whatever damage might be done by publicizing legitimate secrets was regarded as minor compared to the damage that the intelligence agencies themselves, operating beyond public scrutiny, would be likely to cause. Hence, disclosing information about an "unreformed" intelligence agency was unproblematic; it is less clear what the authors of the camp would have said about public discussion of a "reformed" intelligence agency—although one might argue that in the absence of public scrutiny, any such organization was likely to stray.

More recently, the focus of a great deal of academic research and writing has turned to historical accounts of intelligence activities.[4] Discussion of more contemporary matters has been dominated by accounts of specific espionage cases, with respect to which the emphasis has been on allegations of professional incompetence rather than ethical or political malfeasance.[5] These works tended not to have political or ideological points to make (aside, presumably, from the perhaps obvious one that it is better to have a competent intelligence agency than an incompetent one).

Silent Warfare is intended to address a different set of questions. It attempts to discuss the basic concepts involved in an understanding of the world of intelligence. The purpose is to enable the reader to think about the general issues of intelligence policy in a way that does justice to the subject's complexities and ambiguities. Thus, the approach is fundamentally theoretical; publicly available details of actual intelligence activities are used to illustrate general points;[6] no attempt is made to be comprehensive with respect to the history of any aspect of intelligence or to its current condition.

It is for this reason that the book can rely on publicly available information concerning intelligence activities.[7] No attempt has been made to provide data not already in the public record. This in part because we have had authorized access to classified intelligence information in connection with various positions within the U.S. government (not, however, in any intelligence agency). As a precondition of our access, we promised not to disclose such information.[8]

More importantly, we regard secrecy as essential to intelligence operations and, in any case, do not believe that the publication of details about the operations of U.S. intelligence agencies is a good in itself. The vast majority of such details appear not to raise significant issues of public policy or to be necessary for the understanding of the fundamental concepts of intelligence, at which this book aims.

If intelligence is becoming a recognized field of academic study, especially in the English-speaking world, its theoretical treatment remains undeveloped. In this book, we attempt to alleviate that shortcoming. At the same time, we recognize that the book's relatively heavy reliance on the Anglo-American experience precludes it from reaching a truly general "theory of intelligence." This reliance is due in large part to the fact that most of the publicly available information about intelligence concerns, not surprisingly, the intelligence agencies of those countries that have the most open political systems. Nevertheless, where possible, we refer to intelligence activities of other societies and consider the question of how intelligence agencies vary depending on the nature of the regimes they serve.

This book, then, does not provide readers with any secrets or "inside information," either spectacular or humdrum. We hope it provides instead a framework for understanding intelligence itself as well as the many tidbits of intelligence-related data that will, no doubt, continue to find their way into the public domain.

Chapter 1

What Is Intelligence?

In popular fiction and in the public imagination, intelligence has often been synonymous with espionage and skullduggery, with the sexual blackmail of a Mata Hari and the cloak-and-dagger exploits of a James Bond. Although activities of this sort have their place within the world of intelligence, the full concept is much richer. To get a sense of this richness, we can begin by looking at the different categories of phenomena to which the term "intelligence" is applied; these include certain kinds of *information, activities,* and *organizations.*[1]

Intelligence refers to *information* relevant to a government's formulation and implementation of policy to further its national security interests and to deal with threats from actual or potential adversaries. (The term "adversary" is used here in a broad sense. For example, a friendly government, with which one is negotiating a treaty, may be an adversary *in the context of the negotiation;* at a minimum, the sides are presumably competing to maximize the benefits they gain from the agreement, at least in part at the expense of the other.) In the most obvious and often most important case, this information has to do with military matters, such as an adversary's capabilities and plans for military action. Potential or actual enemies typically do their best to keep this type of information secret. Of course, other types of secret information may be equally important—for example, information about another country's diplomatic activities and intentions, as well as about its intelligence activities.

In addition to data of this sort, many other types of information about an actual or potential adversary may be useful to know, even if the adversary does not attempt to keep them secret. These could include internal political affairs and societal developments as well as economic and demographic statistics. How much material of this sort is actually published depends on the nature of the political regime. In a democratic society, it is almost always publicly available. An authoritarian or totalitarian system, on the other hand, often strives to conceal any information about its internal politics, economic developments, or societal trends that an adversary might find helpful. Regardless of whether publicly available ("open source") information should, strictly speaking, be considered "intelligence," clearly there must be some process by which it is systematically made available to government officials in usable form. An intelligence service often performs this function.

Finally, intelligence information typically includes not only the "raw data" collected by means of espionage or otherwise but also analyses and assessments based on it. It is this output, often referred to as the intelligence "product," that is typically of direct value to policy makers. The extent to which this intelligence product strives to present a comprehensive evaluation of a situation, based on all available data, both public and secret, varies from one intelligence service to another.

As an *activity,* intelligence involves the collection and analysis of intelligence information. It also includes activities undertaken to counter the intelligence activities of adversaries, either by denying them access to information or by deceiving them about the facts or their significance.

Intelligence thus comprises a wide range of activities. For example, there are various methods of collecting information, such as espionage, aerial photography, interception of communications, and research using publicly available documents, radio and television broadcasts, and the Internet. There also are different techniques for analyzing the information that has been collected: some of these may be similar to the methods the social sciences use, while others, such as the decoding of encrypted messages, are peculiar to the intelligence world. Similarly, denying information to others involves various activities, some of which are similar to law enforcement work, such as investigating and trailing suspected foreign intelligence agents to learn about their activities. Others are more esoteric, such as using encryption to protect communications (although recent developments in information technology have made encryption capabilities commercially available as well). Finally, there are various means of deceiving adversaries, such as "double agent" operations and the transmitting of fake messages (that is, misleading messages one sends anticipating that an adversary will intercept and believe them).

Given this wide variety of activities, it seems difficult to find a common thread tying them together. They all, however, have to do with obtaining or denying information. Therefore, intelligence as an activity may be defined as the component of the struggle between adversaries that deals primarily with information (as opposed, for example, to economic competition, diplomatic maneuvering or negotiations, or the threat or use of military force).

Finally, the term "intelligence" also refers to an *organization* that carries out these activities. One of the most notable characteristics of such organizations is the secrecy with which their activities must be conducted. Many of their methods of operation, such as the use of undercover agents or strict rules concerning access to information, derive from this requirement. Since intelligence agencies are organized to enhance their capacity for secrecy, they also may be given, along with their information functions, the responsibility of undertaking secret activities to advance their governments' foreign policy objectives more directly.

Such activity, called "covert action" in the U.S. intelligence lexicon, may range from the mundane, such as covertly providing critical assistance to a friendly foreign government, to the spectacular, such as orchestrating the overthrow of a hostile one. Whether such work should be assigned to the same organizations that collect and analyze intelligence information has occasionally been a controversial question. Even if, for practical bureaucratic reasons, intelligence organizations are given the responsibility for covert action, the more fundamental question—from a theoretical, as well as a practical, viewpoint—of whether covert action should be considered a part of intelligence would remain.

THE SCOPE OF INTELLIGENCE

Because not only governments but many other types of organizations operate in an environment characterized by a competitive struggle, the concept of intelligence can be applied to them as well. For example, some researchers extend the concept to business corporations, treating intelligence as "organized information . . . designed to meet the unique policy-making needs of one enterprise."[2] Similarly, one could speak of the intelligence function of a political party or campaign in trying to figure out what the opposition is up to.

These possible extensions of the term "intelligence" are not dealt with in this book, which limits itself to the traditional scope of intelligence—that is, to information and activities relevant to the national security concerns of governments.

But even accepting this limitation, the scope of intelligence remains somewhat unclear, since the term "national security" is itself undefined. Its core meaning has to do with protecting the nation against threats, ultimately military, emanating from foreign nations. When a nation is being invaded or is about to be, its national security concerns clearly center on defeating or preventing the invasion and securing itself against similar situations arising in the future. In less perilous times, it may be much less clear which foreign nations, events, or circumstances threaten national security and therefore require the attention of the nation's intelligence agencies.[3]

The problem is further complicated by the fact that national security interests, and hence threats to them, cannot be considered independently of the nation's type of government (or regime) and its ideological outlook. Although adherents of *Realpolitik* would argue that a nation's interests are determined by the objective factors of the international system, ideological views, and a country's political culture more generally, affect how a government perceives them.[4] For example, a regime's ideological character may determine whether it views a given foreign country as a threat. In particular, status quo and revolutionary powers have typically had different views about what constitutes a threat to national security.

Domestic Intelligence

An even more important area in which the nature of the regime affects the scope of intelligence is what is called "domestic intelligence." Any government must be concerned not only with purely external threats (such as military invasion) but also with threats against its ability to govern, or its very existence, that arise from individuals or groups within the nation's borders. Such threats could come from groups that seek to overthrow the government by illegal means, use violence to change government policies, or exclude from the body politic members of a given ethnic, racial, or religious group. But how a government defines such internal threats depends heavily on the type of government it is.

A regime in which a dynasty or a single political party has a monopoly of power, for example, is likely to regard any domestic political dissent as a security threat, and its intelligence service will focus a great deal of attention on detecting and thwarting that dissent. In the most extreme case, the government of a totalitarian state may regard all nonmembers of the ruling party as actual or potential enemies.[5] By contrast, the notion of a "loyal opposition," as found in parliamentary and other democratic systems, implies that the government's domestic political opponents do not pose a security threat and hence are not suitable targets of intelligence.[6]

In addition, domestic groups that are hostile not merely to the government of the day but to the nation's fundamental system of government (or regime) can relate to foreign powers in many different ways. At one end of the foreign-domestic spectrum would be an individual or domestic group that acts on behalf of, and at the direction of, a hostile foreign power. There could also be groups or individuals who share common objectives with a foreign power and cooperate in the pursuit of them. Finally, there could be groups that share the ideological or other beliefs of a foreign adversary but that do not have actual ties to it. Different regimes would have varying views concerning which of these types of groups are national security threats, against which intelligence must be collected.

Intelligence and Law Enforcement

A related question deals with what are called "transnational" threats, which do not emanate primarily from a foreign government—for example, narcotics trafficking, international terrorism, or certain types of organized crime. These can be serious threats to a nation's well-being, but they appear to fall within the ambit of law enforcement rather than of intelligence. Nevertheless, intelligence is often involved in the fight against them, for several reasons. First, they involve activities in foreign countries, which can be expected to limit strictly the activities of one's law enforcement agencies, and whose own law enforcement agencies may be unable or unwilling to be of much assistance. Intelligence may be called upon for information about the foreign aspect of these activities, information that would otherwise be unavailable.

Second, and more important, the law enforcement approach typically involves waiting until a crime has been, or is about to be, committed and then attempting to solve that particular crime and arrest the perpetrators. This may not be an acceptable approach toward certain transnational threats. A single incident, such as the blowing up of a passenger airplane in flight, may cause so much harm that a government must try to prevent such a crime rather than merely solve it after it occurs. Furthermore, a specific crime, such as a single instance of narcotics smuggling, may be part of a criminal enterprise's operations; if the enterprise is large and well organized, arresting the perpetrators of a single crime may not have much impact. Such occasional arrests may represent, from the perspective of the kingpins, a tolerable cost of doing business. Finally, even if agencies were content to wait until a specific crime occurred, the chances of solving it would depend heavily on their having a great deal of background information available about the organizations involved.

For these reasons, governments often adopt an intelligence approach to these types of activity. Instead of waiting for a specific criminal act on which to focus, agencies gather information over a long time concerning relevant individuals and groups—their motivations, resources, interconnections, intentions, and so forth. Often it is necessary to use informers, who penetrate the groups involved and operate like spies. It may also be possible to intercept communications or to use other technical methods of collecting information. Thus, intelligence agencies are often involved in the fight against transnational groups. Depending on the regime, the agencies' involvement may be limited to the foreign aspects of their activities, while domestic aspects remain in the purview of law enforcement agencies.

Even in dealing with entirely domestic organized crime groups, however, law enforcement agencies often use intelligence techniques. For example, with respect to domestic law enforcement, the U.S. Federal Bureau of Investigation (FBI) distinguishes between criminal intelligence investigations and ordinary criminal investigations. Of the two, the former type of investigation is described as "broader and less discriminate than usual"; it is not focused on a single completed criminal act but rather on a criminal organization of which the size, composition, past acts, intended criminal goals, and capacity to do harm must be determined.[7] The dividing line between the law-enforcement and intelligence approaches is whether the focus is on punishment of a given criminal act or on struggle with an organization engaged in criminal activity.

Economics and Intelligence

Finally, there are questions concerning the function of intelligence agencies with respect to economic issues. Again, much depends on the regime's nature and the nation's economic system. In a system with a government-run economy, intelligence would be concerned with the economic aspects of the government's relations with foreign governments (such as international trade) in much the same way it is with all other aspects of its international relations. In addition, intelligence can be used to enhance the state's economic well-being. Acquiring advanced Western technology, for example, was an important function of the former Soviet Union's intelligence services (and it remains an important goal of Russian and Chinese intelligence). This activity not only increased the technological level of the Soviet and Chinese military but saved both countries the great expense and difficulty of developing technology on their own, whether for military or civilian uses.[8]

In a market economy, however, it is much less clear which economic issues have national security dimensions that justify or require the involvement of intelligence agencies. There are a number of specific areas, such as assessing the economic capability of a potential military adversary or following developments affecting the flow of vital strategic resources, upon which governments are likely to want detailed information. Whether intelligence agencies and techniques are employed to obtain this information depends to some extent on whether or not other countries attempt to keep it secret. In general, however, specific economic questions that have a direct impact on military or other foreign policy aspects of national security fall within the purview of intelligence agencies. For example, in wartime, intelligence means could be used to gain access to strategic materials (or deny the enemy access to them), a key national security goal. Similarly, in the course of negotiations with a foreign country on economic matters, a nation might use its intelligence capability to learn about its partner's negotiating positions.

More generally, a nation's appetite for economic intelligence on industrial, commercial, and financial activity in other countries probably depends on whether its government has an "industrial policy" bureaucracy that could make use of it. As such, questions about the use of intelligence agencies to collect economic information are in large measure surrogates for a more fundamental debate over government's role in directing a country's economic future.

The broader question, however, is whether intelligence should be used to advance the economic well-being of the nation in general.[9] As the end of the Cold War diminished the threat of a military confrontation between major powers, economic strength appeared to gain importance in determining a country's international power and prestige; as a result, there has been a growing interest in the role intelligence could play in enhancing economic strength.[10] However, a nation's economic well-being rises or falls over time because of such factors as rates of capital investment, productivity of labor, management skill, and the education level of its workforce. In addition, while many developments in the international economy may have important national security ramifications, it is not obvious that the government should, or even can, do very much about such developments. Moreover, in a democratic society, economic policy is much more likely to be determined by the interplay of domestic economic interests than by any coherent view (whether or not based on intelligence information) of the future world economic environment. For these reasons, it is not clear whether a government such as that of the United States would be an important consumer of such intelligence. Private economic interests could probably put it to much greater use, but it is not clear that information gathered clandestinely at government expense could be distributed equitably to individuals or corporations to further private interests.[11]

Other "Nontraditional" Issues

Some students of intelligence have advocated that in addition to economics, other "nontraditional" concerns also be considered as within the scope of intelligence—for example, environmental issues. While the argument is made that environmental problems can affect national security, the main motivation seems to be that technical intelligence collection systems developed for other purposes can help track environmental changes over time and across large expanses of territory, and that they can do so at small additional cost.[12]

INTELLIGENCE AND THE INFORMATION AGE

Given that intelligence deals with information, it seems reasonable to suppose that it will be affected in very important ways by the advent of what is called the "information age." The notion of the information age is admittedly a rather ambiguous one. Yet it is clearly very important; it has already changed the way many organizations—especially business corporations—operate, and it is likely to have important effects on government as well.

From the technical point of view, the driving factor is the tremendous technological progress that has been made in the processing and communication of information. However, technological change is only a small part of the picture: more important are the behavioral and institutional changes that result from the focus on information as the key to organizational activity. (In the military arena, what is often referred to as the "revolution in military affairs" depends critically on the enhanced usefulness of information for the targeting of new types of precision-strike weapons, and on the enhanced ability to collect, process, and disseminate that information in a timely manner for operational purposes.)

The effect of these changes shows up in several different forms. At one level, they suggest new ways in which information can be more rapidly circulated and used within government, so as to make policy making and policy implementation more effective. In addition, they focus attention on the increased amount of information available throughout the entire society, within nonintelligence parts of the government and outside the government as well. In other words, intelligence services are finding that other types of organizations are becoming more proficient at the collection, analysis, and transmission of information—that is, the intelligence services have, with respect to some types of information, more "competition" in providing data to policy makers. From the perspective of the government as a whole, a key question becomes how most effectively to exploit the information that is produced and disseminated elsewhere in the society, and how to make sure that the intelligence services' unique product is melded with other sources of information in a way that best meets the government's total information needs.[13]

THE ELEMENTS OF INTELLIGENCE

Whatever its scope in terms of coverage, intelligence can be divided according to the type of activity involved into four parts, often referred to as the "elements of intelligence": *collection, analysis, covert action,* and *counterintelligence.* Since these elements are treated in detail in subsequent chapters, the following discussion is intended only to elucidate the nature of the four types of intelligence activity and to sketch the relationships among them.

Collection refers to the gathering of raw data, through espionage; technical means (photography, interception of electronic communications, and other methods involving technology); exploitation of "open sources" (for instance, publications, and radio and television broadcasts); or in any other manner. While collection is obviously fundamental to intelligence work, opinions differ regarding the relative importance of the various methods. For example, students of intelligence have debated the relative importance of "open source" collection versus methods unique to intelligence services, and the relative importance of espionage versus technical collection.

However good the collected information, however, it almost never speaks for itself. In other words, some *analysis* of the information is necessary if it is to be useful to policy makers and military commanders. In the vast majority of cases, the collected information is fragmentary, ambiguous, and susceptible to widely divergent interpretations. Thus, the process of analyzing the available information to make judgments about the capabilities, intentions, and actions of another party is a vital part of the intelligence process. Even more difficult is the process of forecasting ("estimating," in American intelligence jargon) the future capabilities, intentions, and actions of a foreign government or political organization.

Conceptually, *covert action* differs from the other elements of intelligence in that while the others are concerned with seeking and safeguarding information, covert action seeks to influence political events directly. In terms of intensity, covert action can range from persuasion or propaganda to paramilitary action; it has been described as "an activity midway between diplomacy and war."[14]

While the techniques for exerting this influence are many, they have the common characteristic of anonymity—that is to say, the role of the government conducting the activity is not readily apparent or is not publicly acknowledged. For this reason, an intelligence agency's ability to act secretly often means that it is assigned to carry out covert action as well. But as was discussed above, because this activity involves implementing policy rather than informing policy makers, there have been occasional suggestions in the United States that covert action not be a function of the same agency (i.e., the Central Intelligence Agency) that collects and analyzes intelligence. On the other hand, both the United States and Great Britain have discovered through experience that having two organizations running clandestine operations (one for espionage and the other for covert action) can result in energy-sapping rivalry, duplication of effort, and mutual interference.[15]

In its most general sense, *counterintelligence* seeks to protect a society (and especially its intelligence capabilities) against any harm that might be inflicted by hostile intelligence services. In the first place, counterintelligence involves denying certain information to adversaries. This protection is accomplished by programs of security (actions taken to keep information away from those not authorized to have it); and by counterespionage (actions taken to apprehend or otherwise neutralize foreign agents, so as to prevent them from acquiring and communicating secret information). In addition, counterintelligence can seek to protect against an adversary's intelligence analysis as well as his collection capability; this is done through deception operations that provide false or deliberately misleading information to induce the adversary to reach incorrect conclusions concerning one's own capabilities, actions, or intentions.

However, protecting oneself against an adversary's intelligence capability, understood broadly, requires other activities as well. It may be necessary to take steps to ensure that one is not deceived by misleading information deliberately provided by the other party. Thus, counterintelligence must safeguard the integrity of the collection and analytical functions. One would also want to know about a foreign government's covert action aimed at influencing one's own government or society. Ultimately then, the breadth of counterintelligence activities is determined by the threat that an adversary's intelligence activities pose.

Chapter 2

Spies, Machines, and Libraries: Collecting the Data

We begin our discussion of the elements of intelligence by examining the collection of the raw data that, once correlated and analyzed, forms the basis of intelligence judgments and assessments. The various collection methods (the intelligence "disciplines") can be broadly characterized as (1) collection from human sources (variously referred to as espionage, human intelligence collection, or in U.S. intelligence jargon, *humint*), (2) collection by technical means (technical intelligence, or *techint*), and (3) noncovert collection via diplomatic contacts or generally available sources of information, such as newspapers, Websites and other Internet-based resources, and radio and television broadcasts (open-source collection).[1]

HUMAN INTELLIGENCE COLLECTION

Human intelligence collection, or espionage, is what the term "intelligence" is most likely to bring to mind. Typically, it involves the identifying and recruiting of a foreign official who, by virtue of a position of trust in his government, has access to important information and who is willing, for some reason, to pass it to officers of one's intelligence service. In some cases (especially in wartime), the person providing the information may not be a government official but a private individual who has the opportunity to observe (or hear about) something of interest, such as ships' arrivals in and departures from a harbor. The person to be recruited might also be someone who is privy to important information by virtue of a close relationship (such as friendship, business dealings, etc.) with someone of intelligence interest (for instance, a terrorist or an international arms dealer).

Ordinarily, individuals in two different roles are involved: an intelligence *officer,* who is an employee of an intelligence agency, and a *source,* who provides the officer with information for transmission back to the intelligence service's headquarters. The intelligence officer, or "handler," maintains communication with the source, passes on instructions from the intelligence service's headquarters, provides necessary resources (such as copying or communications equipment), and, in general, seeks to ensure that the flow of information continues.[2]

Types of Intelligence Officers

Since they must avoid the attention of the government of the country in which they operate, intelligence officers cannot simply hang out shingles advertising their willingness to pay cash for secrets. They require what in intelligence jargon is called "cover"—that is, a plausible reason for being in the country, visible means of financial support, a pretext for meeting people with access to sensitive information, and so forth.[3]

In current U.S. parlance, a distinction is made between "official" and "nonofficial" cover. *Official cover* refers to disguising an intelligence officer as a diplomat or some other kind of governmental official who would ordinarily be posted abroad. *Nonofficial cover* refers to any other type of disguise—as a businessman, journalist, tourist, etc.—that could explain why the officer is in the host country. A nonofficial cover officer may also disguise his nationality and pretend to be from a country other than the one whose intelligence officer he is.[4] If the host country is one that routinely accepts immigrants, the officer can enter under that guise.

The use of official cover has several advantages. Most obviously, it can provide the intelligence officer with diplomatic immunity. If his espionage activities are detected, international law limits the host government to declaring him *persona non grata* and expelling him from the country.

In addition, posing as a diplomat improves the intelligence officer's access to some potential sources; as a diplomat, he would, without raising suspicion, meet with host-government officials in the course of his ordinary business, as well as with other countries' diplomats stationed in the same capital. Indeed, since other countries will also use official cover for their intelligence officers, he will have "innocent" opportunities for meeting them as well.[5]

Also, stationing intelligence agents in an embassy under official cover guarantees that if a national of the host country approaches the embassy with sensitive materials or an offer to provide them, the matter can be handled by an intelligence professional. In this sense, the existence of official cover intelligence officers eases attempts by host-country nationals to make contact with the intelligence service; such positions serve as useful and perhaps necessary "mailboxes," especially in countries that strictly regulate or prohibit their nationals' travel to or communication with the outside world.[6]

Finally, official cover has certain administrative conveniences. The officer can be paid, and other personnel matters can be handled, through regular government channels, and secure communication with the intelligence service's headquarters can be conveniently maintained through the intelligence "station" (the group of intelligence officers under official cover).[7]

At the same time, however, official cover has several drawbacks. Most importantly, because of the relatively small number of officials posted to a given host country, that country's counterintelligence service may be able to determine, fairly precisely, which "diplomats" are intelligence officers and which are not. This may be done by the obvious, if laborious, methods of maintaining surveillance on each official and noting his or her movements and contacts, tapping telephones, bugging apartments, and so forth. The practice of hiring nationals of the host country to work in embassies in various support capacities probably facilitates such surveillance, especially in those countries where it must be assumed that anyone allowed to work in a foreign embassy has agreed to cooperate with the host country's intelligence service.[8] In addition, simpler and less expensive methods may be able to accomplish the same goal. For example, materials published by a country might be used to trace the careers of its foreign service officers and thus identify patterns that indicate an intelligence connection.

Furthermore, while official cover may provide easy access to some potential sources (primarily other diplomats and officials of the host-country national security bureaucracies), it may hinder access to others who might be hesitant to deal with foreign officials, either in general or with those from a particular country. In any case, potential recruits are immediately put on notice that they are dealing with an official of a foreign government, and that may make them more cautious. In addition, if diplomatic relations are broken off, as might happen in case of an intense crisis or war—when good intelligence may be most necessary—official-cover officers must leave the country, thereby disrupting the operation of any networks of sources they had established.[9]

The advantages and disadvantages of nonofficial cover are, for the most part, the obverse of the considerations already discussed. On the one hand, since they pose as members of a variety of professions and strata of society, nonofficial-cover officials (NOCs) can have access to a different, and perhaps wider, spectrum of potential sources. Similarly, they can pose as (or, indeed, be) nationals of the country to which they are posted or of some third country. Obscuring the connection with the government for which they work may help them make contact with potential sources and gain access to information. If diplomatic relations are broken off, they may be able to remain and continue to operate. In general, NOCs should also be much harder for the host government to identify.

On the other hand, nonofficial cover suffers from many disadvantages. The expense and administrative difficulty involved in providing nonofficial cover is much greater than in the case of official cover. One method is to persuade a corporation or other private organization to allow an intelligence officer to pose as a member of its staff. Alternatively, the officers may themselves establish businesses or engage in activities that provide plausible explanations for their presence in the target country. The drawback here is that this may not only be expensive but require the intelligence officer to devote a great deal of time to his or her "cover" activity if the cover is to be persuasive, which reduces the time and effort the officer can spend on the primary task of intelligence collection.[10] Communications are likely to be more difficult, since an NOC cannot make regular use of the embassy's communications facilities without raising some of the very suspicions that nonofficial cover is intended to avoid.

One well-known and particularly successful NOC was Richard Sorge, a German citizen and correspondent for a leading German newspaper who spied for Soviet military intelligence in China and Japan from the 1930s until his arrest in the fall of 1941. His close relationship with the staff of the German embassy in Tokyo, including the ambassador, gave him extraordinary access to information about German and Japanese war plans. Shortly before his arrest, Sorge reported to Moscow the critical information that "the Soviet Far East can be considered safe from Japanese attack." According to Sorge's report, Japan had decided not to attack the Soviet Union; instead, it would strike south and east in the Pacific against the United States and the British and Dutch colonies in Southeast Asia. Reassured by Sorge's reporting, Stalin felt free to transfer hundreds of thousands of troops from the Far East to Moscow, where they would help stop the German advance in the winter of 1941–42. In retrospect, halting the Wehrmacht outside Moscow was to be a critical turning point in the war.[11]

Another example of the successful use of nonofficial cover, an example that illustrates the value of being able to disguise one's nationality, is that of Israeli agent Eli Cohen. An Egyptian-born Jew, Cohen emigrated to Israel in 1956 at the age of thirty-two and volunteered his services to Israeli intelligence. He was sent by the Israeli intelligence agency, the Mossad, to Argentina in 1961 to build a cover as an Arab businessman, under the pseudonym Kamal Amin Taabet. After quickly establishing a wide range of contacts in the Syrian expatriate community of Argentina, Cohen moved to Damascus in early 1962. Armed with letters of introduction provided by his new Syrian friends back in Buenos Aires, Cohen was able (with some good luck) to establish himself within Syria's ruling circles. In fact, he was so well connected that at one point he was used as an emissary between a new Ba'athist government and an exiled former president of Syria; at another point, he was thought to be in line for a post in the cabinet of the Syrian government itself. However, after reporting on Syrian political, military, and diplomatic matters for three years, Cohen was caught by Syrian counterintelligence and executed in May 1965.[12]

A particularly ambitious use of nonofficial cover involves officers who enter the host country in the guise of ordinary immigrants. Obviously, it is easier to insert such officers into a country that routinely receives a large number of immigrants and visitors and is relatively casual about controlling its borders than into one that does not receive immigrants, generally keeps a watch on visitors, and guards its borders carefully.

An interesting example that illustrates how much time and effort the Soviet Union was willing to devote to operations of this type is that of Ludek Zemenek, a Czech national recruited by Soviet intelligence (the Committee of State Security, known as the KGB from its Russian initials).[13] Given the identity of a Rudolf Herrmann (the real Rudolf Herrmann having been a German who died in the Soviet Union during World War II), he lived in East Germany for about a year. Then, at the end of 1957, he left with an East German wife (also a Soviet intelligence officer) and an infant son for West Germany, where he appeared to be an ordinary East German refugee.[14]

After four years in West Germany, Herrmann emigrated to Canada, where he eventually established a small business producing advertising and commercial films. He fulfilled various minor tasks for the KGB, such as filing "personality reports" on politicians and journalists he met through his business, and maintaining communications with a Canadian professor who was a KGB agent. His most important mission, however, was to preserve his cover so that he would be able, in case of a break in diplomatic relations between the USSR and Canada, to take control of the network of Canadian sources from the legal "resident" (chief of the KGB station at the Soviet embassy in Ottawa).

After six years in Canada, Herrmann was instructed to move from Canada to the United States, where he performed similar tasks. When his son Peter was seventeen, Herrmann recruited him to work for the KGB as well. Since Peter had been brought to West Germany as an infant and had been raised from the age of four in Canada and the United States, his background would not give rise to any suspicion; he was to prepare himself for a career in the U.S. government, where he could operate as a long-term Soviet source, or "mole." Presumably, he would have been able to do so had the FBI not confronted father Herrmann several years later and, by threatening to arrest him, his wife, and his son, obtained his cooperation.

The mix of official and nonofficial covers a government employs in carrying out its human collection activities will depend on a number of factors. Broadly speaking, the two most important are the type of intelligence being sought and the means available for acquiring it. In the case of the United States and its allies during the Cold War, human collection against the Soviet Union was focused principally on the intentions of the Soviet leadership, the nation's military capabilities, and its intelligence services' efforts against the West. This focus, combined with the close surveillance of all foreigners by Soviet security services, meant that human collection efforts by the United States and other countries came to rely chiefly on intelligence officers operating under official cover.

In contrast, in recent years China has relied heavily on nonofficial cover to carry out its collection program in the United States. Although China's intelligence services do conduct some traditional recruitment and collection using official cover, Chinese humint routinely employs a variety of NOC mechanisms, including front companies, scientific and student exchange programs, and commercial and scientific delegations. Chinese intelligence also uses long-term "sleeper" agents who immigrate from China and establish themselves as residents for an extended period before carrying out intelligence-related activities in the countries to which they have emigrated. This extensive use of nonofficial covers follows from the priority that the Chinese government has given to acquiring advanced American technology and related information, the relatively open nature of U.S. commercial markets, the ease of establishing residence in the United States, and the existence of a substantial American-Chinese ethnic community into which recent immigrants can blend.[15]

Types of Intelligence Sources

Just as we may classify intelligence officers as official cover or NOC, we may make distinctions among types of intelligence sources. One basic distinction is between sources whom the intelligence officer, after preparing the ground, actively recruits into the service of the intelligence agency and *walk-ins,* who volunteer to assist the intelligence agency of a foreign country, sometimes literally by walking into its embassy.

Recruited sources are generally considered more reliable, since the intelligence officer has had a chance to study their character and motivation before attempting to recruit them.[16] In addition, sources to be recruited will have been chosen on the basis of their access to important information. However, the identification and recruitment of sources is a laborious and time-consuming endeavor, and there is no guarantee that even the most carefully chosen and studied potential source will in fact respond positively to the recruitment attempt, or "pitch."

Walk-ins, on the other hand, are inherently suspect, since there is always the possibility that the supposed volunteer has in fact been dispatched by his own country's intelligence service to pass false or misleading information, inform his country about the opposing service's methods of operation, or entrap one of the opposing service's intelligence officers so as to bring about his or her arrest or expulsion. However, an intelligence service that is too suspicious of walk-ins may miss opportunities to obtain information that it could have easily had. Intelligence lore and history contain stories of walk-ins who were at first ignored or spurned but turned out to be valuable intelligence sources.

A famous case of this sort involved Fritz Kolbe, a German foreign ministry official during World War II. Kolbe's job included sorting through the mass of cable traffic that flowed into Berlin daily from German embassies around the world. The cables regularly touched on sensitive strategic, military, and intelligence subjects as well as diplomatic matters. Having managed to be assigned occasionally as an official courier, Kolbe traveled to Switzerland in August 1943 carrying nearly two hundred documents taken from the files of the foreign ministry in Berlin. He first approached the British embassy in Bern. Wary of "agents provocateurs" or German plants, the British rebuffed Kolbe's approach. He then turned to Allen Dulles, the head of U.S. intelligence operations in Switzerland. Cautious, but less so than their British allies, the Americans worked with Kolbe, who in subsequent trips to Bern provided them with more than 1,500 secret German documents. Kolbe was perhaps the greatest espionage success of the war for the United States.[17]

In addition to classifying sources, we can also distinguish among the reasons why they provide information. Sources may be motivated by ideological, ethnic, or religious loyalties that are stronger than their ties to the countries of which they are citizens; they may be disillusioned by the actions or ideologies of their own countries; they may be greedy; they may be somewhat unbalanced people who wish to bring some excitement into their lives; they may desire to avenge what they see as ill treatment by their government; or they may be subject to blackmail. The relative importance of these motives depends on the characteristics of the societies involved and on the tactics of the opposing intelligence services.

For example, the history of Soviet human intelligence collection against the United States and Great Britain since the 1930s shows a substantial shift from ideology toward greed and revenge as reasons Americans and Britons were willing to betray their countries. In the 1930s, the Soviets found that the appeal of communism to many Cambridge University students and instructors, including some from prominent families, made the ideological atmosphere very favorable. Among the students recruited at that time who later became major Soviet agents within the British government were Guy Burgess, Donald Maclean, and Harold ("Kim") Philby.[18]

On the other hand, Americans and Britons who were arrested for espionage on behalf of the Soviet Union in the late 1970s and 1980s appear to have been motivated mostly by greed.[19] In another instance, that of Edward Lee Howard, a former CIA officer who gave the Soviets important operational details concerning the agency's activities in Moscow, the motive was revenge against the CIA, for its having fired him.[20]

In general, the popular imagination probably overestimates the use of sex to gain secrets and the prevalence of blackmail as a reason for espionage, although the potential for blackmail may enable an intelligence officer to keep active a source who had become a spy for some other reason but later on wants to quit. Even so, some cases involving seduction and blackmail of the sort featured in popular spy novels have come to light.

For example, there were the Mata Hari–like exploits of Betty Pack during World War II. Married to a British diplomat, the American-born Pack worked for both British and American intelligence. Her technique consisted largely of having affairs with key foreign government officials. Among her considerable accomplishments, she collected valuable diplomatic information from the Polish foreign ministry before the war, obtained important data on Polish cryptologic efforts to break German codes, completely compromised the internal workings of the French (Vichy) embassy in Washington, and acquired French and Italian naval ciphers.[21]

More typical than seduction, however, is the use of sex to entrap and then blackmail an official who has access to sensitive materials or information. A classic case of this type involved Maurice Dejean, the French ambassador to Moscow in the 1950s and 1960s. Taking note of the married ambassador's roving eye, the KGB assigned a beautiful co-optee (a Soviet citizen pressured to cooperate) to seduce him. Once the affair was well along, the couple was surprised by the "unexpected" return of her "husband." "Outraged," he threatened to make the matter public and take the ambassador to court. Dejean confided in a Russian "friend"—in reality, the senior KGB officer who had orchestrated the operation from the start; the "friend" offered to help keep the whole matter quiet. The KGB's plan was to use this compromising situation to blackmail Dejean into working for them when he returned to France and, they hoped, was given an even more senior post. However, the Soviets' scheme was spoiled by the defection of a Russian film writer who was privy to the plot.[22]

Problems of Human Intelligence Collection

Many problems encountered in human intelligence collection are inherent in the nature of the enterprise, while others are more specific to the nature of the intelligence target. Of the former, the most critical is ensuring quality control—being confident that the information sources provide is genuine.

Sources may, for pecuniary motives, either fabricate information or imaginatively repackage and embellish publicly available material to make it appear to have come from highly placed inside sources (creating, to use intelligence jargon, a "paper mill"). The history of intelligence contains occasional examples of clever paper-mill operators who bilked their clients of large sums of money.

Such paper mills flourished in the late 1940s and early 1950s, exploiting the Western intelligence services' difficulty in operating in the communist countries of Eastern Europe. Often they were run by impoverished émigrés from those countries, who soon discovered they could make a living by selling "information" they claimed to receive from acquaintances among their former countrymen who had risen to important positions in the new communist governments. Since many of these émigrés were well educated and politically sophisticated, they were able to embellish and interpret publicly available information to produce convincing intelligence reports.[23]

A more serious quality-control problem arises from the possibility that an agent has been "doubled"—that he is secretly working for his supposed target and that the information he is providing to his supposed employers is intended to deceive them. Such doubling can occur when an intelligence source is apprehended and chooses to cooperate with his captors to avoid punishment.[24] Alternatively, the source could have been a "double agent" (a supposed intelligence source who is really working for the country he appears to be spying on) from the beginning, as was noted above in the discussion of walk-ins.

Some of the most interesting and remarkable stories in intelligence history concern the use of double agents. For example, in what was called the "double-cross system," the British succeeded in gaining control of, and running, the entire German human intelligence collection effort in Great Britain during World War II. From almost the beginning of the war, the British controlled all intelligence reports transmitted home by Germany's supposed agents in Britain. Among other achievements, these reports helped deceive the Germans about the location and nature of the D-day landings in Normandy. Even as late as June 9, 1944, three days after D-day, a message from a British-controlled source was instrumental in retaining a German panzer division in the Calais area (to repel the supposedly imminent landing of a "main force" that in fact did not exist), thereby helping the real invasion force in Normandy to secure its foothold.[25]

Other problems derive from the nature of the target. The more effective and pervasive a target country's internal security apparatus, the more difficulties it poses for human intelligence collection in that country. A government that maintains close control over international travel and communications, as well as over the movements, communications, and economic activity of its people generally, can make it extremely difficult for nonofficial cover, or "illegal," intelligence officers to travel to the country, set up their "cover" activities, and operate without being detected. Official-cover officers can be subjected to intensive surveillance, making it hard for them to meet with citizens of the target country without being observed. The result is what is termed in U.S. intelligence jargon a "hard target" or "denied area," a country in which intelligence activities can in general proceed only under official cover and then only with great difficulty.

Other targets pose particular troubles as well. For example, the collection of intelligence about terrorism is hampered by the relatively small, secretive, and tightly knit nature of most terrorist groups. (Similar considerations apply to human intelligence collection against organized crime.) To the extent that membership in these groups depends on long acquaintanceships, family ties, or previous criminal acts, it becomes very difficult to insert an intelligence source into them (in intelligence jargon, to "penetrate" them). Similarly, the loyalties existing within such a group (to say nothing of the discipline it can impose on its members) make it difficult to persuade an existing member to betray it.

The difficulties do not come to an end even if a source is inserted successfully into a terrorist group. To remain a member in good standing, the source must provide material support for, or participate in, terrorist actions. Yet most intelligence agencies feel obligated to put some limit on actions an officer or source can take to preserve his bona fides. At the same time, using the information provided by the source to warn against or otherwise thwart planned terrorist acts may make it clear to the terrorists that there is an informant in their midst, thus endangering the source's life. Thus, it is often not until a member has been apprehended that an agency gets an opportunity to look into the inner workings of groups of this type.

Tradecraft

The particular methods an intelligence officer uses to operate and communicate with sources without being detected by the opposing intelligence service are known collectively as "tradecraft." The most serious problem an intelligence officer faces is that the opposing side is likely to keep him under surveillance (that is, watch and follow him) to monitor his activities and identify those with whom he comes in contact. The officer's task, then, is to determine whether he is under surveillance, and if so, to escape that surveillance long enough to contact sources or potential sources without giving away their identities.[26]

A technique for escaping surveillance that the CIA apparently teaches its officers is illustrated by the ruse employed by Edward Lee Howard, the cashiered CIA officer, to escape FBI surveillance in 1985. Returning home at night in his car, his wife at the wheel, and believing he was being followed by the FBI, Howard had his wife make a sharp turn at a dark intersection; immediately after she turned the corner, he opened the passenger-side door and rolled out. At the same time, Howard's wife pushed up a dummy in his place, making it appear to anyone following from a distance that Howard was still in the car. She then drove home, entered the garage, and pulled down the garage door, leaving the surveillance team unaware that Howard had escaped their surveillance and was now able to move freely, without being followed.[27]

More typically, an officer may spend several hours traveling by a circuitous route to a meeting, taking several different forms of transportation. If he notices that the man who sits next to him on a westbound subway also happens to be on his eastbound bus, he may reasonably conclude he is being followed. The surveillance team may try to avoid discovery by using a relay system so the same individual is not tailing the officer all the time. The game of surveillance and counter-surveillance can be complicated almost indefinitely.[28]

Tradecraft also includes techniques for communicating with a source without having to meet with him or her at all. For example, an officer may unobtrusively hand a package or piece of paper to a source as they pass on the street (a "brush pass"). If done correctly, the maneuver may not be observed by the opposing side's surveillance. The officer may place his briefcase on the floor next to his chair as he enjoys a drink in a café; the source takes the table next to his and places his own briefcase, identical in appearance to the officer's, on the floor next to it. When the source leaves, he takes the officer's briefcase instead of his own. Again, unless the surveillance has carefully watched the putting down and taking up of the briefcases, the switch may not be noticed.

Similarly, an officer may leave a note at an arranged location, such as in a hollow tree in the park; some hours later, the source retrieves it (a "dead drop").[29] If the officer places the note without being observed, anyone maintaining surveillance on him to determine his contacts will simply continue following him, not realizing that the meeting has in effect already occurred. Robert P. Hanssen, an FBI counterintelligence specialist recently charged with spying for the Soviet Union and then the Russian Federation for more than fifteen years, communicated almost entirely by means of "dead drops"; evidently, based on his own knowledge of FBI procedures, he considered that the safest method.[30]

Another precaution is for an intelligence service to avoid, if possible, meeting a source in the country against which he is spying. It is likely to be much safer to meet in a third country, where surveillance may be less vigilant or nonexistent. For example, the Soviet Union often preferred to meet particularly important U.S. sources, such as John Walker (who provided the Soviets with vast amounts of classified information relating to naval communications and operations) in Austria, a country that, although a Western-style democracy, was officially neutral in the Cold War.

> The Walker case revealed how carefully the Soviets handle an important agent. Most of his meetings with the Soviets were in Vienna, Austria. . . . During these meetings Walker and his KGB contact would walk the streets[,] . . . [never using] a safe house to meet in, as his contact had come directly from Moscow and the Vienna *rezidentura* (residency, the group of KGB officers working out of a Soviet embassy) was unaware of the operation.[31]

In other cases, intelligence services operating against the United States have preferred to meet sources in Canada or Mexico. These are logical choices, given the ease with which Americans can visit these countries and the large numbers who do so. For example, CIA linguist and analyst Larry Wu-tai Chin, a long-time spy for the People's Republic of China, made frequent trips to Toronto to be debriefed by his handler and to pass undeveloped film to him.[32]

Other classic means for intelligence officers and sources to communicate without having to meet in person involve "secret writing" and "microdots." These techniques are useful in cases in which the officer and source have an innocent ostensible reason for communicating with each other but suspect that their letters are likely to be opened and read by the opposing side. To use secret writing, the officer or source would first write an innocuous cover letter. He would then write, typically using a specially treated piece of carbon paper, a secret message on top of the original letter. The message is invisible to the naked eye and becomes legible only when treated by a particular chemical agent known only to the intelligence service for whom the officer and source are working. Microdots are a second means of communicating; in this case, photographs are shrunk to microscopic size and hidden somewhere on the letter, perhaps under the stamp, the flap of the envelope, or on top of punctuation marks in typed letters.

Defectors

So far, the discussion has dealt only with intelligence sources who remain in place—that is, who report information while retaining the official position that gives them access to it. This is obviously the best situation from the point of view of intelligence collection, since it implies continuing access to information, as well as the potential to "task" the source to obtain specific documents or pieces of information that are particularly necessary or useful. But it requires that the communications between the source and his handler remain hidden, and it exposes the source to the risk of being caught.

In a denied area, these difficulties are magnified. As a result, human intelligence collection against such countries often depends heavily on defectors. From the intelligence point of view, these are sources who do not remain in place but rather flee their countries, typically illegally, and are granted asylum. In the post–World War II period, human intelligence collection by the West against the Soviet Union depended heavily on such individuals. For example, in the early 1950s, Western intelligence services had little success in recruiting Soviet intelligence officers. However, in 1954, in the space of four months, five officers defected to the West. These defections resulted in a wealth of information about Soviet intelligence operations in the decade following World War II. Through the defections, important new intelligence was learned about the KGB's security practices and operational tradecraft, its efforts at breaking the codes of other governments, its penetrations of Western governments, and its involvement in assassinations.[33] Similarly, the defection of Hussein al-Kamal, Iraqi dictator Saddam Hussein's son-in-law, in August 1995 provided valuable information about Iraq's covert program to develop biological weapons that had not been uncovered by the United Nations inspection commission (UNSCOM) during the previous four years.[34]

Despite their importance, defectors present the same problems as walk-ins. It is difficult to be certain that they are genuine defectors rather than loyal citizens sent out by their government to deceive the opposition. Some skepticism is obviously required in dealing with them, at least initially. The conflicting information provided by several major Soviet defectors to the United States—in particular, concerning the presence or absence of a highly placed Soviet mole in the American government—has never been completely sorted out; it bedeviled U.S. intelligence for a quarter of a century.[35]

TECHNICAL INTELLIGENCE COLLECTION

Technical intelligence collection (or *techint,* in U.S. intelligence jargon) refers to a group of techniques using advanced technology, rather than human agents, to collect information. Ultimately limited only by human ingenuity and the laws of physics, these techniques have for the most part involved long-range photography and the interception of various electromagnetic waves, although other phenomenologies are also exploited (for example, acoustic signal

Photographic or Imagery Intelligence

Photographic or imagery intelligence (*photint* or *imint*), as the name implies, involves photography to collect intelligence. More specifically, it uses long-range photography to obtain images of places or things to which direct access is not possible. It began as aerial surveillance, which came into being almost at the same time as aviation itself.[36]

At the beginning of the First World War, in August 1914, the British Royal Flying Corps conducted aerial surveillance of the German troops advancing through Belgium.[37] Once the initial period of movement ended and the German and allied armies faced each other along a continuous front from Switzerland to the North Sea, aerial surveillance was seen as a substitute for the cavalry reconnaissance patrols that could no longer roam the area alongside and behind the enemy army. As Brig. Gen. William Mitchell, the American apostle of airpower in the interwar period, wrote, "One flight over the lines gave me a much clearer impression of how the armies were laid out than any amount of traveling around on the ground."[38] From this it was a relatively short step to placing cameras on these reconnaissance planes and developing an aerial photoreconnaissance capability.

With the further development of aviation and photography, aerial photographic reconnaissance became an important source of intelligence information during World War II. It was used not only to track the deployments and movements of enemy forces but to follow major technological advances as well. Thus, the British used aerial photography, as well as other intelligence sources, to follow German technical developments, such as the radio-beam systems the Germans developed to guide their bombers to targets in England, new air defense radars, and the V-1 and V-2 missiles.[39]

So far, the examples given of aerial photoreconnaissance have all been from wartime; this is hardly accidental. In wartime the military incentive for conducting this sort of activity is greater, and the political obstacles to it are fewer. Not only is it more important to know what is happening in the enemy's country during wartime, but alternative methods of learning about it are fewer. One cannot rely solely on reports from journalists, travelers, diplomats, or attachés; in general, press coverage is tightly controlled, borders are closed, and travel within the target country is restricted, even for the country's own nationals and the nationals of neutral countries. At the same time, the international-law prohibition against overflying another country without its consent no longer poses a political obstacle.

Even so, the difficulties the United States faced in trying to conduct human intelligence collection activities against the Soviet Union during the years immediately after World War II led it to consider the possibility of using photoreconnaissance in peacetime. This interest was reinforced when in 1950 it was feared that the North Korean invasion of South Korea might be the prelude to a Soviet invasion of Western Europe. Given the paucity of human intelligence sources, the United States feared that Soviet preparations for such an invasion might not be detected. In addition, basic intelligence information about the Soviet "order of battle" (size and composition of the armed forces) was often lacking, and it was accordingly difficult for the American government to make reasonable judgments about what its own military expenditures should be.

An example of the lack of hard data on Soviet forces was the supposed "bomber gap" of the mid-1950s. The United States had very little information on Soviet plans or capabilities for building a strategic, or "heavy," bomber (a plane capable of carrying a nuclear weapon over intercontinental ranges). But at Soviet Air Force Day ceremonies in July 1955, immediately before a "Big Four" (United States, Soviet Union, France, and Britain) summit meeting in Geneva, an American air attaché saw twenty-eight heavy bombers of a relatively new type fly over. It appeared that the Soviets had undertaken a crash program to build strategic bombers that would, given U.S. defense plans, open a significant gap—dubbed the "bomber gap"—between American and Soviet capabilities in this area. Yet, the attaché had been deceived by a simple ruse: he had seen not twenty-eight new bombers but a smaller number making multiple passes over the reviewing stand.[40] Absent more reliable information, however, the attaché's reporting became the basis for calls for increased American defense spending.

Various attempts were made to overcome this deficiency in knowledge about the Soviet military. One project, code-named "Moby Dick," involved launching balloons in Western Europe equipped with downward-pointing cameras. The idea was that these balloons would then drift across the Soviet Union on the prevailing westerly winds until they reached Japan or the Pacific Ocean. At that point, their camera pods would be released in response to a radio signal and recovered. In reality, many of the balloons came down over the Soviet Union, enabling the Soviets to assess the camera's technology. In any case, because of the random movement of the balloons over the vast landmass of the Soviet Union, the photographs developed from the recovered film probably yielded minimal intelligence.[41]

On July 21, 1955, at the "Big Four" summit, President Dwight D. Eisenhower proposed an "Open Skies" plan for mutual aerial surveillance of the United States and the USSR. According to this plan, the two countries would "give to each other a complete blueprint of [their] military establishments . . . from one end of [the] country to the other," and each country would have the right to conduct aerial surveillance over the other's territory as it saw fit.[42] Eisenhower believed the plan would deter any attempt at launching a surprise attack; in his judgment, a potential attacker could not hope to achieve surprise if it were subject to unlimited aerial surveillance. The surveillance would also facilitate future disarmament agreements, since it would help determine whether the other party was living up to its obligations.

Eisenhower, however, was not willing to condition his plans for improved intelligence collection on Soviet agreement. Eight months earlier, on November 24, 1954, he had secretly approved the development of a new reconnaissance plane, the U-2, which could fly above the reach of Soviet fighters and surface-to-air missiles (SAMs). In addition, it was foreseen that photographic reconnaissance from satellites would become feasible.[43] In any case, the Soviet premier, Nikita Khrushchev, rejected the "Open Skies" proposal, characterizing it as an attempt to legalize espionage. On June 21, 1956, Eisenhower secretly approved the first U-2 flight over Soviet territory.[44]

During the next four years, the U-2 flights, both over Soviet territory and along its periphery, yielded a rich intelligence return, providing the United States for the first time routine coverage of important Soviet military test facilities and bases. The Soviets lodged confidential diplomatic protests against the overflights, but they were at first unable to do anything about them. Yet it was just a matter of time before the Soviets developed some means to attack the U-2. On May 1, 1960, they succeeded in shooting down one of them, capturing the pilot, Francis Gary Powers, in the process.

Even before the U-2 incident, however, the United States had begun work on a satellite photoreconnaissance capability.[45] Although this capability was openly discussed during its developmental stage,[46] its existence was, during the early years, regarded as highly classified.[47] This policy remained in effect until 1978, when President Jimmy Carter, wishing to assure the American people of the verifiability of the second SALT (Strategic Arms Limitation Treaty) treaty, publicly confirmed that the United States possessed a capability; its existence had been by that time an open secret for many years. With the end of the Cold War, the existence and identity of the National Reconnaissance Office (NRO)—the agency charged with "the research and development, acquisition and operation of spaceborne and airborne data collection systems" designed "to meet U.S. Government intelligence needs"—was declassified.[48]

The key to photographic reconnaissance from space is the quality and power of the optical equipment used to collect and focus the light reflected from objects on earth. Choosing the altitude at which the satellite will orbit involves a trade-off between the quality of the picture (other things being equal, the lower the orbit, the better the quality) and the length of time the satellite can remain aloft (if the satellite traverses the upper reaches of the earth's atmosphere, the atmospheric drag will slow it down and cause it to plummet to earth). Other factors determining the orbit include requirements to maximize the ability to photograph certain parts of the earth's surface and to position the satellite with respect to the sun so that photographs may be taken under optimal lighting conditions. A particular difficulty encountered by space-based photography is that the light must pass through the entire atmosphere, which tends to diffuse it, hence blurring the image. On the other hand, space-based cameras, unlike those on planes, are not exposed to the vibrations of a jet engine or atmospheric turbulence.[49]

Initially, all photoreconnaissance satellites used high-powered cameras that upon command from earth ejected the exposed film in a capsule; the capsule was recovered as it descended from space, and the film was developed and analyzed. For some purposes—such as following long-term trends or identifying and locating fixed military installations—the delay between the taking of the photo and its development and analysis was not a problem. The difficulty with the film-recovery system, however, arose in connection with targets that were mobile or events that were fast breaking. A few days' delay, for example, might mean the difference between a surprise attack that was successful and one that was not.

To speed up the process, the film can be replaced by an array of light-sensitive semiconductors known as a charge-coupled device (CCD). As light hits one of these semiconductors, an electrical charge is produced proportional to the intensity of the light. By measuring the magnitude of these charges on the individual elements of the CCD and noting precisely where on the grid each element is, a processor can reconstruct from this information a picture either on film or in a computer terminal. Because there is little delay in transmitting that data electronically from space to a ground station, imagery taken of a target can be reproduced on earth virtually in "real time"—that is, with negligible delay.[50]

Despite this improvement, any photographic reconnaissance capability still depends on sunlight and the absence of cloud cover. To get around these limitations, other types of imagery, using radar or infrared waves (emitted by warm or hot objects), may be employed. For example, instead of relying on the sunlight naturally reflected from an object on earth to produce an image, a radar reconnaissance system transmits its own radio waves to the target area below, recovers the waves reflected by various objects and, by a complex process, converts that data into an image.[51] By "illuminating" targets independently of the sun and using wavelengths that can penetrate clouds, fog, or precipitation, radar reconnaissance systems potentially provide a twenty-four-hour, all-weather imaging capability.

Similarly, another part of the electromagnetic spectrum, the infrared, can be used to detect objects that are hotter (or cooler) than their backgrounds. During the day, for example, infrared imaging allows one to distinguish real foliage (which has one heat "signature") from most camouflage (which has another). At night, because objects heated during the day cool at different rates, an infrared system may enable an analyst to detect various kinds of objects and targets. For example, at nightfall, metallic objects, such as tanks, cool more slowly than the surrounding terrain or vegetation; this difference can be captured by an infrared imaging system, enabling one to locate those tanks at sundown.[52]

As impressive and potentially useful as these more exotic imaging reconnaissance capabilities may be, they have a major drawback—the quality of the imagery they produce. In general, the resolution (generally speaking, the size of the smallest object that can be detected) of photos taken with visible light is better than those taken by means of radar waves or some other part of the electromagnetic spectrum. For some purposes, such as the mass movement of troops, low-resolution imagery of a wide area may be sufficient. However, for other requirements, such as ascertaining the technical characteristics of a particular weapon system, greater precision is required. A key factor in effectively employing these different kinds of imaging systems is knowing what level of resolution is needed to answer the questions a government might have about its potential adversaries or battlefield opponents.

It has been a long time since space-based photoreconnaissance was the exclusive preserve of U.S. and Soviet intelligence. Additional countries have launched their own photoreconnaissance satellites for intelligence purposes, and as the relevant technologies mature, more and more countries may be able to do so, if they are willing and able to expend the necessary resources. Countries that have launched their own satellites or are actively considering the possibility of doing so include China, France, and Japan.[53]

A related development has been the development of photoreconnaissance capabilities for commercial purposes. In 1986, a French government agency launched a commercial photoreconnaissance satellite (Satellite pour l'Observation de la Terre [SPOT], or "earth observation satellite") that offered ten-meter-resolution black-and-white photos for public sale. In 1999, Ikonos, a U.S. company, entered the market with one-meter-resolution photography; the company plans to offer even more precise photographs (half-meter resolution) starting in 2004, and it has already received U.S. government permission to do so.[54] Other commercial reconnaissance services are offered or planned by companies or government agencies in Russia, South Africa, Canada, India, Australia, Israel, China, and Brazil.[55]

Signals Intelligence

Signals intelligence (or *sigint*) is the generic term given to the process of deriving intelligence from intercepted electromagnetic waves, generally referred to as signals. It may be subdivided according to the type of electromagnetic wave being intercepted:

- The interception of, and derivation of information from, foreign communications signals (radio messages) by other than the intended recipients is known as communications intelligence, or *comint.*
- The interception, processing, and analysis of foreign telemetry (radio signals that relay to engineers information from sensors on board a test vehicle concerning its flight and performance characteristics) is known as telemetry intelligence, or *telint.*
- The interception, processing, and analysis of noncommunication-related electromagnetic radiations coming from a piece of military equipment (such as a radar) while it operates are known as electronic intelligence, or *elint.*[56]
- In principle, any electromagnetic wave, emitted either as a necessary part or as a by-product of the functioning of a piece of electrical equipment, is subject to interception by a receiver that is properly placed, tuned, and sufficiently sensitive.[57]

Communications Intelligence (Comint)

Of these varieties of signals intelligence, the oldest is comint, which is practically contemporaneous with the use of radio for military and diplomatic communications.[58] Through the end of World War II, comint (combined with cryptanalysis—the breaking of the codes and ciphers in which the valuable messages are transmitted)[59] was, as far as available information allows us to judge, more important than any other source of intelligence for the major powers, both in peace and in war.[60]

One of the earliest publicly documented uses of comint was the effort by the British navy during World War I to gain advance warning of any bid by its German rival to venture out into the North Sea. In addition, at the beginning of the war, the British severed German-owned underwater telegraph cables that linked Germany with the Americas, Africa, and Spain. As a result, Germany's diplomatic "cables" to those areas had to be sent by radio and were vulnerable to interception by British monitoring stations.[61]

Whatever the earlier successes, it was World War II that marked the heyday of British, as well as American, communications intelligence. Under the rubrics "Ultra" and "Magic," German and Japanese communications were intercepted and decrypted, and vast amounts of accurate and timely information were made available to British and American political and military leaders. While measuring the precise extent of its impact on the course of the war remains a huge historical task, it is obvious that comint played an invaluable role in the Allied defeat of the Axis powers.[62]

One of the clearest cases in which comint's contribution was crucial was the U.S. Navy's victory over the Japanese at the Battle of Midway. Japan hoped to exploit its remarkable success at Pearl Harbor in December 1941 by seizing the strategically located island of Midway and, in the process, destroying what remained of U.S. naval forces in the Pacific. Had the Japanese plan worked, Hawaii would have been open to invasion, and the United States might well have had to seek peace on Tokyo's terms. For the Japanese, a quick victory in the Pacific was vital, since fighting a protracted war with the more populous and potentially more powerful United States invited eventual disaster.

Unknown to the Japanese, U.S. Navy cryptologists in Hawaii were intercepting and decoding the Japanese navy's encoded communications. As a result, American forces knew in advance Japan's plan for attacking Midway.[63] Armed with that intelligence, Adm. Chester Nimitz ambushed the Japanese naval armada north of the island on June 4, 1942, destroying four enemy carriers and virtually eliminating Japan's ability to carry out further large-scale operations in the Pacific. The Battle of Midway was a decisive defeat for the Japanese and a turning point in the war; it ended any hope on Japan's part that the war could be won quickly, if at all.[64]

While we would expect that a country's most sensitive radio messages would be encrypted to protect their confidentiality, some areas of communications intelligence are independent of cryptanalysis. Because of the expense and difficulty involved, some radio traffic is not encrypted; for example, tactical voice communications, such as between airplanes and ground control stations, are often broadcast "in the clear." In other cases, message traffic is not encrypted because it is believed, rightly or wrongly, that an adversary does not wish to, or cannot, intercept or (because of the large volumes of information involved) process it. For example, commercial traffic is typically not encrypted, although some of it could be of value to a potential adversary. Finally, one should not underestimate the importance of simple inertia: for example, the United States made only a belated response to the discovery that long-distance telephone traffic transmitted via microwave towers was being intercepted by countries from their various diplomatic sites in the country.[65]

In addition, a technique known as "traffic analysis" can derive useful information from fluctuations in the volume and other external characteristics of radio communications, even when the content of the messages cannot be understood. For example, if an army headquarters and its subordinate command posts exchange an unusually large number of messages, an analyst might conclude that an important operation is about to take place.[66] Similarly, by means of "direction finding," or "DF-ing"—a technique for determining the geographic origin of a radio signal—one can determine the location of the ship, plane, or command post that is transmitting it.

In World War II, for example, German submarines (U-boats) operating on the high seas used their radios to communicate with each other and with the naval high command on land. The German navy's use of "wolfpack" tactics against the Allied convoys required a significant amount of signaling among the U-boats and their headquarters to coordinate and concentrate attacks. However, this left the submarines vulnerable to "DF-ing" by British and American radio intercept posts and by the warships escorting the convoys. While not as valuable as the actual decryption of German naval communications, Allied DF operations were an important intelligence tool in the Battle of the Atlantic. Combined with code breaking, they made it possible for many of the Allied convoys to avoid the German wolfpacks altogether, and as time went on, they assisted in American and British efforts to hunt and sink U-boats.[67]

While most comint involves interception of radio messages, messages being transmitted by wire also can be intercepted. This requires physical access to the wires and so is of less general application than comint involving radio traffic, although in particular cases it may be important. For example, wiretaps may readily be maintained on telephone lines to an adversary's embassy or consulate in one's own country.

On occasion it may be possible to gain surreptitious access, even outside one's own country, to telephone or telegraph wires that an adversary is using. For example, in the divided cities of Vienna and Berlin in the early and mid-1950s, British and American intelligence managed to tap wires used by the Soviet military authorities. In Berlin, this involved elaborate secret tunneling from a point in the American sector of the city under the sector border to intercept cables running entirely within the Soviet sector.[68]

A related technique is the tapping of undersea cables used by an adversary. For example, in the 1970s, divers operating from a U.S. submarine were able to tap beneath the Sea of Okhotsk a Soviet undersea cable that connected the Soviet naval base at Petropavlovsk on the Kamchatka Peninsula with Vladivostok and Moscow. The divers attached a device that recorded the conversations; the recordings would be picked up during periodic visits to the site.[69]

By surreptitious means it may also be possible to gain access to the very equipment used in sending or receiving encoded communications. For example, a former British intelligence officer recounts his service's success in compromising Egyptian diplomatic communications with the placement of an electronic listening device in close proximity to the enciphering machine located in Egypt's London embassy. Posing as telephone repairmen, British intelligence officers were able to plant in a nearby phone a device capable of picking up the distinct sounds made when the Egyptians configured the machine's initial settings. With this information, British code breakers were able to duplicate those settings on their own model of the widely used machine, and in short order they were breaking the enciphered Egyptian communications. Similar operations have involved the bugging of electric typewriters while they were being shipped to a country's embassy.[70]

Technological advances in telecommunications have posed new problems for communications intelligence collection. Whereas the interception of traditional radio transmissions depends on the ability to place a receiving antenna of sufficient sensitivity at the right location, and the tapping of standard telephone lines is a matter of obtaining physical access, the interception of newer communication methods poses harder problems. For example, fiber-optic cables, which have been adopted commercially because they provide much greater bandwidth (that is, ability to transmit more information per unit of time), are also much harder to tap than the wires that they replace.[71] Similarly, cellular telephones, despite the fact that they transmit via the airwaves, pose difficult problems because of the complex algorithms according to which individual phone calls are handled as the caller moves from one location to another.[72]

Telemetry Intelligence (Telint)

The other forms of sigint are newer than comint, and they reflect the expanding military use of electromagnetic phenomena. Telemetry intelligence, or *telint,* is similar in concept to comint except that the communications on which one is eavesdropping are between a test vehicle (such as a missile) and a ground station, and they consist not of words but the readings from various sensors and other on-board equipment. (These communications are known as telemetry—"measuring from afar.") The values of such variables as the acceleration the vehicle is undergoing, the temperature at various points within the vehicle, the rates of flow of fuels, and so forth, taken together, give engineers on the ground a picture of what is happening on the test vehicle. This helps the engineers troubleshoot any problems that may have occurred during the test and perfect the vehicle's performance.

At the same time, such information is obviously valuable to potential adversaries. If they can intercept and interpret these data streams, they will gain insight into new weapon systems when they are still in the test stage. (The analysis of telemetry data is a very challenging task; along with cryptanalysis, it is discussed in the next chapter as a type of intelligence analysis.) Thus, just as in the case of comint, the country conducting the test may seek to deny others access to telemetric information by broadcasting it back to ground stations in encrypted form. Alternatively, the telemetry data may be recorded and kept on board the test vehicle to be recovered and extracted later. This process, called "encapsulation," secures the data against interception; however, it may be a risky procedure, since in the case of a catastrophic failure of the test vehicle, precisely when the telemetry data would most useful, the "capsule" containing it may be destroyed or hard to locate.

Electronics Intelligence (Elint)

Electronics intelligence, or *elint,* involves monitoring and analyzing noncommunication electromagnetic emanations from foreign military equipment. At its most basic level, elint enables a country to keep track of key elements of another country's armed forces (such as its air defense radars, command and control centers, etc.), providing what is sometimes referred to as an "electronic order of battle." The EORSAT (Elint Ocean Reconnaissance Satellite) system used by the former Soviet Union, and now Russia, is an example of this kind of monitoring. For years, these space collectors have been used to locate and track U.S. warships by intercepting the routine electronic (such as radar) signals emitted by the ships as they travel on the high seas.[73]

However, elint collection involves more than just detecting the presence of an emitter. By intercepting a radar signal, for example, one can determine various operating characteristics of the radar, such as its beam width (how much space it can scan at one time) and its maximum operational range. For example, the range of a radar that emits discrete pulses can be determined from the pulse repetition rate (the number of discrete pulses, or "bundles," of radio waves emitted per second). Thus, British scientific intelligence during World War II was able to deduce from the fact that the German Freya air defense radar operated at a pulse repetition rate of five hundred pulses per second that its maximum range was three hundred kilometers.[74]

A more recent case of elint's value was exhibited during Israel's 1982 offensive into Lebanon. As the Israeli army moved into Lebanon in an effort to eliminate Palestine Liberation Organization (PLO) forces operating from there, the Israeli high command was concerned about a possible attack on its flank by a concentration of Syrian troops and tanks in the Bekaa Valley in eastern Lebanon. Protecting those forces was an array of Syrian SAM batteries. Using small, pilotless, slow-flying drones, the Israelis were able to trick the Syrian batteries into turning on their fire control radars, by having the drones emit signals that made them appear to be planes; the Syrian emissions were then collected by a second set of drones. Based on this information, the Israelis were able to determine the operational characteristics of the SAM radars and pinpoint their locations. As a result, within a few short hours, the Israeli air force was able to destroy virtually all the Syrian batteries, gain uncontested control of the sky over Lebanon, and eliminate any serious possibility that the now exposed Syrian forces would join the battle on the side of the PLO.[75]

Measurements and Signatures Intelligence (Masint)

The possibilities for technical intelligence are limited only by the laws of physics and human ingenuity. In addition to photint and sigint, other techniques have been used to collect intelligence. These have been grouped together under the heading of measurements and signatures intelligence, or *masint,* although they do not have much in common with each other (aside from their being neither photint nor sigint).[76]

For example, special sensors have been developed to detect and characterize nuclear detonations. These include seismometers, which measure the shock waves associated with underground nuclear tests; devices to detect the radioactivity associated with nuclear materials or the fallout of above-ground nuclear tests; and sensors for the remote detection of the flashes of light produced by above-ground nuclear tests.[77] A different kind of sensor, sonar, uses another natural phenomenon, sound waves, to detect submarines under the ocean's surface; aside from its location, other characteristics of the submarine may be determinable from an analysis of the sounds it emits or reflects.[78]

Platforms for Intelligence Collection

In public discussion and in our survey so far, the emphasis has been on collection by satellite-based systems. Satellites have the obvious advantage of being able to overfly any part of the world, without respect for international boundaries.[79] For this reason, they are particularly valuable for collecting intelligence against countries to which other forms of access are effectively barred by their isolation and strict security measures. However, they have certain drawbacks as well:

- They are, in general, much more expensive than other reconnaissance platforms.[80]
- They cannot get very close to their targets (satellites in low earth orbit generally remain at altitudes well above a hundred miles, while those in geostationary orbit must be at an altitude of 22,400 miles).
- They are relatively useless a large part of the time even if their orbits are calculated to maximize the intelligence they gather (in other words, a photographic reconnaissance satellite that earns its keep by taking pictures of Russia or the Middle East must nevertheless, because of the laws of orbital physics, spend a great deal of less productive time over the Southern Hemisphere as well).
- Their orbits are predictable, so the adversary may be able to warn his troops and sensitive installations of when they will be vulnerable to observation by a reconnaissance satellite.[81]

Thus, while the advantages of space reconnaissance are many and substantial, other kinds of platforms continue to play important roles in the area of technical collection. Airplanes, for instance, can fly missions along the periphery of an adversary's territory; they can intercept communications that cannot be intercepted from space; they can take pictures of areas near territorial boundaries, while remaining safely out of the target country's airspace; and they can intercept radar signals from the adversary's air defense radars, some of which may have become active precisely to determine the airplane's course. Pilotless aircraft (unmanned aerial vehicles, or UAVs) may be used in areas where enemy air defenses pose an unacceptably high risk to pilots and crew of manned vehicles. Aircraft have many advantages (corresponding to the disadvantages of satellites listed above): they are cheaper than satellites, they can get closer to their targets, they can hover over areas of interest, and, perhaps most important, their trajectories cannot be predicted.

In the 1990–91 Gulf War, AWACS (Airborne Warning and Control System) and J-STARS (Joint Surveillance Target Attack Radar System) surveillance aircraft flying behind American lines allowed U.S. commanders to track and target Iraqi air and troop movements on virtually a real-time basis. J-STARS in particular provided critical data on the disposition of Iraq's ground forces just prior to the start of the coalition's offensive, reassuring the coalition that its surprise maneuver around the enemy's right flank would go virtually unchallenged. During the Battle of Al-Khafji on January 29, 1991, J-STARS detected an Iraqi convoy of follow-on forces moving south from Kuwait City. This information was immediately passed to coalition commanders, who ordered air strikes against the advancing Iraqi troops. Within hours, fifty-eight of the convoy's sixty-one vehicles had been destroyed.[82]

The NATO operation in Kosovo in 1999 (Operation Allied Force) saw an "unprecedented" used of UAVs for reconnaissance purposes, "reducing the need to send manned aircraft into hostile airspace."[83] The flexibility of UAVs was underlined by the following observation by senior U.S. officials: "While a significant number of UAVs were lost, their ability to loiter over hostile territory enabled them to provide surveillance information unavailable otherwise and avoided the risk of losing aircrews. Moreover, UAVs are designed deliberately to be expendable, with acceptable cost a higher priority than survivability."

Platforms other than aircraft can also be useful for technical intelligence collection. Vans and trucks can clandestinely monitor communications and signals of military, diplomatic, or scientific installations while parked nearby. Similarly, ships can intercept radio signals from off an adversary's coast. Seaborne or ground-based radars, if they can be located close enough to a site where test missiles are launched or where warheads reenter the earth's atmosphere, can track an adversary's missile flight tests and determine some of the missile's characteristics. Ground-based sites, depending on location, also can be used to intercept various radio signals, including even signals that may have inadvertently bounced off the surface of the moon.[84] Finally, miniaturization of listening devices and other sensors allows intelligence services to collect technical intelligence when a human agent can get close enough to the target and surreptitiously "plant" the sensor.[85]

In short, collection platforms can range from the mundane to the exotic. For a modern, technologically advanced intelligence community, the decision about which platforms to use and in what combinations is principally a product of two assessments: Which platforms can best collect the desired intelligence? Second, what are the relative costs and risks involved in using particular platforms?

COMPARISON OF HUMINT AND TECHINT

Over the years, there has been a continuing debate in the United States concerning the relative importance of humint and techint. On one side are those who view technical intelligence as primary and as likely to keep increasing in relative importance as technology advances; on the other are those who think technical intelligence has been overemphasized at the expense of traditional espionage and that it is necessary to right the balance.

Perhaps the most striking contribution to the debate has been the spirited defense of techint's primacy in the memoirs of Adm. Stansfield Turner, President Carter's director of central intelligence (DCI):

> Now that we have technical systems ranging from satellites traveling in space over the entire globe, to aircraft flying in free airspace, to miniature sensors surreptitiously positioned close to difficult targets, we are approaching a time when we will be able to survey almost any point on the earth's surface with some sensor, and probably with more than one. We can take detailed photographs from very long distances, detect heat sources through infrared devices, pinpoint metal with magnetic detectors, distinguish between barely moving and stationary objects through the use of Doppler radar, use radar to detect objects that are covered or hidden by darkness, eavesdrop on all manner of signals from the human voice to electronic radio waves, detect nuclear radiation with refined Geiger counters, and sense underground explosions at long distances with seismic devices. Most of the activities we want to monitor give off several kinds of signals. Tanks in battle can be detected by the heat from their engines, the magnetism in their armor, or photographs. A nuclear weapons plant emits radiation, has a particular external physical shape, and receives certain types of supplies. One way or another, we should soon be able to keep track of most activities on the surface of the earth, day or night, good weather or bad.[86]

The sheer technological prowess involved in creating these sorts of technical collection devices is indeed breathtaking. Nevertheless, admiration for the technology can easily lead to an overestimation of what techint can accomplish and a concomitant depreciation of human intelligence. In the United States, this view was particularly prevalent during the middle and late 1970s; since that time, however, humint's importance has received renewed recognition.

The strengths of techint are well described in the passage quoted above. Technical intelligence was indispensable to the United States for the collection of the major part of the information it obtained about the Soviet Union. It should be noted, however, that in many other countries a large part of such information is publicly available. Information about the size and general composition of the armed forces and the development of major new weapon systems, for example, is available in most countries from official (especially budgetary and parliamentary) documents. However, elaborate and costly technical intelligence methods were required to collect such information about the Soviet Union, because of the regime's pervasive secrecy on military issues in particular, and national security affairs in general. Much of the technical collection effort that was developed over the years was devoted to countering the effects of this secrecy.

Nevertheless, since the collapse of the Soviet Union and the Warsaw Pact, the number of "hard targets" has been substantially reduced and, with it, the need to rely so heavily on technical collection for the bulk of intelligence. Of course, closed societies still exist, and some of them, such as North Korea, are of major intelligence interest; in this case, the heavy reliance on techint is likely to continue. A more interesting case would be that of the People's Republic of China, which remains a difficult country in which to conduct espionage but that is vastly more open in terms of travel and communication than the Soviet Union ever was.

Moreover, with respect to many of the categories of information that all countries keep secret—such as political and military intentions and plans—human intelligence collection always was, and still is, required. Proponents of humint stress that despite technological progress, traditional espionage remains necessary to provide information about the intentions, political activity, and strategic concepts of an adversary's leadership. Technical intelligence, for example, clearly showed Iraq's army massing on the Kuwaiti border in July 1990; what it could not illuminate was Saddam Hussein's intention: Would he invade Kuwait, or was he trying to scare it into making financial concessions? By contrast, one well-placed agent on the Polish army's general staff was able to report on the Polish government's secret decision in late 1981 to impose martial law in order to crush Solidarity, the independent labor movement.[87] In short, understanding the adversary's intentions, his strategy, and his perception of the situation in which he finds himself is often the most important intelligence information we could have.

Interception of communications among the adversary's political and military leadership (high-level comint) can also provide intelligence of this sort; it would be similar to having a human agent with excellent access to the adversary's leaders. Obtaining this information through comint, however, is much more difficult than the Turner statement suggests. First of all, an adversary may be expected to encrypt its most sensitive communications. In this connection, it should be noted that human intelligence collection can be useful and even critical in this regard as well: it can provide codebooks or other information that facilitate the decrypting of messages. For example, in the early 1930s, French intelligence obtained from an agent in Germany important information about the German coding machine known as "Enigma," including instructions for its use, some details of its construction, and the "keys" specifying how the machine was to be configured on a daily basis. This information was shared with the Polish intelligence service, which achieved major cryptanalytic breakthroughs that formed the basis of the eventual British success with Ultra during World War II.[88]

Second, most comint capabilities can be defeated by keeping messages off the air—that is, transmitting them via wire instead. Intercepting "landline" messages requires gaining access to the wires, which is likely to be difficult in most cases. Furthermore, as already noted, wires are being replaced by fiber-optic cables, which use coherent light (laser beams) to carry messages and are far less vulnerable to wiretapping.

In addition, all types of technological intelligence collection, including comint, suffer from a potential "embarrassment of riches." Because of the global reach of the technical collection systems, there must be some method by which they are told which targets to observe and which to ignore.[89] While it may be correct that "we [soon] will be able to survey almost any point on the earth's surface with some sensor," no one could survey them all at the same time, and even if one could, one would not be able to process and analyze all the data the sensors could collect.

Thus, the existence of technical capabilities like those described by Turner does not imply that nothing of importance on the earth's surface can escape the notice of a well-equipped intelligence service. As became evident from inspections conducted after the Gulf War, American technical collection before the war had not been, in and of itself, sufficient to keep track of Iraq's effort to build a nuclear weapon.[90] The issue is not whether technical collection is valuable; obviously it is. Rather, the point is simply that the earth is a large, diverse, and in some areas, busy place. Accordingly, much depends on the ability to target sensors appropriately. Human intelligence collection can provide the essential first indication that something of interest is occurring or will occur at a given location. This makes it possible to target the technical systems on that area. Without such clues, the systems would be less efficient and might miss important developments either for long periods or altogether.

A human intelligence source can also provide the clues necessary to interpret the raw data gathered by a technical collection system. Even with a good picture of a building, for example, an intelligence analyst may not be able to determine its function. However, a human source familiar with it may be able to explain that the presence of a certain detail, not otherwise remarkable, indicates that the building was designed for a specific purpose connected with a specific military program. Without the human source, the detail might not have been noticed or its significance understood. But once this "signature" is recognized, pictures of similar buildings can be examined to see if the same detail is present.

In a number of cases, however, the signatures of possible collection targets are getting more difficult to identify or, if identifiable, to track. In some instances, this is because targets have gotten smaller, more mobile, or have gone underground. In other cases, this is because the activity that is of intelligence interest (such as biological or chemical weapons research) is not readily distinguishable from related but legitimate functions (such as the production of pharmaceuticals or pesticides). In addition, it may be possible in some instances to eliminate key telltale signatures altogether. After the Gulf War, for example, the UN team sent to Iraq to find and dismantle that country's nuclear weapons facilities discovered that Iraq had carefully constructed many of the buildings in the program to avoid detection by satellites and other technical collection systems. Some had been built to prevent radioactive emissions, while others had been designed to draw as little attention as possible to themselves, by aping the physical appearance of legitimate industrial plants. Apparently, it was not until an Iraqi engineer knowledgeable about Saddam Hussein's effort to build a bomb defected after the war that these facilities were identified as belonging to Iraq's nuclear weapons program.[91]

With respect to some kinds of intelligence information, however, the problem of correctly targeting technical intelligence collection systems may be virtually insoluble. For example, humint is likely to be necessary to collect crucial information about nongovernmental targets (such as terrorist organizations) that lack the fixed facilities or communication networks that are vulnerable to technical collection. In other words, the fewer known locations that a group can be associated with, the harder it is to target technical sensors on it. Intelligence collection against such groups is likely to depend heavily on the ability to infiltrate the group or to recruit its members as informants. If groups of this sort become important intelligence targets, human intelligence collection will become more important as well.

Humint and techint, then, can serve complementary roles; separately, they can provide distinct kinds of information. The collapse of the "Iron Curtain" has, of course, eliminated the original reason behind the development by the United States of a sophisticated system of technical collection. However, continuing obligations to monitor the arsenals of other states, especially states with closed societies and active programs to develop weapons of mass destruction, along with a growing demand from the American military for technical intelligence to support its operations, suggests that a substantial shift away from technical intelligence collection is not likely. On the other hand, requirements for intelligence on new states, new political actors, and new concerns are perhaps best addressed by human collection. While the correct mix of humint and techint will be, as it has been in the past, a matter of debate, there is little doubt that a global power like the United States will continue to require both.

This discussion of humint and techint has addressed their relative importance in strategic intelligence—intelligence directed at national-level decision makers. However, it is also important to note that advances in telecommunications and computing capability have made it possible for the information collected by techint systems (including those developed for national-level purposes) to be made available to commanders on the battlefield in real time—or at any rate, sufficiently quickly to be useful for tactical purposes. This development is still in its early stages, but it promises to become an important use for techint systems.[92]

OPEN-SOURCE COLLECTION

Publications and Broadcasts

No discussion of intelligence collection would be complete without reference to the gathering of information from open sources—that is, newspapers, books, radio and television broadcasts, the Internet, and any other public source of information.

The importance of open sources in the intelligence process is a matter of dispute and is ultimately tied to basic questions about the nature of intelligence. One view, exemplified by Sherman Kent, is that the bulk of "high-level foreign positive intelligence . . . must be through unromantic open-and-above-board observation and research."[93] The more traditional view, on the other hand, is that while open sources may provide important context and background, the key facts, such as an adversary's specific intentions, must be obtained primarily, if not solely, from nonpublic sources, by means of espionage or technical collection.

This question is discussed at length in chapter 7. At this point, the focus will be on the various uses to which open-source information can be put. For example, a standard task of military intelligence officers has been to prepare vast compendia of information concerning countries in which future military operations may have to be conducted. Such compendia ideally include all information that might be useful to a military staff. Information concerning the country's geography, its communications and transportation networks, key military and economic facilities, and so forth would have to be included in sufficient detail to allow the planner to make a wide range of decisions, such as determining how quickly troops and supplies could be moved from point A to point B.

Except in the case of the most secretive countries (such as the former Soviet Union, which admitted in 1988 that it had falsified maps as a security measure),[94] much of this information will be available in open-source literature: road and railroad maps and timetables, newspaper and magazine articles, government economic and statistical reports, and even old travel guides. Collecting and cataloging it are other matters. Huge amounts of information are involved, and the resources needed to collect it for every relevant country are unlikely ever to be available. If, as discussed in the next chapter, the U.S. military force that invaded Grenada in 1983 was not supplied with adequate maps and other information about the island, this was not due to any difficulty in collecting the information but rather to the failure to allocate sufficient resources to what had probably seemed to many a small, out-of-the-way island.

Similarly, a vast profusion of statistical sources throughout the world publish economic data. Deciding what should be collected, however, requires some sense of what intelligence requirements are likely to be. Economic data may be needed to support the formulation of policy on international trade or economic sanctions, to deal with the effects of shortages and international cartels (such as the Organization of Petroleum Exporting Countries), and so forth. Other kinds of economic data, such as might result from the monitoring of cash flows, could shed light on the international drug trade. Finally, economic intelligence may be needed to support political and military analyses. During World War II, for example, economists of the Office of Strategic Services, or OSS (working for the U.S. air staff in Europe) employed a wide array of largely unclassified economic data to help plan a strategic bombing campaign; the goal was to destroy the parts of the German industrial infrastructure—such as oil and ball bearing plants—that were believed to be vital to sustaining the Nazi war effort.[95] In more recent times, predictions of Soviet behavior in the late 1980s were dominated by questions of how its economic situation would affect other areas of policy. Each of these intelligence requirements calls for different sorts of economic data.

In addition to these obvious types of open-source materials, intelligence analysts require the same sorts of information—speeches by prominent political figures, texts of laws and resolutions, census and other demographic data—that would be required for any academic analysis of the political or social conditions in a foreign country; indeed, the end product may be similar.

Depending on the available resources, an intelligence agency may be able to collect specialized data in amounts that would overwhelm an academic researcher. For example, an important technique for understanding the policies and policy-making processes of "closed" political systems involves tracing the careers of a large number of individuals to determine which midlevel officials are the protégées, or "clients," of which senior executives. Once these patron-client relationships have been identified, an analyst can, by noting the promotions and demotions of the clients, determine the relative standings of their high-level patrons. To do this, however, requires the collection and maintenance of an extensive biographical data base. It would involve scanning all major newspapers and news broadcasts; recording every news item that indicates the promotion, demotion, or transfer of an official or that links two officials; and computerizing the resulting data base to make it useful for researchers. A scholar, even an academic institute, might be hard pressed to undertake such a task.[96]

Diplomatic and Attaché Reporting

Another means of collecting information—one that might be regarded as a composite of humint and open source, because it is obtained by human agents but in a straightforward and aboveboard manner—would be the reports diplomats and military attachés file concerning events in the countries to which they are posted. Indeed, the line between diplomat and intelligence officer has not always been clear-cut. As one historian of diplomacy primly puts it, "Ambassadors sometimes readily crossed the nebulous line between legitimate gathering of information and espionage and other ill-reputed activities."[97] But even today, when the two functions are separate, diplomatic reports on the political situation in the host country can be important inputs to any political analysis. A diplomat who has good access to major political figures in a country or a sophisticated appreciation of the country's history and political makeup should be able to provide insights into the internal political situation that would not be found in the media.[98]

Similarly, military attachés, to the extent they have access to military officers of their host country, can gain insights into its military establishment, such as the personalities and competence of the leading military officers, as well as their characteristic ways of thought, views on military doctrine, and relations with the civilian leadership. In addition, attachés may be invited to observe military exercises or attend reviews or ceremonial occasions where new military equipment is paraded or flown. They also may be able to travel in the host country and thus observe airfields, harbors, and other military and civilian installations of interest.[99]

Other Overt Human Sources

Diplomats and attachés are not the only foreigners who visit countries and report their observations. For example, the 1987 agreement between the United States and the USSR on the elimination of intermediate-range and shorter-range missiles (the INF Treaty) and, more recently, the Strategic Arms Reduction Treaty (START) provides that each party send inspectors to specified military facilities of the other party to ascertain whether the country is complying with the treaty's terms. The inspectors have greater access to those facilities than attachés or other visitors would have. Obviously, their reports will contain valuable information concerning their host's military forces.

Similarly, businessmen, scientists, and other travelers learn information about the countries they visit—information that while not officially secret is not available in the public media. Whether this information makes its way to their country's government depends, in a country whose citizens do not need special permission to travel abroad, on the willingness of such travelers to report it. But the general increase in international trade, travel, and research has meant that the opportunities for such overt human collection have grown substantially in recent years.

Chapter 3

What Does It All Mean? Intelligence Analysis and Production

WHAT IS ANALYSIS?

Analysis refers to the process of transforming the bits and pieces of information that are collected in whatever fashion into something that is usable by policy makers and military commanders. The result, or "intelligence product," can take the form of short memorandums, elaborate formal reports, briefings, or any other means of presenting information. This section indicates the breadth of analytical techniques. In describing these activities, standard intelligence terminology is not always used; indeed, analysis does not have any standard categories. Furthermore, the categories that do exist are neither precise nor mutually exclusive. An attempt has been made here to arrange the techniques from the most technical, such as the decryption of encrypted messages, to the most speculative, such as the prediction of future social and political trends. A subsequent section discusses the variety of intelligence products and the functions they serve.

Technical Analysis

We use the term "technical analysis" here to refer to analytical methods that transform highly specialized data, totally or virtually incomprehensible to everyone but the specialist, into data that other intelligence analysts can use. The examples discussed are cryptanalysis (which transforms seemingly random strings of letters or numbers into the text of a message in a known language), telemetry analysis (which transforms a radio signal into a group of time series describing the performance of a missile or other test vehicle), and photo interpretation (which identifies and measures objects in a photograph).

Cryptanalysis Cryptanalysis refers to the solving, or "breaking," of enemy codes and ciphers, thereby enabling analysts to transform an intercepted encrypted message into its original, meaningful form. In most cases, the interception involves the reception of radio signals by someone other than their intended recipient. However, the cryptanalytic problem is the same in the case of an encrypted message taken from a captured courier, an encrypted letter opened by postal censorship, or an encrypted telegram obtained by tapping a telegraph cable.

In technical usage, the terms *code* and *cipher* refer to different methods of encryption. In a code, a word or phrase (signifying a thing, concept, or location) is replaced by the group of digits or letters (which may or may not form an actual word) that is found opposite that word or phrase in a given codebook. Thus, the message "Attack on Saturday" would be encrypted by finding the code group for "attack" (say, FGHJ) and that for "Saturday" (say, ADFK), thus producing the encrypted message FGHJ ADFK. If a word is not found in the codebook, the sender can either reword the message to use words and phrases that do appear in it or spell out the missing word using special code groups for individual letters or syllables.

In a cipher, on the other hand, each letter in the original message—called the *plaintext*—is replaced, following some formula or algorithm, by another letter, thereby forming the *ciphertext.* (In a "transposition" cipher, the letters of the original message are retained but are transmitted in a jumbled order, according to some scheme.) For example, a cipher might consist of the rule that each letter be replaced by the letter following it in the alphabet. In this extremely simple cipher, the message in the example used above would be enciphered as BUUBDL PO TBUVSEBZ.

A more complicated cipher (still much too simple to offer any security) might consist of the following algorithm: replace the first letter of the message by the letter following it in the alphabet; the second letter, by the letter two places down in the alphabet; and so forth. (For the purposes of such a cipher, the alphabet would be envisaged as written in a circle, with the letter A immediately following the letter Z. Thus, the twenty-sixth letter of the message would be unchanged, while the twenty-seventh, like the first, would be replaced by its immediate successor, and so on.) The message would now read BVWEHQ VV BKEGERPO.

These techniques can be combined in various ways. For example, a coded message may itself be enciphered in the same way a plaintext might be. Thus, our sample message—encoded as before and then enciphered by the first method discussed—would yield the following "superenciphered" text: GHIK BEGL. The advantage of such a procedure is the greater security it offers: To recover the original message, an adversary must break both the code and the cipher. Typically, the code would remain in effect for a long time, while the cipher algorithm would change frequently. The reason is that while the former is quite difficult to change (each change of code means new codebooks must be distributed to each embassy, headquarters, or post that might send or receive messages), it is a simpler matter to change the cipher algorithm.

Cryptanalysis is the process of solving ("breaking") codes and ciphers—that is, reconstructing the adversary's codebook or figuring out the method he is using to encipher messages—using primarily the encrypted messages themselves. (*Decryption,* on the other hand, usually refers to the process by which the intended recipient—who, of course, already knows the code or cipher being used—recovers the plaintext.) *Cryptology* is the more general study of these matters, both for cryptanalytic purposes and for the devising of more secure codes and ciphers. *Cryptography* is sometimes used to refer specifically to the latter activity (the devising of codes and ciphers) but is sometimes used synonymously with cryptology.

The typical raw material with which cryptanalysis begins is a collection of encrypted messages. The task of cryptanalysis is to discern whatever patterns exist in the apparently meaningless jumble of letters or numbers and to relate those patterns to the known patterns that exist in the language in which the messages were presumably written. For example, in ordinary English text, the letter E appears more frequently than any other; therefore, in a group of messages enciphered in the simple substitution cipher discussed above (in which each letter of the plaintext is replaced by the one immediately following it in the alphabet), the letter F would probably be the most frequent.

Noticing this fact, the cryptanalyst would begin by postulating that F stands for E. He then might notice that UIF appears more frequently than any other three-letter word and assume that it stands for THE. At this point, he might well guess that each letter in the ciphertext stands for the letter immediately preceding it in the alphabet and, trying it out, would discover that this was indeed the case.

As may be seen by even this simple example, the amount of raw material a cryptanalyst can obtain is an important factor in determining whether a solution can be achieved. In a short message, E may not be particularly frequent: In our example ("Attack on Saturday"), it does not appear at all. In a longer message or series of messages, however, the laws of probability take over, and it would be extremely unlikely for the frequencies of the various letters (or small groups of letters) in the plaintext to differ much from the frequencies with which they appear in ordinary English text.[1]

The history of cryptology is a fascinating one, but it is impossible to go into it in detail here.[2] For our purposes, it will be sufficient to divide that history into three periods, according to the technology that was available for encrypting messages.

In the first period, running from antiquity to the 1930s, messages had to be encrypted by hand. Various techniques were available, including codebooks and substitution and transposition ciphers. By the end of this period, codebooks had grown to be cumbersome affairs, with thousands of entries. However, since they tended to be used for long periods, cryptanalysts could eventually reconstruct them. Similarly, cryptanalysts were helped by the fact that the complexity of ciphers was limited by the fact that all the steps involved in producing the ciphertext had to be performed by hand. Because the possibility of an encryption or decryption mistake increases as the cipher algorithm becomes more complex, it was not always practical to make ciphers harder to "crack."

Of course, the easiest way to break a code is to steal, capture, or otherwise obtain a copy of the codebook without letting the enemy know about it. Since producing a new codebook and distributing it to everyone who would need it is not an easy matter, a code was likely to remain in use for a long period of time, thus enhancing the usefulness of the captured book.

Before and during World War I, all the major European powers had special offices for decrypting foreign diplomatic and military messages. At the beginning of World War I, for example, the British managed to obtain (from captured or sunken ships) copies of the major German naval codebooks. The Germans took the precaution of further enciphering the coded messages, but the British decrypted them nevertheless.[3]

However, probably the most important British cryptanalytic success involved German diplomatic, rather than naval, codes. On January 17, 1917, British cryptanalysts decoded a message, known to history as the "Zimmermann telegram," in which the German foreign minister directed the German ambassador to Mexico to propose a German-Mexican alliance against the United States, in case the Americans reacted to German initiation of unrestricted submarine warfare (scheduled for February 1) by declaring war on Germany. Subsequent publication in U.S. newspapers of the telegram, which envisaged Mexico recovering Texas, New Mexico, and Arizona, created a firestorm that did much to make President Woodrow Wilson's decision to go to war inevitable. The release of the telegram was handled so skillfully that the Germans did not suspect that their code had been broken.[4]

In contrast to the European experience, American cryptography was in its infancy at the outbreak of World War I. The story of American cryptography during the war and in the following decade illustrates how, despite the immense intellectual challenge involved, it was still possible for an individual, working by himself or with a small group, to discover the basic principles of the art and to solve codes and ciphers used to encrypt the most sensitive messages. Indeed, Herbert Yardley relates how he was able, working for several hours on his own, to cryptanalyze a message to President Wilson from Col. Edward House, Wilson's personal representative, then on a diplomatic mission to Germany.[5] Yardley's account of his leadership of the U.S. Army's cryptanalytic unit once the United States entered the war, as well as of the State Department's "Black Chamber" after the war's end, indicates the extent to which cryptography was at that time an art rather than a science and how much it depended on the insights and intuitions of individuals working essentially by themselves.

However, in cryptology, as in many other areas of milit[illegible] and intelligence activities, World War I marked a crucial stage. According to [illegible] historian of the subject,

> The First World War marks the great turning point in the history of cryptology. Before, it was a small field; afterwards, it was big. Before, it was a science in its youth; afterwards, it had matured. The direct cause of this development was the enormous increase in radio communications.[6]

Increased radio traffic meant a greater advantage to be gained by breaking an enemy's code or cipher. At the same time, the increased amount of traffic meant that, other things being equal, codes or ciphers of the same complexity became more vulnerable to cryptanalysis, since the more raw material (encrypted in the same code or cipher) available, the greater the chance that the cryptanalyst will detect the repeating patterns that make a solution possible.

More radio traffic also meant that manual systems for encrypting and decrypting messages were more and more overloaded. This, plus the desire for more secure encryption systems, led to a second period, in which mechanical or electromechanical devices, such as the American Hagelin, the German Enigma, and the Japanese "Purple" (Alphabetical Typewriter 97) machines, were used to encipher texts.

Such machines could incorporate much more complicated enciphering algorithms or formulae than were feasible when enciphering had to be done manually. More complicated cryptanalytic techniques and procedures were therefore needed to solve these ciphers. Breaking them involved the development and use of primitive computers as well as advances in statistics and other branches of theoretical mathematics.[7] An extensive literature has evolved concerning the solving of electromechanical cipher machines such as Enigma and "Purple" during World War II.[8]

We are today in the third period, which is characterized by the use of computers both to encipher and decipher messages and to support cryptanalytic efforts. For obvious reasons, this subject is very sensitive, and not much information is publicly available about it. The rise of "public cryptography"—the study and use of cryptography by independent scholars and businessmen—has brought some information about it into the public domain.[9] However, it is not possible from unclassified sources to determine how the sophistication of public cryptography's methodology compares to that of intelligence agencies.

Nevertheless, a few things can be said about the current situation and the relative cryptologic strengths of various countries. Given the centrality of computers, it would seem likely that the U.S. lead in the area of supercomputing gives it an important advantage in breaking codes; to some extent, this may be balanced by other states' (for instance, Russia's) strengths in the area of theoretical mathematics.

At the same time, it would appear that advances in computer power (in terms of the speed with which the basic arithmetic operations may be performed) favor the defense. In other words, although an increase in computer power enables both the encrypter to use ciphers of greater complexity and the cryptanalyst to solve ciphers of greater complexity, the net effect is to favor the encrypter: A given increment in computer power allows complexities to be introduced into the cipher that the same increment in computer power cannot unravel. If this is so, the long-term prospects for cryptanalysis, at least as it attempts to break the ciphers of major powers using the most advanced technology, are in principle not very good. In practice, of course, a given cipher, because of some error in its construction, may not take full advantage of the available computer technology and therefore be weaker than it should have been. In addition, mistakes in using the cipher may allow cryptanalysts to solve it.[10] Finally, human agents may provide an adversary's codebooks, enciphering algorithms, etc., thereby enabling an intelligence agency to decrypt messages that had been encrypted using cryptologic systems that cryptanalysis was unable to crack.[11]

The Fragility of Cryptanalysis Cryptanalysis is among the more fragile of intelligence methods, since a country can change its cryptographic system once it realizes that an adversary can read its encrypted messages. Thus, it is not surprising that the American and British cryptanalytic successes during World War II were considered to be among the most vital secrets of the war, worthy of the most careful security arrangements that could be devised. The British success in mastering the German Enigma machine was kept secret for about thirty years, despite the large number of people involved in the operation.

The American experience was far different. In what might have been the worst security breach of the war, the *Chicago Tribune* published on June 7, 1942, an article on the U.S. victory at the Battle of Midway. Headlined "Navy Had Word of Jap Plan to Strike at Sea," it cited materials derived from decoded Japanese messages. In particular, it included the names of not only the Japanese carriers involved but also the light cruisers that had supported the would-be occupation forces. Furthermore, it asserted that when the Japanese fleet moved toward Midway, "all American outposts were warned" and that U.S. naval intelligence had been able to predict "a feint at some American base [Dutch Harbor, in the Aleutians], to be accompanied by a serious effort to invade and occupy another base [Midway Island]."[12]

A Japanese intelligence expert would probably have concluded from the article that the United States had been reading coded Japanese naval messages. The matter was referred to a grand jury in Chicago; however, no indictment was brought. It appears that the key U.S. officials ultimately decided against prosecution on the grounds that a trial would only call attention to the article and probably require a public confirmation of the fact that the United States was reading coded Japanese naval messages. (Ironically, on August 31, 1942, this very fact was mentioned by a congressman in a floor speech castigating the *Tribune*'s "unthinking and wicked misuse of the freedom of the press.")[13]

As for whether or not the Japanese benefited from this "leak," the jury is still out. It is true that on August 14, 1942, the Japanese navy introduced a new version of its code (dubbed JN-25d by U.S. cryptanalysts). The appearance of a new version of the code so soon after the previous version (JN-25c) had been introduced (on June 1) was suspicious.[14] However, the new version of the code "retained the characteristic of the broad JN-25 formula," thus allowing the United States to regain access to the Japanese message traffic more easily than if the Japanese had instituted an entirely new system.[15] Nevertheless, it did take the United States about four months to become as familiar with the JN-25d code as it had been with previous versions.[16]

A more clear-cut example, involving Britain this time, of the fragility of cryptanalysis occurred in 1927. During the preceding years the British cryptanalytic bureau, the Government Code and Cypher School, had been able to decipher messages between the Comintern (Communist International) headquarters and the Soviet government in Moscow, on the one hand, and the various Soviet representatives in London—the Soviet embassy as well as a trade delegation and a trade office of Arcos, the All-Russian Cooperative Society—on the other. By this means, the British government tracked the activities of the Soviet diplomats and trade representatives, activities that included espionage and involvement in British trade union affairs. In 1927, the British cited these departures from diplomatic decorum when they broke off diplomatic relations with the Soviet Union. Pressed in Parliament to defend their action, the British ministers revealed publicly their ability to read encrypted Soviet messages. The predictable result was that the Soviet Union introduced new ciphers, which the British were unable to break.[17]

A similar case, in which a democratically elected government revealed sensitive cryptanalytic capabilities in order to build support for its policies and thereby lost access to encrypted messages, seems to have occurred in the United States in 1986. Apparently to justify its eventual decision to bomb government facilities in Tripoli, Libya,

> President [Ronald] Reagan [the *Washington Post* reported] and his top advisers made an extraordinary disclosure of sensitive intelligence information . . . to demonstrate that United States has hard evidence that Libya . . . was directly responsible for the bombing of a West Berlin nightclub. . . .
>
> The specifics cited by the president[,] . . . sources said, will make it clear that the United States has the capability to intercept and decode Libya's sensitive diplomatic communications.[18]

The predictable result in fact occurred: "The public disclosure of decoded Libyan diplomatic cables has caused American intelligence analysts to lose a valuable source of information that may take weeks or months to replace, Administration officials said today."[19]

These examples demonstrate a general point about intelligence, a point that applies to other collection and analysis techniques as well: The better the available information, the more inhibited one is in using it and perhaps alerting the adversary to one's intelligence capabilities. This dilemma is strongest in the case of a democratic government that finds itself pressed to reveal detailed intelligence information to persuade the public that its policies are reasonable. But a form of the same dilemma exists for any government, under any circumstances, whenever it possesses specific intelligence information upon which it wishes to act.

The problem is most likely to come up in wartime, when the incentive for acting on the intelligence may be very great. For example, during World War II the British knew, from intercepted and deciphered communications, the precise schedule of the German ships bringing supplies across the Mediterranean to Gen. Erwin Rommel's forces in North Africa. Nevertheless, to prevent the Germans from becoming suspicious about the security of their communications, the British adopted the rule that no ship could be attacked before it had been overflown by reconnaissance aircraft, thus providing the Germans with an apparent explanation of how the British had been able to target it.

This point is also illustrated by the story that British Prime Minister Winston Churchill knew in advance about the particularly destructive German air raid on the English city of Coventry but did nothing to alert its air defenses or emergency services for fear of compromising the British ability to read encrypted Luftwaffe messages. Historical research, however, seems to have established that this story is not true: the available comint did not allow the British to identify Coventry as the raid's target.[20] Nevertheless, the tale provides a particularly dramatic illustration of the moral and strategic dilemmas that a government *could* face in deciding whether to risk an intelligence source by acting on the information it provides.

Telemetry Analysis Telemetry is the radio transmission of information from a test vehicle to a ground station—information on the vehicle's operation (for instance, its acceleration or the thrust generated by its engine), its condition (such as the temperature of various components or the amount of vibration it is undergoing), or other characteristics. The purpose is to provide the data that engineers conducting the test need to assess the vehicle's performance or, in case of failure, to determine the cause. Using this information, the engineers reconstruct the vehicle's flight profile and assure themselves of its reliability or make any necessary modifications.

The same radio signals, however, can be intercepted by a foreign intelligence service through a type of collection known as telemetry intelligence, or *telint*. Telemetry analysis is the process by which telint data are used to deduce the basic characteristics of the test vehicle. Of course, when the test engineers begin to interpret this data, they already know, from the design of the telemetry system, precisely to which missile characteristic each part of the data stream (or telemetry "channel") refers. The telemetry analysts working for a foreign intelligence service, on the other hand, begin with none of this information; they must figure out, from the raw radio data themselves, what characteristic of the missile is being measured by each channel.[21] Once the analysts have made these determinations, they can attempt to use the data to create a computer model of the missile, from which such characteristics as initial weight (launch weight) and payload (warhead "throw weight") can be derived.

Telemetry analysis was a particularly important tool for keeping abreast of developments in the Soviet Union's strategic weapons programs and for monitoring Moscow's compliance with arms control agreements. However, like cryptanalysis, telemetry analysis is fragile. Once a government understands the value of telemetry to an adversary in analyzing its weapons programs and understands how its own telemetry might be collected, it can take steps to deny that information. During the debate over the ratification of SALT II in 1979, for example, it became clear that the United States relied heavily on access to Soviet telemetry to monitor Soviet missile programs and to verify Soviet compliance with the treaty's provisions. In addition, by the late 1970s, Soviet intelligence had probably obtained, through espionage, a fairly thorough understanding of how the United States could collect Soviet missile telemetry from space. Whatever the precise reasons, from that period on, the Soviet Union increasingly encrypted telemetry from its strategic missile tests, concealing that data from U.S. intelligence.[22]

It is not clear what the prospects are for the successful cryptanalysis of encrypted telemetry. In any case, there are methods other than encryption that can be used to deny telemetric information to an adversary's intelligence service. As noted in the previous chapter, the data may be recorded on tape inside some kind of hardened capsule (similar to the "cockpit voice recorder" on commercial aircraft) that can survive reentry into the atmosphere and the impact of the landing and then be recovered. Similarly, telemetric data from a cruise missile or experimental plane can be broadcast at very low power to a "chase" plane flying near it and recorded on board the plane; if the radio signal is sufficiently weak, it might prove impossible to intercept outside the test range.

Photo Interpretation Despite the sophistication of the equipment that can take pictures deep within otherwise inaccessible territory, no substitute has been found for the human eye when it comes to figuring out what those photographs show. This is not as simple a task as it might seem; while it is often said that photographs are a particularly persuasive form of intelligence (in the sense that senior officials feel more confident about the intelligence they are getting when they can "see it for themselves"), the average surveillance photograph is likely to be unintelligible to the layman. It is only after the photo interpreter (PI) points out and labels the interesting items that ordinary viewers can understand what they are seeing.[23]

The quality of a photographic reconnaissance system is typically measured by what is called the "ground resolution distance." While the precise meaning of this term is quite technical, it may be thought of as the size of the smallest object that can be distinguished from neighboring objects or from the background. Although many other factors must be taken into account to determine how well a photograph can be interpreted, ground resolution distance is "nevertheless . . . a convenient measure useful in making gross comparisons and evaluations."[24] As ground resolution improves, so too will the amount of information that potentially can be derived from a photograph. In general, a photograph's quality is judged on the basis of the range of analysis that can be undertaken with respect to a particular target. For example, can an aircraft be detected (as a plane), generally identified (as a particular kind of plane), precisely identified (as a particular variant of that kind of plane), or (for purposes of technical analysis) described in detail?[25]

The actual ground resolution distances an intelligence service's photographic surveillance satellites can obtain are classified, because this information would tell adversaries what details (of military equipment, facilities, and so forth) the service could, or could not, see. Such information would be useful to any military planner who wants to keep certain details of new weapons systems secret. Planners of deception efforts would also find this information useful, since it would tell them how closely a decoy would have to resemble the real object to make the two indistinguishable in photographic surveillance.

However good the resolution, all sorts of important information cannot be learned directly from a photograph. PIs must often work from what are called "signatures"—specific details that, on the basis of experience or logic, are associated with certain pieces of equipment, certain activities, intention to take certain steps in the future, and so forth.[26] For example, the lengthening of an airfield runway would suggest the pending arrival of a new type of aircraft requiring the longer runway; from experience, a PI might know that a given runway length is correlated with a given type of airplane and could predict that such an aircraft type was to be stationed at that airfield. Similarly, in a lighter vein, it was thought possible to distinguish a military base for Soviet troops from a Cuban base by the presence of a soccer field as opposed to a baseball diamond.

One method of using signatures that the United States has relied on goes by the fanciful name of "crateology"—the correlation between military equipment and the type and size of crates in which it is usually shipped. Once it has been determined that, for example, a particular plane or missile has been shipped in crates of a certain size, crateology suggests that other boxes of the same size whose contents have not been observed directly may be assumed to contain that type of plane or missile.[27]

The usefulness of such signatures derives from the tendency of most organizations—military ones in particular—to follow routines, to do things "by the book." Thus, when the Soviet Union decided to deploy medium-range and intermediate-range ballistic missiles (MRBMs and IRBMs, respectively) in Cuba in 1962, it first prepared the island's defenses by deploying antiaircraft batteries along Cuba's coast in a (trapezoidal) pattern that PIs immediately recognized as the standard deployment arrangement for Soviet SA-2 (surface-to-air) missiles. It was this discovery that alerted U.S. intelligence to the possibility that, in one participant's words, "something extraordinary was happening" on the island. Similarly, photos from a subsequent U-2 mission showed a significant amount of excavation and construction under way just west of Havana. While no missiles or missile-related equipment were actually seen at the site, the PIs were certain that the Soviets were building an IRBM site, based on the pattern of construction and excavation found there. Indeed, when one of the PIs "was shown the photos of the sites in Cuba, he opened one of his books and there was a photograph of an identical [IRBM] site in Russia."[28]

The use of signatures can be very productive, but it can also be misleading. During the Cuban missile crisis, for example, a critical piece of information being sought was the location of the missiles' nuclear warheads. Had they already been delivered to Cuba, and if so, where were they? Using signatures developed from photos of nuclear installations in the Soviet Union, American PIs had associated the storage of nuclear weapons with extensive and elaborate security measures. Because these weapons were being deployed outside the Soviet Union for the first time, it made sense to conclude that the warheads would be held under even tighter control. As a result, absent any signs of especially strict security at the launch sites or the weapons storage bunkers then under construction, the PIs believed that the warheads were not yet in Cuba.

However, in the aftermath of the crisis, a more thorough analysis of the photos revealed that the warheads had been at these sites all along, stored in rather innocuous-looking vans. Seeing no special security or activity around them, analysts had left the vans unidentified or had categorized them generically as miscellaneous missile-support vehicles. Only later would these vans become signature elements, tied to Soviet nuclear weapons facilities in Russia and Eastern Europe.[29]

In addition, if one's adversary identifies the signatures on which one's PIs are relying, he can use this knowledge to his own advantage, including possibly for schemes of deception. According to some accounts, the Indian government relied on knowledge of this sort to hide the preparations for its 1998 nuclear weapons tests from U.S. intelligence. Indian knowledge of the signatures on which the United States was relying has been traced to an incident three years earlier when India had been planning to conduct nuclear tests. As part of a diplomatic effort to forestall them, the United States, of course, had to explain the basis of its concern that tests were imminent; American specialists showed Indian officials U.S. satellite photos revealing the specific indicators (signatures) of a forthcoming nuclear test. Thus, in 1998, India had a much better idea of how to hide nuclear test preparations (for instance, by burying the cables connecting the control center to the test site).[30]

Data Banks (Basic Research)

As already noted in the section on open-source collection, a frequent major function of an intelligence service is the assembly and maintenance of large databases covering many topics of value to a government's foreign and military policy. This work can take the form of compiling encyclopedias of relevant information on all countries where military activity could conceivably take place.[31] Such compendia are designed to support a military planner, who would be looking at the country as a potential combat zone, and hence would contain detailed information about existing military forces, transport and military facilities, and military geography, as well as information about the country's politics, demographics, industry, agriculture, and so forth.

Although the analytical problems confronted in compiling such an encyclopedia are minimal, it is a major task to try to sort out what information is important and what is not. Decisions on which countries to cover and to what degree of detail can be very difficult to make, yet have important consequences should the information be needed to support a military operation. For example, the plan for the invasion of Grenada in October 1983 by the United States and the countries of the Organization of Eastern Caribbean States was developed very rapidly. One consequence was that adequate military maps were not available. According to Adm. Wesley McDonald, commander in chief of U.S. forces in the Atlantic, "The Army, particularly the troops on the ground, were operating initially from roadmaps or other types of maps which made it very difficult for them to determine . . . their grid coordinates. That is one of the lessons learned."[32]

Other types of data banks serve the needs of intelligence analysts themselves. For example, as already noted, collating and analyzing vast amounts of unclassified data can provide insight into a closed society such as the former Soviet Union, and China and North Korea today. Biographical data files (containing all newspaper references to party and government officials, their positions, promotions, travel, and so forth), for instance, can be analyzed to shed light on the relationships among officials, factional struggles within the leadership, and the like.

Production of Finished Intelligence

The types of analysis described above are the necessary initial steps of the analytical process; for the most part, the results of this work serve as sources for other intelligence analysts but do not go directly to the policy maker or military commander (the ultimate consumer of intelligence). This section discusses the kinds of finished intelligence produced. The analytical techniques used are neither as technical as cryptanalysis or telemetry analysis, nor unique to intelligence work. In some cases, such as the production of economic or political intelligence, the techniques are not distinguishable from those of corresponding social sciences.

Scientific and Technical Intelligence In the years immediately before and during World War II, the pace at which new scientific and technological principles were incorporated into weaponry increased substantially. A nation's ability to compete militarily became as dependent on its technological level, and its ability to manufacture weapon systems embodying that technology, as on its overall productive capacity, the size of its military forces, or any other measure of military strength. This was particularly true of air warfare, which saw the development and introduction of air defense radar, sophisticated navigational systems for guiding bomber aircraft to their targets, jet aircraft, ballistic and cruise missiles, and finally, the atomic bomb. Understanding new weapon systems that the enemy was developing thus became an important objective of each nation's intelligence agencies. In many cases, it was important to obtain fairly detailed information about the way a system worked in order to develop methods of countering it.

This imposed a new task on intelligence systems: to predict the emergence of new weapons and to understand them well enough when they did emerge to enable one's own armed forces to defend against and to counter them.[33] This required that the intelligence agencies have access to specialized scientific and technical knowledge and that this capability be integrated into the intelligence process.

Collection requirements for scientific and technical intelligence have to be more precise than for other forms of intelligence; it is not obvious to someone unfamiliar with the new technology what is to be looked for and where. This in turn means that close coordination is needed between the analysts and the collectors. To some extent, the process must be similar to the scientific method, in which hypotheses (formulated by the analyst) are tested, albeit by directed observations rather than by experiment. For example, R. V. Jones, the head of the British Air Ministry's intelligence section during World War II, recounts how his theory concerning the nature of the first system of radio signals *(Knickebein)* that the Germans used as a navigational aid for bombers was confirmed when an aircraft fitted out with special receivers and flying in an area designated by him picked up the radio signals he had predicted would be there.[34]

Analysis in the area of scientific and technical intelligence requires the blending of intelligence and scientific or technical expertise. Although the scientific principles themselves are, of course, universal in nature and known to experts throughout the world, the ways in which they are put to use in technological developments can differ widely between countries. Thus, this type of analysis requires enough familiarity with scientific and technical developments to understand what an adversary is doing, combined with enough imagination to realize that the adversary might solve technical problems that the analyst's own country had not been able to solve, or might reach a different but nonetheless valid solution to them.

Military Intelligence Military intelligence deals with information about foreign military establishments and is needed for planning one's own military forces in peacetime or conducting military operations in time of war. The most elementary military intelligence is what is known as the "order of battle," a tabulation of the basic information about a nation's military forces—amount of manpower, numbers and types of weapons, organizational structure, and similar data. Characterizing this information as elementary does not, of course, imply that it is easy to get or even that it is a simple matter to know which types of auxiliary or reserve troops, for example, should be counted and which should not. The revision of the North Korean order of battle by U.S. intelligence in the late 1970s is a case in point; over one year, intelligence estimates of the number of North Korean ground troops increased by a third. Similar adjustments were made for the number of tanks, rocket launchers, and artillery "tubes."

Not, strictly speaking, part of the order of battle but a necessary complement to it would be information about the qualitative aspects of a foreign military establishment: how good the training is, what the quality of the leadership is, and so forth.

One step up from this fundamental level would be information about how the forces could be expected to fight: what tactics they have adopted and trained for, what they envisage the nature of a future war to be, and what their strategy would be for fighting it. The raw data for this intelligence can come from open sources (such as military publications), attachés' or diplomats' overt contacts with the adversary's military, observation (either directly or via technical collection systems) of deployments and exercises, or human intelligence sources with direct access to military plans. As with scientific and technical intelligence, this sort of analysis calls for blending the intelligence perspective (with its concentration on all available bits and pieces of evidence about the adversary and what they indicate about how he thinks) with that of the military specialist (with its understanding of weapon systems' capabilities and the kinds of warfare that can be waged with them).

But above all, open-mindedness is needed to be able to imagine that the adversary has adopted different solutions to common military problems and that his solutions may well be appropriate for his circumstances and resources or even superior to one's own. In summary, "strategic planners need intelligence on the *otherness of the enemy*—intelligence that will reveal the enemy's methods of operation, internal disputes, and ways of doing business, as well as the ways in which the enemy differs from [oneself]."[35]

A simple but important example of the need (and failure) to understand the "otherness of the enemy" is provided by the French with respect to German battle plans on the eve of World War I. The German strategy (the Schlieffen Plan) was to avoid a frontal assault against France by conducting a flank attack through Belgium and then across the largely unguarded Franco-Belgian border. However, to implement this plan, the Germans had to use reserve units in the front lines; otherwise they would lack sufficient manpower for both the flanking attack and the defensive positions along the Franco-German border. The French had intelligence reports indicating what Germany intended to do, but they dismissed them as improbable: since they themselves would not use reserves as front line troops at the outbreak of war, they did not believe the German army would do so. Thus, the French misjudged where the Germans would attack—not for a lack of intelligence data, but because they failed to understand that the German military might operate in a manner different from their own.[36]

Finally, when military operations appear imminent or are actually beginning to take place, there must be information about the disposition and movement of military forces. This type of information is the primary data for what is known as "indications and warning," which addresses the task of avoiding strategic surprise.

Political Intelligence Political intelligence consists of information concerning the political processes, ideas, and intentions of foreign countries, factions, and individual leaders. The analysis that produces this intelligence is similar to that underlying all academic and journalistic writing and speculation on both international politics and the domestic politics of foreign countries. One obvious difference, of course, lies in the existence of secret intelligence sources, human or technical (primarily communications intelligence), that provide information not available to the public commentator.

How important these additional sources are depends on both the nature of the regime of the country being studied and the number and quality of intelligence sources one has with respect to that country. The more democratic and open a society is, the easier it is to study its political life without recourse to intelligence sources. In contrast, for states in which key political decisions are made by single individuals (or families, or parties), intelligence sources become both more important and in all likelihood more difficult to obtain. Nevertheless, even in the case of a closed society, there may be open-source data that, properly analyzed, reveal much more about political life than would appear at first glance. For example, as noted in the discussion of open-source collection, biographical data (such as the fact that A seems to have been beholden for past promotions to B) about a country's leaders can be analyzed to gain insight into factional struggles within the élite; even in a regime that makes a point of presenting a public face of unity, it may be possible to understand the internal struggles by noting whether protégés of one leader have gained status at the expense of protégés of another.

In addition to the question of the availability of non-open sources of information, another (and perhaps more) important difference between political intelligence analysis and academic or journalistic work has to do with their different purposes and modes of work. This difference shows itself in various ways, aside from the content of the work. For example, intelligence analysts must provide answers in a timely fashion. Their work is useless unless it reaches policy makers before they have been forced by circumstances to act. Academic authors, by contrast, generally have the luxury of taking as much time as they feel is necessary to reach conclusions. Similarly, academics typically work alone and on subjects of their own choice; intelligence analysts, for their part, are largely guided in their choice of topics by the requirements of others, and their work must be coordinated with that of others before it is completed.

Differences in purpose and process also affect the content of intelligence and academic analyses. For one thing, intelligence analyses must emphasize the aspects of a situation that underlie the immediate issues facing the policy makers; the focus in an academic work is presumably determined by the aspects the researcher deems the most fundamental. This question is discussed at greater length in chapter 6, on the overall relationship between intelligence and policy.

Economic and Social Intelligence Economic and social intelligence deal with the same phenomena as do the various social sciences, at least as far as they are concerned with major contemporary issues. As with political intelligence, the focus of the intelligence analysis should be determined by the information that policy makers require. Intelligence analysis here is often less sophisticated—theoretically and mathematically—than corresponding academic studies, and the problem does not seem to be differences in work circumstances or goals.

Not only are the methods of academic and intelligence research in this realm the same (at least in principle), but the scholar is more likely in this area than those in any other to have access to the same data as the intelligence analyst, since little of it is acquired by intelligence methods. As such, an estimate done by an intelligence analyst on the future of a country will not be very different from what might be produced by a scholar in an university or think tank. Nevertheless, sometimes intelligence methods are necessary. Much important economic data about the former Soviet Union was kept secret; this included, for example, the size of its gold reserves and the annual sales of gold on the world market. While intelligence analysts are often forced to estimate these numbers in the same way any other economist might, an intelligence source might be able to provide important clues or the official Soviet numbers themselves. In general, however, the contribution of intelligence sources to economic and social analysis is small.

As a practical matter, the intelligence agencies cannot expect to attract the highest-quality analysts in these areas. The freedom of academic life proves more attractive to talented social scientists, even if salaries are typically lower. In addition, multinational corporations, banks, and brokerage firms can easily outbid intelligence agencies for the services of highly qualified economists. In general, there is no reason to expect that analyses by intelligence personnel of economic issues not involving societies that keep basic economic data secret will be superior to those of economists in the business world.[37] Of course, much economic analysis done in the business world is treated as proprietary information and is not available to policy makers in the government, but at least some of it could be, via consulting services and newsletters.

THE INTELLIGENCE PRODUCT

The product of the intelligence process can be any means, from a formal report to a hurried conversation, by which an intelligence analyst transmits processed information to the policy maker or military commander who needs it and can use it. In this section we discuss the various forms of intelligence product and the functions they serve. The categorization is general rather than precise; the terminology reflects ordinary usage among U.S. intelligence agencies, but it is not completely standardized.

Broadly speaking, we divide intelligence output into three groups: *current intelligence, basic intelligence,* and *intelligence estimates.* In this we follow Sherman Kent's lead; he speaks, using his own coinages, of the "current reportorial form" of intelligence, the "basic descriptive form," and the "speculative-evaluative form"; he describes them as relating to information about the present, the past, and the future, respectively.[38] We use primarily U.S. examples to illustrate the different intelligence products, because more detailed information is available for them than for those of other nations. The distinctions, however, are generally valid, although the emphases placed on the different products vary from one intelligence service to another.

Current Intelligence

Intelligence agencies have a variety of products designed to inform policy makers of major new items of information that might affect policy. In this regard, agencies serve a function similar to that of the news media.[39] The range of information that should be covered depends on the scope of the nation's intelligence interest. Obviously, some priorities must be established on the basis of what is, in Kent's words, "positively germane to national problems which are up now and other problems which appear to be coming."[40] While a formal system of priorities may exist, it must be supplemented by the intelligence producers' own judgments about what is important to their consumers. This judgment, in turn, depends not only on the intelligence analysts' common sense but also on the closeness of their contact with the policy makers.

In the United States, the best known product of this type is the *President's Daily Brief* (PDB). It is intended to include "intelligence items of the highest significance necessary for the President to perform the national security duties of his office" and "is distributed only to the President, the Vice President, and a select group of executive branch officials designated by the President."[41] According to Cord Meyer, a former career CIA official, writing in 1980,

> It is designed to be read in ten or fifteen minutes by the President at the beginning of each working day. It does not attempt to recapitulate what the news media have reported in the last twenty-four-hour period, but rather to summarize the significance of what secret sources have reported that bears on current world developments.[42]

Less restricted in circulation is the *Senior Executive Intelligence Brief* (SEIB), which has apparently replaced an older publication called the *National Intelligence Daily* (NID). The SEIB is "compiled in consultation with other intelligence agencies" and includes "key current intelligence items[,] . . . tailored to the needs of senior officials throughout the United States Government responsible for national security."[43]

From time to time, the view is expressed that U.S. intelligence agencies spend too much time and effort fulfilling this "current intelligence" function, to the detriment of their ability to analyze situations in greater depth. For example, a Senate committee report dealing with the CIA's analytical branch, the Directorate of Intelligence (DI), made the following comments under the heading "The 'Current Events' Syndrome":

> The task of producing current intelligence—analyzing day-to-day events for quick dissemination—today occupies much of the resources of the DI. Responding to the growing demands for information of current concern by policymakers for more coverage of more topics [*sic*], the DI has of necessity resorted to a "current events" approach to much of its research. There is less interest in and fewer resources have been devoted to in-depth analysis of problems with long-range importance to policymakers. . . .
>
> According to some observers, this syndrome has had an unfavorable impact on the quality of crisis warning and the recognition of longer term trends. The "current events" approach has fostered the problem of "incremental analysis," the tendency to focus myopically on the latest piece of information without systematic consideration of an accumulated body of integrated evidence. Analysts in their haste to compile the day's traffic, tend to lose sight of underlying factors and relationships.[44]

The very persistence of this criticism over the years probably indicates that the pressure for a current events approach—the source of which is the desire of policy makers to be kept informed of the latest hot news—is inherently strong and will often predominate over the intelligence analyst's own desire to conduct in-depth studies.[45] The same pressures are probably at work in the intelligence agencies of other countries as well.

Indications and Warnings

One of the most important functions an intelligence agency can perform is to provide timely warning of hostile military action; in the nuclear era, the importance of this function is all the more evident. In fact, the character of the post–World War II U.S. intelligence system as a whole was probably determined more by the failure of the prewar intelligence organizations to provide effective warning of the Japanese attack on Pearl Harbor than by any other factor.

Because of its importance (especially during the Cold War, when the United States and the USSR and their respective allies had large armies and thousands of nuclear arms facing each other), and because judgments might have to be made quickly, this intelligence function has been (in the United States, at least) systematized to a much greater extent than any other. The system, known as *indications and warnings* (I&W), is based on an analysis of the steps an adversary would either necessarily or probably take to prepare for an armed attack. These hypothetical events—the calling up of reservists, forward movement of military forces, changes in communications patterns, and so forth—are called "indicators"; when the event actually occurs and is observed, it is referred to as an "indication." Analysts determine how great the threat is by the totality of indications and issue warnings at various threshold levels.[46]

Oleg Gordievsky, a KGB officer who spied for British intelligence from 1975 to 1985, has provided a glimpse into the I&W procedures used by the former Soviet Union. According to him, the Politburo in 1981 ordered the KGB and Soviet military intelligence (called the GRU, after its Russian initials) to cooperate on a new worldwide monitoring system to watch for signs of a possible Western nuclear attack. The GRU was responsible for monitoring the purely military indicators, while the KGB was to watch for signs that the political decision to launch a nuclear attack had been taken. Among the indicators that the KGB residency in Britain was responsible for monitoring were:

- The pattern of work at 10 Downing Street (the prime minister's residence), the ministry of defense, the foreign office, the U.S. embassy, and the headquarters of the British intelligence and security services (for example, were the lights on at night?)
- The frequency with which couriers traveled between those establishments
- The comings and goings of the prime minister and other key ministers (for example, was the prime minister making an unusual number of trips to Buckingham Palace?)
- The existence of any unusual civil defense measures, such as stockpiling food or preparing emergency blood banks.

Routine reports were to be made every two weeks, but any particularly striking events were to be reported immediately.[47]

This type of formalized system, in which indicators are determined in advance and can thus guide the collection process to some extent, ensures that intelligence is fed into the policy-making process and is not ignored. However, it exists only with respect to the most important questions, such as the possibility of hostile military action. In most other areas, no automatic system is set up to guarantee that the available intelligence is brought to bear when decisions are made.

Following what was widely regarded as the CIA's failure to provide adequate warning of the Iranian revolution of 1978–79, proposals were made to establish a political I&W system to warn of political instability in foreign countries. This would require establishing indicators comparable to those used to warn of military attack. This is much more difficult for politics than with military matters, as the rapid and unexpected collapse of communist regimes of Eastern Europe in 1989 and the Soviet Union in 1991 have once again shown; it is unlikely that the current state of the social sciences allows this to be done with sufficient reliability to be of real use. Nevertheless, a more formal system would clarify the extent to which intelligence is responsible for warning of potentially serious events, even when the policy-making community is not focusing on that country or region of the world.

Basic Intelligence

Another general type of intelligence product may be termed the "basic intelligence report." Such a report tries to provide as full a picture of a given situation as possible, drawing on publicly available data and relevant information from all intelligence sources ("all-source" intelligence). In the military arena, for example, such products might be an order of battle. Similarly, a basic intelligence report on a nation's political system could include an account of all the major political forces and personalities, their traditional views and interests, the ways in which they have related to each other, and so forth.

Periodic Reports

Just as I&W represents a systematized form of current intelligence to deal with a specific question of great importance, there may be special series of reports to deal with specific issues. For example, during the Cold War, U.S. intelligence produced semiannual reports on Soviet compliance with strategic nuclear arms agreements; these reports present the best intelligence judgments concerning that country's strategic nuclear forces relevant to the agreements' provisions. In 2001, the CIA's Directorate of Intelligence (DI) provided on its Website the following list of its periodic reports:

- Regional Reviews. Periodic assessments (ranging from daily to monthly) of foreign political, economic, military, and societal issues relevant to US interests . . . deal[ing] with regional and national events in Africa, Europe, Latin America, the Middle East, Asia, and the Slavic and Eurasian states of the former Soviet Union.
- The Terrorism Review. A monthly publication [that] addresses current trends in international terrorism activity and methods[,] . . . includ[ing] a chronology of international terrorist incidents.
- The Narcotics Monitor, [which] assesses narcotics-related developments worldwide.
- Proliferation Digest, published monthly [containing] articles on proliferation themes.
- The International Arms Trade Report, published bimonthly.

Intelligence Estimates

The most ambitious type of intelligence product is that which not only describes the current situation but also attempts to predict how it will evolve. Such works are referred to in U.S. intelligence parlance as *estimates*. In particular, a *national intelligence estimate* (NIE) represents the most authoritative statement on a subject by U.S. intelligence agencies collectively.

These estimates are supposed to take the broadest view of their subject and project the current situation into the future. In the United States, they are produced by a special staff, with the support of analysts throughout the intelligence agencies. The estimates are supposed to incorporate the views of all the agencies in the intelligence community.[48] A good deal of effort is devoted to finding a consensus position, but when this is not possible, a dissenting view may be expressed in what is traditionally called a "footnote," even though the dissent is in fact sometimes included in the text.

NIEs on certain topics of major importance are produced annually (or at some other fixed interval); other topics are covered in response to specific requirements, either self-generated (that is, the idea for the estimate arises within the intelligence community itself) or from elsewhere in the government, most often the National Security Council (NSC). Shorter, more topical estimates, known as Special NIEs (or SNIEs), may be produced in response to more urgent requirements.

In contrast to the U.S. practice, estimates in Israel during the period before the 1973 Yom Kippur War were a monopoly of Military Intelligence, a branch of the armed forces. Although other intelligence services existed—the Central Institute for Intelligence and Security (Ha-Mossad), which operated covertly in foreign countries; the Shin Beth, which was responsible for counterintelligence and counterterrorism; and the Foreign Office research department—only Military Intelligence had access to all intelligence information and was responsible for analyzing and distributing it. Furthermore, the cabinet's staff had no intelligence expertise, and there was no mechanism by which the political leadership tasked Military Intelligence to provide evaluations of specific subjects. This concentration of power was later criticized as contributing to the failure of Israeli intelligence to warn of the Egyptian-Syrian attack on October 6, 1973 (discussed in the "intelligence failure" section of this chapter).[49]

Variations among Intelligence Services

While current and basic intelligence functions seem essential to the work of any nation's intelligence services, how integral is the estimative function to the intelligence process? Its importance varies from nation to nation and time to time. For example, in the United States, preparing estimates is seen as the peak of the intelligence process. In the Soviet Union of the 1930s, by contrast, Stalin wanted to keep the estimative function in his own hands; he ordered the NKVD (a predecessor of the KGB) not to send him estimates or assessments of the foreign situation but to confine itself to reporting the secrets (high-level informant reports) it had obtained.[50] This point has to do with the relationship between the intelligence and policy-making functions of a government, discussed further in chapter 6.

INTELLIGENCE FAILURE AND SURPRISE

Types of Failure

Surprise Attack The possible failure of intelligence to assess a situation correctly is a danger coeval with intelligence itself. In this section, we examine the causes of intelligence failure that can reside in one's own intelligence apparatus; in chapter 5, we will examine how failure may be induced by deception efforts undertaken by an adversary.

The most dramatic, and potentially most damaging, intelligence failure occurs when an attack happens without warning, and a nation's military forces are taken by surprise. Indeed, as already noted, the U.S. intelligence community in large measure owes its current configuration to an effort to remedy the intelligence deficiencies thought to have contributed to the nation's being surprised by the Japanese attack on Pearl Harbor on December 7, 1941.

The literature on successful surprise attacks is extensive. The German attack on the Soviet Union on June 22, 1941, and the Egyptian-Syrian attack on Israel in 1973 (which started the Yom Kippur War) are, aside from the Pearl Harbor attack, among the most frequently discussed cases.[51] Even during a war, when military forces are presumably at higher levels of alert than during peacetime, substantial surprise can be, and has been, achieved. Examples are the German attack in the Ardennes in December 1944 (the Battle of the Bulge), the Chinese entry into the Korean War in November–December 1950, and the North Vietnamese and Vietcong offensive (the Tet offensive) throughout South Vietnam in late January 1968.[52]

Closely related to the failure to anticipate an attack is the situation in which a nation expects an attack but, because of a significant misestimation of where or how it will occur, responds disadvantageously. An impressive example of this kind of intelligence failure is the German reaction to the Allied landings in Normandy on June 6, 1944 (D-day). The Germans certainly expected an attack, but they were so convinced that the main thrust would be against the Pas de Calais region that they treated Normandy as a diversion and passed up a good opportunity to counterattack in force while the beachheads were most vulnerable.[53]

Other Kinds of Surprise Although an unanticipated attack may be the most damaging surprise a nation can suffer, it is not the only one. For example, an unexpected political event (such as a shift in alliances or a coup d'état that overthrows a friendly foreign ruler) also may be a serious blow to a nation's foreign policy interests. The American underestimation in 1978 of the shah of Iran's political troubles and of the depth of the opposition to his rule is one of the best-known examples of this type of intelligence failure.[54]

Similarly, the absence of warning of a sudden, major economic change, such as the failure of U.S. intelligence agencies to foresee the 1973 "oil shock"—a rapid increase in the world price of oil—also may be accounted an intelligence failure, depending on one's opinion of the field of view and responsibilities of intelligence agencies. As has been noted, intelligence's role with respect to economic questions is less settled and more complicated than with respect to political or military matters. In any case, the 1973 oil shock is an example of the complexity of this type of problem, since the underlying causes were economic (the previous low price of oil had encouraged oil consumption and discouraged exploration and development), while the immediate cause was political (the Arab oil states' support for Egypt and Syria in the October 1973 Yom Kippur War).[55]

While the disasters that can flow from being surprised on the battlefield are obvious, the harm caused by the failure to foresee political or economic events is more difficult to assess. In large part, it depends on whether the government would have been prepared to take action had it been warned and whether there were strategies that could have averted the event or mitigated its unfavorable consequences.

For example, it is not clear what, if anything, the U.S. government would have done had it been warned of the 1973 oil shock. Similarly, correctly assessing the shah's political troubles is a vastly different task from determining what, if anything, could have been done about them; success in the former respect would not have necessarily guaranteed success in the latter.

Other Kinds of Failure Most of the well-known cases of intelligence failure sooner or later involve surprise, since a mistaken view of the external world is likely to cause unexpected misfortune at some point and in some manner. (However, there are also cases in which, through faulty intelligence, an army or country, unaware of an adversary's vulnerability, has lost an opportunity to take advantage of a favorable situation.[56] In such cases, of course, there is failure but no "surprise.") In any case, the notion of surprise is perhaps not the most helpful one for understanding the harm intelligence failure causes.

An intelligence failure is essentially a misunderstanding of the situation that leads a government (or its military forces) to take actions that are inappropriate and counterproductive to its own interests. Whether it is subjectively surprised by what happens is less important than the fact that the government or the military is doing or continues to do the wrong thing. Thus, the German intelligence failure with respect to the Normandy D-day landings resulted not so much in the German army's being surprised as in its false assessment of the Normandy landings as feints meant to distract attention from the "real" invasion force targeted on the Pas de Calais region.[57] Similarly, the primary cause of the Chinese rout of the UN forces in Korea in December 1950 had more to do with a fundamental misunderstanding of Chinese doctrine and tactics than with "surprise" as usually understood.[58]

Furthermore, examples of surprise involving failures to foresee what action a hostile force would take or with what success it would meet apply particularly to nations that are on the defensive, strategically or tactically. A nation on the offensive, however, also can suffer through misestimating the opponent's strengths or misunderstanding some other relevant factor. For example, the Allied attack on the bridge at Arnhem, Holland—the "bridge too far"—in September 1944 was unsuccessful in large part because of intelligence's failure, due to overconfidence and a negligent analysis of the available information, to realize that two German armored divisions were present in the immediate area.[59]

Finally, the intelligence failures discussed above involve a misunderstanding that is revealed quickly once one side or the other takes action. Another sort of failure involves mistaken estimation of a continuing process or condition in which, because nothing occurs to reveal the truth of the situation, it is possible to remain in error for a longer time. For example, in estimating the size of the strategic arsenal of the former Soviet Union, the U.S. intelligence community made both major overestimations and underestimations that colored American strategic views for years. The major overestimations of Soviet strategic weaponry, which produced American perceptions of a "bomber gap" in the mid-1950s and a "missile gap" from the late 1950s until 1961, are perhaps the better known of these errors.[60] But at least equally important was the tendency throughout the mid-1960s, and ending only in the early 1970s, to underestimate the extent to which the Soviet Union was building up its strategic forces.[61]

Causes of Failure

Aside from instances in which relevant information cannot be obtained at all, intelligence failure refers to a disorder of the analytical process that causes data to be ignored or misinterpreted. Therefore, it is similar to a mistake in any other intellectual endeavor—for example, a mistake by a historian in interpreting an ancient text, leading to an incorrect description of some aspect of antiquity; or a mistake by a meteorologist in assessing the importance of a low-pressure system, leading to an incorrect prediction about the next day's weather.

In addition, however, some peculiarities of the intelligence analysis process introduce further sources of error. While intelligence analysis is an intellectual activity, it is one that, unlike the work of an individual academic, takes place in an institutional setting and according to standard procedures, so that the final result is more the product of a system than of any individual. As such, it is vulnerable to certain pathologies that can be addressed in institutional or bureaucratic terms. This section addresses some of the causes of intelligence failure, looking first at institutional ones and then at those that relate more directly to the intellectual content of the intelligence work.

Subordination of Intelligence to Policy The possibility that intelligence judgments will be made to produce the results superiors wish to hear instead of what the evidence indicates is perhaps the most commonly discussed source of error or bias in intelligence analysis. It is, however, extrinsic to the intelligence analysis process itself (assuming that the analyst realizes he is going against his own best judgment). As such, it is an issue in what may be called the management of intelligence—the way in which intelligence relates to the higher-level policy makers whom it serves; it is dealt with in the discussion of intelligence and policy in chapter 6.

Unavailability of Information When and Where Needed Given the large size of the organizations involved in collecting and analyzing intelligence, a possible source of problems is unavailability of information that is in the system to those who need it, when they need it. This unavailability has various causes: for example, security regulations that restrict the circulation of sensitive information, bureaucratic jealousies and power struggles in which control over information becomes a weapon, or simple lack of awareness in the office possessing the data of another office's information needs.[62]

Similarly, a problem can arise if no central office has both the responsibility to do analysis in a given area and access to all information relevant to it. In this case, while different offices work on different parts of the problem, a key piece of information may be ignored if its significance can become apparent only in the context of all the available data.

Typically, the Pearl Harbor intelligence failure is explained in terms of a lack of communication between the various intelligence and operational units involved. However, while there may have been some communication problems between the army and navy commands in Hawaii, it is not clear that a corresponding difficulty existed between the two services in Washington. A more important difficulty stemmed from the lack of a centralized analytical office with the resources and the responsibility to analyze all relevant intelligence. Instead, intelligence seemed to be handled on the fly by a few people who worked directly for high-level policy-making officials—an effect of the small size of the U.S. military establishment at that time as much as anything else.

Received Opinion The success of any intellectual endeavor (scientific discovery, for example, as well as intelligence analysis) can be compromised by the force of received opinion, often referred to as "conventional wisdom"—those opinions about a subject that are generally regarded, without sufficient investigation, as true. While, in one sense, we obviously cannot do without it (we could hardly afford the time or effort to reinvestigate and rethink all our opinions every day), relying on received opinion poses the real danger that we will either misunderstand or perhaps ignore evidence that suggests the truth is otherwise.

Conventional wisdom, for example, among U.S. intelligence analysts and diplomats in the summer of 1990 was that Iraq would not invade Kuwait. Even though overhead satellite photos captured a large-scale buildup of Iraq's elite army divisions on the Kuwaiti border in late July, the prevailing view was that Iraq's leader, Saddam Hussein, was engaged in "saber rattling" in an effort to intimidate Kuwait's leaders in disputes concerning oil production and pricing and over the repayment of Iraq's debts to Kuwait. This assessment was based on the view that Iraq was too worn down by its just completed war with Iran (1980–88) to undertake a major military operation and that, in any case, it was unprecedented for one Arab nation to invade another. But on August 2, Iraq invaded and conquered Kuwait.[63]

As another example of the power of received opinion and resulting failure to assess an adversary accurately, one can examine the British expectation in the 1930s that the German rearmament would be limited in scope. According to Wesley K. Wark,

> the general [British] expectation was that the German armed forces would be rearmed well above Versailles treaty levels but only to a strength sufficient to satisfy the demands of national security. Thus no aggressive intent was assumed from the evidence of Versailles infractions. . . . Coupled with the overall assumption that Germany's rearmament goals were limited in conception and defensive in orientation was the notion that the pace of rearmament would be governed by the dictates of efficiency. In British eyes this meant that German rearmament would proceed at a moderate pace to maintain high standards of professionalism and the best possible utilization of weapons systems. This conservative outlook on rearmament, which showed little understanding of the Nazi dynamic, was perhaps the most flagrant contribution to what proved to be a set of grievous underestimates of future German military strength.[64]

However pernicious the effect of received opinion on an individual's thinking, its impact can be heightened by the bureaucratic environment in which an intelligence service carries out its analysis. While an individual's thought can be influenced by particularly striking evidence that does not fit the preconceived pattern, or even by a chance insight that suggests another interpretation of the evidence, it is unlikely that many people will be affected in the same way at the same time. Thus, individuals challenging the received view are likely to encounter the resistance of the much larger number who remain comfortable with it.

If individuals economize on time and effort by not rethinking all their opinions all the time, organizations may be said to do the same. Given the size and complexity of the organizations involved and the consequent need to obtain the consent (or at least the acquiescence) of many people to the judgments reached, fundamental reevaluation of the evidence with a view toward rethinking all basic assumptions is a very difficult and time-consuming process.

Thus, if an analyst has to write a report, he is likely first to review what was written the previous year and then merely update it as necessary. This not only saves labor but also offers a degree of security. Because last year's report was approved, if the analyst limits himself to the changes indicated by new evidence, the underlying reasoning does not have to be duplicated, and the sources of controversy can be minimized.

Clearly this creates a tremendous vulnerability to error in situations involving gradual change. Because intelligence evidence is almost always spotty and incomplete, the accumulation of various bits and pieces of new information may not force a change in the underlying analysis. This may be true even if the preponderance of evidence at some point would suggest to someone starting afresh that a different framework would make more sense. In this manner, an older way of viewing the situation may survive much longer than it should.[65]

Mirror-Imaging The two problems discussed above apply primarily to intelligence analysis conducted in a bureaucratic setting. Another source of error in intelligence analysis, however, reflects a more common intellectual failure not tied to the setting in which the analysis is conducted. It may be termed "mirror-imaging," by which is meant the judging of unfamiliar situations on the basis of familiar ones.[66] In the case of intelligence, it typically means assessing or predicting a foreign government's actions by analogy with the actions that the analyst feels he (or his government) would take were he (or it) in a similar position.

For example, the failure of Israeli intelligence to foresee the Egyptian-Syrian attack that started the October 1973 Yom Kippur War appears to have been due in part to this phenomenon; Israel's intelligence services did not imagine that the Arabs would begin a war that they seemed sure to lose.[67] For example, less than two months before the outbreak of war, Moshe Dayan told the Staff College of the Israel Defense Forces that "the balance of forces is so much in our favor that it neutralizes the Arab considerations and motives for the immediate renewal of hostilities."[68]

In retrospect, however, it appears that Egyptian president Anwar Sadat wanted the war to break the stalemate that had developed in Israeli-Arab relations and that he did not, in fact, count on winning it. The initial Arab victories (in particular, the Egyptian crossing of the Suez Canal and penetration of the Israeli defensive line on the other side), although reversed on the ground later in the war, provided the psychological backdrop for the eventual regaining of the Sinai Peninsula. Discounting the possibility of this sort of aggressive risk taking, foreign to Israeli and U.S. military experience, would seem to be an example of mirror-imaging.

Another striking example may be found in the report of the Church Committee, the special committee of the U.S. Senate formed in 1975 to investigate the intelligence community. That report cites the following paragraph from a draft of the 1969 national intelligence estimate on the offensive nuclear forces of the Soviet Union:

> We believe that the Soviets recognize the enormous difficulties of any attempt to achieve strategic superiority of such order as to significantly alter the strategic balance. Consequently, we consider it highly unlikely that they will attempt within the period of this estimate to achieve a first-strike capability—that is, a capability to launch a surprise attack against the United States with assurance that the USSR would not itself receive damage it would regard as unacceptable. For one thing, the Soviets would almost certainly conclude that the cost of such an undertaking along with all their other military commitments would be prohibitive. More important, they almost certainly would

> consider it impossible to develop and deploy the combination of offensive and defensive forces necessary to counter successfully the various elements of U.S. strategic attack forces. Finally, even if such a project were economically and technically feasible, the Soviets almost certainly would calculate that the United States would detect and match or overmatch their efforts.[69]

Aside from the context in which the Church Committee cites this passage (the Nixon administration in general, and Secretary of Defense Melvin Laird in particular, are being taken to task for successfully pressuring the director of central intelligence, Richard Helms, to delete this paragraph from the final version of the NIE), its report does not indicate that the judgments in the passage were based on inside information about strategic thinking in the Kremlin. Indeed, the wording (for example, "would almost certainly") suggests instead that the paragraph contains analytical judgments about Soviet thinking rather than direct evidence drawn from documents or high-level informants.

As such it is an example of mirror-imaging, not only in the three major assertions (the last three sentences) it offers to support its main thesis but also in the entire way in which it frames the question. The first assertion implies that U.S. intelligence understood what costs the Soviets might have considered prohibitive, a judgment that rested essentially on a sort of mirror-imaging—the United States itself had concluded that this goal was not economically feasible. The second reflects a conclusion common among the theorists of the U.S. strategic community but not necessarily believed by Soviet military thinkers at the time. Finally, the third attributes to the Soviets a mechanistic, apolitical view of the arms race (as an action-reaction cycle) that was common in the United States but not necessarily in the Soviet Union.

Perhaps even more important, the entire manner in which the question is framed in the first two sentences—that is, the equating of "strategic superiority [that] significantly alter[s] the strategic balance" on the one hand, with "first-strike capability" on the other—reflects the U.S. doctrine of mutual assured destruction (known as MAD) rather than an attempt to understand what the Soviets at the time considered significant. It implies that the Soviets would see partial solutions to the problem of countering U.S. offensive strategic forces as insignificant and not worth developing and deploying.

But since this view is merely implied rather than stated, it is not examined on the basis of the evidence. (For example, a careful evaluation of this view would have had to deal with the emphasis the Soviets placed on strategic air defenses, deep underground bunkers for its leadership, and the Moscow antiballistic missile system, even in the absence of a nationwide ballistic missile defense.) Instead, its attribution to the Soviets seems to be a case of mirror-imaging by analysts who believed that the logic behind the U.S. view was so strong that the Soviets must have accepted it.

Another common form of mirror-imaging, one that affects the ability to assess correctly scientific or technological developments within an adversary's military establishment, is often referred to as the "not invented here" syndrome. This syndrome is characterized by an unwillingness to take seriously the possibility that an adversary has developed a weapon or device that one's own military-technological establishment has not thought of, has dismissed as infeasible, or has simply judged its effectiveness as less than optimal. We would expect this syndrome to be more common with respect to an adversary who is regarded as technologically inferior.

R. V. Jones discusses this phenomenon in his account of British scientific and technical intelligence during World War II. In an epilogue to an intelligence report concerning the V-2 ballistic rocket, which the Germans developed toward the end of the war and first fired against London on September 8, 1944, Jones lists the four possibilities that can exist with respect to a technical development: in this case, the British either do or do not succeed with respect to it, and the Germans either succeed or do not. The "not invented here" syndrome obtains when

> our experts either fail or do not try, [and] the Germans succeed. This is the most interesting Intelligence case, but it is difficult to overcome the prejudice that as we have not done something, it is impossible or foolish. Alternatively, our experts in examining the German development are no longer experts but novices, and may therefore make wilder guesses than Intelligence [that is, intelligence analysts who are not, as such, experts in the relevant technology], which at least has the advantage of closer contact with the enemy.[70]

Jones's solution to the problem is for the intelligence analyst to be wary of technical experts' views, while trying to make use of their expertise:

> From an Intelligence point of view, it must always be borne in mind that the advice comes from a British, and not from a German expert. If this difference in background is not continually appreciated, serious misadjustments can be made. In the tactical field, Napoleon knew this danger well: he called it, "making pictures of the enemy." In the technical field the same danger exists.[71]

"Solutions" to the Problem of Intelligence Failure

What Is Failure? More frequently than the popular myths of omniscient intelligence services would lead us to expect, intelligence reports or estimates contain erroneous statements, and important events occur without intelligence agencies having predicted them. Determining whether such situations constitute intelligence failures requires a standard against which it is reasonable to measure intelligence achievement.[72] Often, it is assumed in discussions of this sort that intelligence performance should be measured against an ideal of clairvoyance. Typically forgotten is that for the most part, intelligence involves not a metaphorical struggle with nature (as is the case with scientific research, which seeks to force nature to reveal its secrets) but a real struggle with a human adversary.

For example, the victim's failure to anticipate a surprise attack is the reverse side of the coin of the attacker's success at achieving surprise. In intelligence work, one opponent is most often trying to frustrate his adversary's attempts to understand the situation accurately. To do so, he will use a whole array of intelligence techniques, including deception, as is discussed in chapter 5 on counterintelligence.

Thus, we cannot compare progress in intelligence techniques to, for example, progress in chemistry. The consequence of progress in chemical research, and the dissemination of the knowledge and insight gained thereby, can be that chemists throughout the world achieve better results in their work. The same is not the case with respect to intelligence; that new insights or procedures enable one group of intelligence officials to achieve better results in its work means, in general, that its adversaries' intelligence officials are not performing their own tasks as well as in the past and, in a sense, have fallen down on the job. This is obviously true with respect to questions of deliberate surprise, but is applicable more generally.[73]

Taken to an extreme, speaking of intelligence failure is similar to speaking of "chess failure," defined as the failure to win chess games. Obviously, to improve our chess-playing abilities, it makes sense to critique styles of play, as well as individual moves, as thoroughly as we can. The result should be better individual chess play and, if we share the insights we have gained, better play by others as well. There cannot be, overall, an increase in the number of games of chess won per number played. Of course, as citizens, we are not concerned with better intelligence in the abstract; we seek to improve our own country's intelligence capabilities and, in so doing, to devalue those of our adversaries.

Institutional Solutions Among the most frequently discussed institutional solutions—solutions that require the restructuring of the institutional framework in which intelligence analysis is carried out—are *competitive analysis* and the establishment of a *devil's advocate.*

"Competitive analysis" refers to the deliberate fostering of separate analytical centers within a government, each of which has the right to formulate and distribute its own intelligence assessments. In principle, each center would have equal and comprehensive access to the raw data, whichever intelligence agency collected it. (In practice, because of the extreme sensitivity of certain types of intelligence information—for example, information that might identify a human source—this situation may well be difficult to achieve.)

Typically, some or all of these centers are constituent parts of major departments and agencies of government or military services and exist primarily to serve the specialized intelligence needs of their parent organizations. For example, in the United States, the Defense Intelligence Agency is a part of the Department of Defense, reporting to both the Joint Chiefs of Staff and the secretary of defense; each military service has its own intelligence command or service; and the State Department has its Bureau of Intelligence and Research. To some extent, the resulting competition among them reflects the fact that they are subordinated to different government departments, which are themselves at times in competition.

Alternatively, it might be possible to create separate analytical centers explicitly to compete, most likely on an ad hoc basis, to examine specific issues. Two American examples for which information is publicly available are the A-B Team exercise of 1975–76 and the Rumsfeld Commission of 1998. In the first, a separate team of experts (the B Team) was established to review evidence concerning Soviet strategic developments and determine if it supported conclusions other than those of the writers of the previous year's national intelligence estimate (the A Team).[74]

In the second, a commission chaired by Donald Rumsfeld assessed the possible ballistic missile threat to the United States from countries other than Russia and China. The commission was formed because of a suspicion, in Congress and elsewhere, that an earlier NIE on the topic had been overly sanguine.[75]

Whether done on a regular or ad hoc basis, the virtue of competitive analysis resides primarily in allowing differing points of view to be expressed at high levels, thereby sharpening the debate and focusing attention on whether available evidence unambiguously supports one or the other position. In this way, competitive analysis can act as an antidote to the problems caused by the easy acceptance of conventional wisdom. With competing analytical centers, it is more likely (although not guaranteed) that at least one of them will be skeptical of the received opinions on a subject and will be able to force the other agencies to mount an explicit defense of them. Competitive analysis is an attempt to imitate, within the limiting confines of the government and its regulations concerning security of information, the free marketplace of ideas that exists in a democratic society and that presumably furthers the advance of knowledge generally.

From this perspective, the possibility that the competing centers may take positions that are biased in favor of their parent agencies' policy preferences or budgetary requests is not such an important drawback. Vigorous debate among the multiple centers will, according to this line of argument, expose the invalidity of positions the evidence does not support, while providing a greater chance that new, unconventional ideas will receive a serious hearing.

Of course, it could happen that a particular strong opinion will pervade the different parts of the government more or less to an equal degree. In that case, we could not expect the mere existence of competing analytical centers to challenge the conventional wisdom, since they would all be infected by the same orthodoxy. This consideration has led to proposals to establish a "devil's advocate"—that is, an analytical entity whose explicit purpose is to challenge accepted views.

The B Team and the Rumsfeld Commission are also examples of ad hoc devil's advocates, established to look at one particular problem and motivated by an already-existing sense that the previous understanding of it had been flawed. The devil's-advocate proposal is an attempt to institutionalize this type of practice and, in so doing, protect it from some of the political controversy that surrounded the B Team, which some critics regarded as exerting illegitimate outside (that is, political) pressure on the intelligence analysis process.[76]

While both of these institutional devices have something to be said for them, neither can be regarded as a panacea, or even as necessarily a step in the right direction. In an article provocatively subtitled "Why Intelligence Failures Are Inevitable," Richard K. Betts has argued that neither institutional solution discussed above—or any other institutional solution, for that matter—can prevent intelligence failure.[77]

Competitive analysis, for example, may air disagreements with the conventional wisdom that would otherwise be suppressed; at the same time, however, it presents the policy makers with a spectrum of views, which may leave them confused or may lead them to ignore intelligence altogether and follow their own prior opinions instead. Similarly, the objections of an institutionalized devil's advocate may lose any real power to force others to rethink their positions precisely because, in dissenting, "he is just doing his job." Indeed, the perverse result may be that otherwise powerful challenges to the orthodoxy are ignored because they are seen as routine and predictable.

This is not to say, however, that institutional arrangements do not matter or that changing them may not be beneficial. Rather, it suggests that the optimal bureaucratic organization of intelligence cannot be determined until we have a sense of what the characteristic problems or deficiencies of a nation's national security apparatus are; the organizational structure should be determined by what would best counteract those bad tendencies. The same solution—for example, competitive analysis—may be helpful or harmful, depending on whether the system suffers from too much conformity with the conventional wisdom (in which case competition might be able to introduce needed new ideas) or from a tendency to allow domestic political concerns to dominate national security questions (in which case a strong, unified intelligence voice may be necessary to bring international realities to the fore).

Intellectual Solutions Institutional solutions have the advantage that they can be implemented from the top down through managerial decisions and directives; they do not, however, attack the heart of the problem of intelligence failure, the thought processes of the individual analyst. Improving thought processes is not a matter that administrative means can deal with directly. Indeed, when we try to be specific about what would be involved, it is not even clear we know what "the improvement of thought processes" means, aside from a general and not very useful admonition to be "smarter."

While it may not be possible to lay down rules that will inevitably guide us to analyze intelligence information correctly, it is nevertheless useful to try to identify intellectual errors or deficiencies that may be characteristic of the analytical process, either generally or as it exists at a certain time and place. In so doing, we can become aware of these tendencies and subsequently try to correct them.

The previous discussion of the intellectual causes of intelligence failure listed mirror-imaging as an important error that must be guarded against. While any intelligence analyst is vulnerable to this error, cultural reasons may make it a particular problem for the U.S. intelligence community. Americans are more open to a belief in the basic similarity of people throughout the world, perhaps because of America's experience in successfully absorbing and assimilating immigrants from diverse cultural and religious backgrounds. Thus, U.S. intelligence analysts risk being more likely than other analysts to understand and predict the actions of others on the basis of what they would do under similar circumstances.

Thus, an emphasis on knowledge of foreign societies and cultures is an important corrective to this error. Expertise can be fostered by a study of the language and history of a country, by an awareness of its religious and cultural traditions, and so forth. A deliberate attempt must be made to see the international situation from other countries' leaders' points of view, rather than our own.

Chapter 4

Working behind the Scenes: Covert Action

Covert action—especially in its more sensational forms, such as the overthrow of a government or the assassination of its leader—looms large in the public's view of what intelligence is; for professionals and students of intelligence, however, it is something of a question whether covert action should be considered a part of intelligence at all. This issue arises because covert action involves taking action to implement a nation's foreign policy, while collection and analysis are limited to providing the information on which that policy may be based.

WHAT IS COVERT ACTION?

Covert action, in the U.S. intelligence lexicon, refers to the attempt by one government to pursue its foreign policy objectives by conducting some secret activity to influence the behavior of a foreign government or political, military, economic, or societal events and circumstances in a foreign country. As the term implies, the defining characteristic of covert action is that the government conducting the activity conduct it in a secret or covert manner. However, what secrecy means precisely can vary according to the particular circumstances.

In some cases, the need for secrecy is absolute, and governments try to act so that the details or even the existence of activities remain unknown outside a very small circle. This would be true, for instance, if the covert action involved helping a group of conspirators prepare a coup d'état in a foreign country by smuggling weapons into the country for it. In other cases, the actions themselves are public knowledge, but governments conceal their involvement in them. An example would be a government's secret financing of a newspaper or radio station that supported its policies or was hostile to those of its adversary. Finally, there may be cases in which a good deal of information about operations becomes public, but for diplomatic or other reasons, governments involved avoid officially acknowledging their connection with them.

In the United States, covert action is now defined by law as "an activity or activities of the United States Government to influence political, economic, or military conditions abroad, where it is intended that the role of the [government] will not be apparent or acknowledged publicly, but does not include . . . traditional counterintelligence . . . diplomatic . . . military . . . [or] law enforcement activities."[1]

By this definition, covert action is distinguished from the collection and production of intelligence information, which is to say, from what in the United States is typically regarded as the heart of the intelligence function.[2] The distinction is that the goal of covert action is not knowledge but is instead the direct furthering of national foreign policy objectives. In this respect, it more closely resembles the nation's other foreign policy tools, such as diplomacy or military force, than the rest of intelligence. On the other hand, insofar as it is activity undertaken covertly, involving the secret employment or support of agents or allies, it resembles human intelligence collection more than it does the overt policy means a government might use.

While this definition is clear enough for most practical purposes, it is not absolutely precise. For example, although the law explicitly excludes "traditional" "diplomatic," "military," "counterintelligence" and "law enforcement" activities from the ambit of covert action, it neither defines those activities nor specifies the dividing line between them and covert action. Diplomacy, for instance, also involves attempting to influence the behavior of other governments and their officials, and it is often carried on secretly; for example, it is often important to keep negotiations between two countries secret from other countries and the public. It may even be that conversations with some officials of a foreign government are not shared with other officials of that same government.

Similarly, "traditional counterintelligence" comprises the use of double agents, as discussed in the next chapter. While these agents are involved in defeating an adversary's human collection efforts, they may also be used to pass bogus information that may deceive him, possibly altering his behavior. (In any case, the double agent must deceive the adversary about his own activity, and the adversary's intelligence collection activities are of necessity influenced.) At what point this "traditional" activity should be regarded not as counterintelligence but as covert action is not clear.

In addition, it should be noted that the term "covert action" appears to be an American invention, not used in the lexicons of all other intelligence services.[3] For example, the nearest equivalent Soviet term of art, "active measures" *(aktivnye meropriiatiia),* was broader than covert action—it referred to both "overt and covert techniques of influencing events and behavior in, and the actions of, foreign countries."[4] As such, it did not fall entirely within the sphere of intelligence. Instead, it included other foreign political activities of both the Soviet government (for example, diplomacy and the use of official media, such as Radio Moscow) and the Communist Party of the Soviet Union (conducted, for example, through foreign communist parties or such front groups as the

World Peace Council). The term focused attention on the goal sought—political influence—rather than on the secrecy or openness of the means used.[5]

Regardless of the terminology used, it is important to keep in mind that what is called covert action in the United States is only one tool of foreign policy among many. Because of its unique features and flamboyant past, it has attracted a great deal of attention, and because of its secrecy, it does pose some particular problems for a democratic government. Nevertheless, the term may be unfortunate in that it emphasizes a characteristic of the means used (their secrecy) while obscuring the fact that the ends sought are, or should be, those of foreign policy as a whole. Because of this focus on the form rather than the substance of the activities involved, the debate in the United States about covert action has largely emphasized questions of legality and propriety at the expense of more fundamental questions concerning foreign policy goals and strategy.

This chapter will treat covert action as an element of intelligence that is also a foreign policy tool; in chapter 6, the specific issues connected with the use of covert action by a democratic government will be addressed. Because of the ambiguities inherent in past and current U.S. definitions of covert action, the discussion in the remainder of this chapter deals with activities more inclusive than the covert action category in order to clarify its limits. A theoretically more satisfying definition of covert action would not, to be sure, be tied so closely to the vagaries of U.S. law and practice; such a definition, however, remains to be achieved.

TYPES AND EXAMPLES OF COVERT ACTION

In its most general sense of the secret influencing of foreign behavior events, or circumstances, the term "covert action" covers a wide spectrum of activities, running from the most pedestrian, such as secretly providing technical assistance (such as security or communication equipment or training) to a friendly foreign government to the most spectacular, such as assassination or supporting or fomenting a coup d'état. It is therefore difficult to provide a comprehensive list of the types of covert action that intelligence agencies have conducted. In addition, the U.S. intelligence agencies have not developed a standard typology of covert action, nor have those who study them. This section attempts to develop such a categorization.

The purpose of covert action is to influence the actions of foreign governments or events or circumstances in foreign countries. These attempts can be directed at the government of a country, at the society as a whole, or at a particular segment of it. In democratic countries, influence successfully brought to bear on the society may be felt quickly by the government as well; however, such influence also can have important effects in the long run in nondemocratic or even totalitarian countries.

Influencing political behavior, circumstances, or events in foreign countries is the very stuff of foreign policy; diplomacy is as much directed toward this goal as covert action. In addition, military forces may be developed or deployed in order to influence foreign behavior; this is common in peacetime but may occur during war as well. Thus, it is not surprising that many of the covert action techniques discussed below can be, and are, carried out in a noncovert manner as well. What is or is not considered covert action, for U.S. government purposes, often depends less on the nature of the case than on the peculiarities of the applicable legal and administrative definitions of covert action.

Covert Support of a Friendly Government

In many cases, covert action is carried out through a tacit alliance with individuals or groups with whom one shares common objectives. It is least difficult to do this when the ally in question is a friendly foreign government. In this instance, covert action can be limited to such unsensational activities as secretly assisting the allied nation with personal security for its leader or equipment for secure (encrypted) communications.

Nonintelligence Assistance There is some reason to call such an activity covert action. The support provided to a friendly government helps it stay in power and, in that sense, influences the course of events in that country. In addition, the action takes place in secret, in that information is not released to the public concerning the support, nor would there be any public acknowledgment of it if word should leak out. But we could just as easily consider the action a form of secret diplomacy. In fact, the term "covert action" would probably be applied to this sort of activity only if it were undertaken by an intelligence agency; supplying secret aid via diplomatic or military personnel might not be so considered.

Such activities are often small in scale and relatively noncontroversial, and hence they are unlikely to make their way into the newspapers. They may, however, be important both technically (by providing capabilities that the friendly government could not have provided for itself) and psychologically (as an indication to the receiving government of the reliability and effectiveness of its patron's support). However, this absence of visibility and controversy need not always be the case.

First of all, the same disputes about which governments should be considered friendly and worthy of assistance would be likely to occur as in the case of noncovert foreign aid. The secrecy involved does not change the nature of such disagreements, although it may lead opponents of a program to suspect that it was kept secret primarily to avoid any challenge to it.

Second, a dispute might arise from the nature of the assistance, especially if the recipient has an unsavory reputation.[6] For example, in 1974 the U.S. Congress banned the use of foreign aid funds for police training; this came about because of controversy concerning the human rights records of Latin American regimes that were recipients of such assistance.[7]

Intelligence Support Another common type of support rendered to a friendly foreign government may be noted in particular: the providing or sharing of intelligence information. In part because this activity is routine, it would not typically be considered covert action. In cases involving an exchange of information of more or less equal value, in which the purpose of providing the other government with information is to receive valuable intelligence in return, it seems more reasonable to view the activity as intelligence collection than as covert action.

In other cases, however, where the exchange is one-sided, the major motivation of the party providing the bulk of the intelligence may well be the desire to help the other government. In this case, it seems reasonable to consider it covert support of a friendly government, since it enables another government to achieve objectives it could not reach on its own, and it is, of course, carried on secretly.[8]

While intelligence would typically be shared only with friendly governments (i.e., the intelligence provider regards the recipient's well-being as being in its own interest as well), cases crop up in which a government would pass specific information to a government not regarded as friendly in order to induce or enable the latter to take a specific step in the interest of both. This possibility, where the motivation is less to help the other government than to make it take a specific action, is discussed below as a method of influencing how a foreign government perceives its situation in the world.

Influencing Perceptions of a Foreign Government

Unlike the situation discussed above, where one is interested in supporting a foreign government whose well-being one regards as furthering one's own interests as well, the more common and characteristic covert action tries to influence perceptions so as to *change* foreign behavior, events, or circumstances to further one's interests. This is done either by influencing the foreign government's actions or by influencing the foreign society, or groups or sectors of it, independently of its government's actions and often against its government's wishes. The ultimate goal is to influence the government's policy or to create the conditions for a change of government. This section and the one following discuss how actions, events, or circumstances can be affected by influencing (1) a foreign government's perceptions or (2) the perceptions of elements of a foreign society, about political, military, or economic matters.

Agents of Influence The simplest and most direct method of affecting a foreign government's actions is to use an *agent of influence*—an agent whose task is to influence directly government policy rather than to collect information. Since an agent who is a high-level official in another government would be in a position to do both, this distinction could be a more theoretical than practical one. In such cases, using an agent whose prime function was intelligence collection to influence its government's policy might not be considered covert action. However, an intelligence service might not wish to jeopardize a good source by having that person try to influence his government's policy if, by so doing, he might call unfavorable and potentially dangerous attention to himself.

An agent of influence could be an official of the target government or a prominent member of the target country's political class (an insider, so to speak) who has good access to government officials, opinion leaders, and the media. If an agent of influence is a high official in the target government, he might, by himself, be able to take actions that benefit another government. The more frequent situation in a large, bureaucratic government, however, is that he will be most useful in persuading colleagues to adopt policies congenial to another government's interests. Obviously, he cannot openly advocate policies on the grounds that they are beneficial to some foreign, presumably unfriendly, power; he must seek to influence his colleagues' perceptions of the political situation in such a way that they are naturally led to take positions useful to the government whose agent he is.

For example, Soviet intelligence in the 1930s and 1940s ran a number of agents who worked for the U.S. government.[9] Among the most important of these was Harry Dexter White at the Department of the Treasury. In time, White rose to become assistant secretary of the treasury, the department's second-highest position. In addition to supplying Soviet intelligence with information and secrets, White acted as an agent of influence. Thus, in preparation for the Yalta conference between Stalin, Roosevelt, and Churchill in February 1945, White took the lead in drafting a Treasury Department proposal to extend a large, thirty-five-year, low-interest loan to Moscow and to grant it half of the proposed German war reparations of twenty billion dollars. In addition, White urged (in line with the Soviet position) that Germany's chemical, electrical, and metallurgical industrial capacity be completely dismantled: "There is nothing I can think of that can do more at this moment to engender trust or distrust between the United States and Russia than the position this Government takes on the German problem." However, in this instance, White's efforts on behalf of the Soviets were partially frustrated by opposition from the Department of State. In the end, no massive loan was made, nor was Germany deindustrialized. Yet Roosevelt did agree, along the lines proposed by White and against Churchill's wishes, to the Russian-set figure on war reparations and their share of it.[10]

A Cold War example of an agent of influence operating within government was Arne Treholt, a Norwegian foreign ministry official and, for more than a decade, a Soviet agent. Using various assignments within the ministry and at the United Nations, Treholt would, as opportunities arose, attempt to moderate or change his country's policies to the benefit of the Soviet Union. Early in his career, for instance, Treholt was given a relatively prominent position in law of the sea conferences and was a member of the Norwegian delegation negotiating with Moscow over boundaries and fishing rights in the Barents Sea. According to one account, "Treholt not only kept the KGB fully informed of the Norwegian negotiating position but also acted as a Soviet agent of influence in the Norwegian negotiating team," helping to produce a treaty "heavily criticized in Norway for being tilted in the Soviet interest." More generally, Treholt used his various positions within the ministry to push policies—such as a Nordic Nuclear Weapons–Free Zone—that were in line with Soviet efforts to weaken Norway's ties to the North Atlantic Treaty Organization (NATO). Treholt was especially effective in dealing with the Norwegian press, using his many contacts in the media to promote stories with an anti-American or anti-NATO slant. When arrested in 1984, Treholt was chief of the foreign ministry's press and information office.[11]

A second Cold War example of an agent of influence, one not a member of the government, was Pierre-Charles Pathé, a politically well-connected Frenchman who in 1979 was convicted of espionage for the Soviet Union and sentenced to five years in prison. As a political insider, he knew a great deal about high-level politics in Paris as well as about the personal lives of major political figures, although he did not have access to classified information. It appears, however, that his real crime was not espionage but being an agent of influence.

In 1976, partially funded by the KGB, he started a political newsletter called *Synthèse* (Synthesis). During the next three years this newsletter, which reached a large part of the political elite in France (at one point, 70 percent of the members of the Chamber of Deputies were among its subscribers), denigrated and attacked Western interests and policy; exaggerated differences of interest and policy between France and other members of the North Atlantic Treaty Organization (in particular, West Germany and the United States); and defended the USSR and its allies. Pathé was arrested after he was observed receiving money from a KGB officer at a clandestine meeting in the suburbs of Paris.[12]

The nature of the relationship between an intelligence service and an agent of influence varies according to the circumstances. In the case of someone like Pathé, a sophisticated journalist and political insider whose sympathies for the Soviet Union predated any clandestine connection with the KGB (it is likely that he first came to its attention when he published an article favorable to the Soviet Union in 1959), the relationship was probably a flexible one, based on shared interests, rather than a strictly disciplined one, based on detailed instructions.

Using categories devised by the intelligence and international departments of the former Soviet Union as a general guide, one can distinguish the different kinds of agents of influence by measuring the degree and type of control exercised by the intelligence service. First, there is the "trusted contact"—that is, someone who is willing to work with a foreign government to advance goals he shares with it but who is not receptive to detailed instruction and would typically not be paid. He may be contrasted with a "controlled" agent, who receives and executes precise orders and who would normally be compensated financially. At the other end of the spectrum would be someone who is manipulated (for example, via aides or his social contacts) to act in a way that serves the foreign government's interests but is unaware of this manipulation.[13]

Use of Information and Disinformation Another method of influencing a government's actions is by providing it with bits of information (or misinformation) designed to induce it to act in a desired manner. An example of this is the reported case in which the United States in 1983 passed to Ayatollah

Khomeini specific information about "Soviet agents and collaborators operating in Iran." This resulted in as many as two hundred executions and the "closing down [of] the communist Tudeh party," which "dealt a major blow to KGB operations and Soviet influence" in Iran. The United States reportedly obtained this information when a Soviet "diplomat" in Teheran, Vladimir A. Kuzichkin, defected to Britain in 1982; Kuzichkin was in fact "a senior KGB officer . . . whose job it had been to maintain contacts with the Tudeh party."[14]

Although, in this case, the CIA reportedly participated in the activity, there is no inherent necessity for intelligence channels to be used to pass such information. Absent any intelligence service involvement, such an activity would probably not be considered covert action, although its nature would remain essentially the same. A historically significant example of this type of activity, one that would not be considered covert action at all, would be British Prime Minister Winston Churchill's effort in April 1941 to warn the Soviet Union of the impending German attack.

Under the circumstances of the time, it is easy to see why Stalin might have suspected Churchill's motives. Stalin, probably possessing an exaggerated sense of English duplicity to begin with, certainly understood that it was in Britain's interest for relations between the Soviet Union and Germany to worsen. Churchill might well have hoped that Soviet defensive measures taken as a result of his message would be misinterpreted by Germany as threatening, thereby provoking further German military measures along the Soviet border, and so forth. As a result, Stalin regarded this well-founded warning as a deception effort and ignored it.[15]

While the two examples cited above involve the passing of true information, there is no reason why misinformation, as long as it is plausible, cannot serve the same purpose. For example, during the Vietnam War, the United States tried to create the impression that an anticommunist guerrilla movement was operating in North Vietnam. The purpose was to cause the North to doubt the efficacy of its own internal security apparatus. In fact, the so-called Sacred Sword of the Patriots League (SSPL) consisted of abducted North Vietnamese villagers who were taken to a purported "liberated" village (actually, a South Vietnamese–controlled island), indoctrinated into the SSPL, trained, and then infiltrated into the North to "spread the word" about the league. Over a four-year period in the mid-1960s, more than one thousand North Vietnamese were captured and then returned to North Vietnam with SSPL materials, documents, and information designed to support the ruse.[16]

Another technique for propagating misinformation is called "silent forgery," which is a forged document that is passed privately to a foreign government but is not made available to the media. In the best case, the target government (the government the forgery is designed to influence) accepts the forged document as genuine and does not investigate the matter. The government whose document the forgery purports to be never learns about it and is hence unable to deny its authenticity.

An example of this technique, one that failed because the target government did in fact investigate, is provided by Ladislav Bittman, a former Czech intelligence agent. He claims that in 1977 the Soviets prepared a forged memorandum, purportedly from the U.S. embassy in Teheran, and arranged for it to be sent anonymously to the Egyptian embassy in Belgrade. The memorandum, stamped "Top Secret," discussed a supposed plot by the United States, Iran, and Saudi Arabia to overthrow Egyptian President Anwar Sadat. The covert action failed when the Egyptian government made an official inquiry to Washington and received a reply that persuaded it that the memorandum was a forgery.[17]

This sort of disinformation effort may be directed specifically against the target's intelligence service rather than the government as a whole. In this case, the misinformation, instead of being given to the target government, is, so to speak, left lying around for its intelligence services to discover; for example, deliberately misleading conversations may be held over telephone lines the target government's intelligence is known to have tapped. This type of disinformation campaign is usually referred to as a "deception operation" and is considered part of counterintelligence rather than covert action. To some extent, this distinction is arbitrary, since the operation's basic purpose and method remain the same. On the other hand, a deception operation is a means of defeating the target's intelligence collection and analysis activities; it depends on, and makes use of, a detailed knowledge of the target intelligence service's sources and methods. In these respects, it is reasonably considered a part of counterintelligence.

Influencing Perceptions in a Foreign Society

As opposed to the techniques already discussed, those discussed below are predominantly directed at influencing currents of thought within a foreign society rather than its government. This is a more amorphous task, and it is harder to measure what effect some of these techniques have in any given case. While many of the examples may seem insignificant taken one at a time, the cumulative effect on public opinion over a long period may be large. These techniques, then, are more suitable for use by a government that understands it is engaged in a long-term struggle than by one that deals with each problem or crisis as a separate event.

Agents of Influence Although this technique would ordinarily involve agents who can more or less directly influence governmental perceptions and policies, one could imagine agents whose main task is to affect a foreign country's public opinion. According to a former KGB officer, France was an especially fertile ground for these types of activities: "A majority of the most highly rated French agents in the mid-1970s . . . were journalists or involved with the press." Employing agents and collaborators in the French media, Soviet intelligence was active in exploiting existing communist and Gaullist tendencies within French public opinion to undermine France's ties to NATO and to increase popular support for friendlier relations with the Soviet Union.[18]

Stanislav Levchenko, a KGB major who defected to the United States in 1979, has recounted several examples of the Soviet use of agents of influence to affect the Japanese media and politics.[19] They include the following: the use of a prominent member of the Japanese Socialist Party to prevent another party member, whom the KGB considered to be a Chinese agent, from achieving a leadership position; the use of a senior correspondent of the Tokyo newspaper *Yomiuri* to promote the publication of an article designed to obtain the release of a Soviet military intelligence (GRU) agent who had been arrested in a double-agent operation; and the use of a young American stringer for the Associated Press to surface a letter purportedly from the wife of a Soviet air force pilot who had defected from Siberia to Japan in his MiG-25 imploring him to return to the Soviet Union.[20]

Unattributed Propaganda One of the more direct ways of attempting to influence a society is by disseminating opinions, information, or misinformation through the available media—that is, by propaganda (as it is pejoratively called). For example, nations with active foreign policies usually have radio stations (such as the Voice of America, Radio Moscow, and so forth) that openly express their views on international questions, much as newspaper editorials express the views of the newspaper's editor or publisher.

At times, however, a government may wish not to be officially associated with the material contained in its propaganda. In these cases, it may put certain opinions or facts into circulation in a manner that does not make their origin apparent. This may be accomplished either by planting them in news media it does not own or control, or by means of media that appear to the public to be independent but that are in fact controlled by the government.[21]

There are two major reasons a government might resort to such unattributed (or "black") propaganda. First, the target audience may be more disposed to believe the propaganda if its origin is disguised and the ulterior motive of the propagandist is not evident. For example, British propaganda in the United States before America's entry into the First and Second World Wars was often disseminated through covert mechanisms in order to appear to be objective and independent news reporting. For example, using emigrés from Central Europe, British intelligence was able to penetrate a number of German clandestine operations being run in the United States. In order to lessen isolationist sentiment and generate antipathy toward Germany in the mind of the American public, information about these operations was passed by the British to the sympathetic editor of the *Providence (R.I.) Journal*. Based on this information, the *Journal* then published stories that were syndicated and run by other newspapers throughout the United States; presumably these papers believed that the accounts were based on American investigative journalism.[22]

A second reason for using "black" propaganda mechanisms is that for diplomatic reasons, a government may not wish to be associated with certain opinions it nevertheless wishes to propagate to a given audience. For example, during the Iranian hostage crisis of 1979–81, the Soviet government took a diplomatically correct position by condemning the hostage-taking at the UN, while its "black" radio station, the National Voice of Iran, implicitly approved it and sought to inflame anti-American opinion in Iran.[23]

In addition to "black" propaganda media, whose origin is meant to be concealed, one may also speak of "gray" propaganda, whose origin, while not totally or effectively concealed, is nevertheless not publicly acknowledged. For example, the U.S. government established Radio Free Europe and Radio Liberty in 1949 and 1951, respectively, to broadcast to the peoples of Eastern Europe and the Soviet Union. Unlike Voice of America, these stations were not to convey official American views but were designed to provide the target populations with information about their own countries that was not available in their own government-controlled media, as well as with information about the West. They were set up as private U.S. organizations; to support this cover, they even made public appeals for contributions. In fact, the stations were run by the CIA. According to Ray Cline, "The CIA organized this effort . . . because it was thought the broadcasts would be more effective if their connection with the U.S. Government would be concealed."[24] But while the U.S. government connection was unacknowledged, it was clear that the radios were an American operation.[25]

Another method of conducting propaganda in an unattributed fashion involves planting stories in independent news media or arranging for books to be written and published by authors and publishing houses that have no visible connections with the government or its intelligence agencies. For example, in a covert action campaign directed during the Cold War against communist influence in Western Europe, the CIA used unattributed propaganda, including secret subventions for publishing books and newspaper articles planted via agents of influence working for wire services or newspapers.

One of the most famous CIA activities of this sort was the publication in various non-U.S. newspapers of a CIA-supplied copy of Khrushchev's 1956 "secret speech" attacking Stalin's "cult of personality."[26] Another example is the CIA's support for the writing and publication of *The Penkovsky Papers,* an account based on the actual case materials of the CIA's premier spy in the Soviet Union in the late 1950s and early 1960s.[27]

A related technique is the use of a front group as a propaganda medium. These groups, while ostensibly broadly based, are in fact under the control of a government and can be relied on to take positions consonant with that government's objectives. They thus serve the same function as unattributed propaganda—they express views that serve a government's interest but in a format more likely to make them acceptable to the intended audience. Before World War II, for instance, the British established a number of front groups intended to counter and harass "America First," the largest and most important of the isolationist organizations within the United States.[28]

Forgeries Another technique for putting material into circulation without taking any responsibility for it is the preparation and circulation of forged documents.[29] As with those discussed above, this technique serves the same general purpose: to influence a target audience's perceptions so it will take desired actions. The material used to do this—the arguments advanced by an agent of influence; the content of the propaganda, attributed or unattributed; or the text of the forgery—must be plausible to those whom one is attempting to influence. In general, therefore, one would expect the false material to be mixed in with elements of truth in order to enhance its plausibility. The resulting amalgam, which has the effect of misleading the target audience in some important respect, is often referred to as "disinformation."[30]

Of course, it is possible that a totally true message (or one that was believed to be true by those propagating it) could have the desired effect on a target audience. The most effective part of the Khrushchev secret speech (in the sense of reducing communism's prestige in Western and Eastern Europe) consisted of the revelations concerning Stalin's crimes and of the "cult of personality." Publicizing it was an effective CIA covert action even though that part of the text was undeniably authentic. Similarly, the British release of the authentic Zimmermann telegram, discussed in the previous chapter, was a masterstroke of unattributed propaganda.

Support for Friendly Political Forces

Another way of influencing events in foreign countries is the provision of material support to friendly political forces, such as political parties, civic groups, labor unions, and media. While this can be, and sometimes is, done openly, covert aid may be more palatable to the recipient groups, since it is less likely to lead to politically damaging charges of foreign interference in the target country's internal affairs.

Certainly this was the case with American covert assistance to the independent Polish labor union Solidarity in the 1980s. Working in conjunction with the Catholic Church and American labor, the U.S. government developed a program intended to help keep the labor organization and Poland's democratic movement alive after Poland's communist government declared martial law in December of 1981. Among the kinds of support secretly provided Solidarity were money, printing presses, and clandestine communication equipment.[31]

Traditionally, the former Soviet Union facilitated this type of activity by a fictitious distinction between the Soviet government and the Communist Party of the Soviet Union. While the former could pursue correct diplomatic relations with other states, the latter, through such organizations as the Comintern, the Cominform (or Communist Information Bureau, which from 1947 to 1956 disseminated the "party line" to foreign communist states and parties), and the International Department of the Central Committee, maintained relations with, and provided support for, "progressive" forces throughout the world.[32] In response to Soviet activity of this sort in Western Europe after World War II, the United States engaged in a covert action program of aid to democratic political and cultural groups and trade unions.[33]

The immediate impetus was fear in the Harry Truman administration (in late 1947) that the communists would win the Italian elections scheduled for the following spring. To support overt U.S. propaganda efforts, the CIA conducted such activities as providing financial and other support (for example, training in electoral campaign techniques) to noncommunist political parties. It also attempted to influence the Socialist party against cooperation with the communists. As Ray Cline, former deputy director of the CIA, explained,

> These kinds of financial and technical assistance to the Christian Democrats and other noncommunist parties, as well as the efforts to split off Socialists from the united front group dominated by the Communists, had to be covert. Italian party leaders could not afford to let Communists obtain evidence that they were supported by foreigners because it would blunt public anger at the Communist Party for its own financial and policy dependence on the Soviet Union. Hence CIA got the job of passing money and giving the technical help needed to get out the vote and win the election.[34]

Following the electoral success of the noncommunist parties, the CIA "was instructed to propose specific information programs and other political action that would negate communist efforts to expand Soviet political influence in Western Europe."[35] As described by the Church Committee, the resulting program involved "subsidies to European 'counterfront' labor and political organizations" that were

> intended to serve as alternatives to Soviet- or communist-inspired groups. [There were e]xtensive . . . labor, media and election operations . . . in the late 1940s. . . . Support for "counterfront" organizations, especially in the areas of student, labor and cultural activities, was to become much more prevalent in the 1950s and 1960s.[36]

As Ray Cline has emphasized, much of this funding went to organizations of the noncommunist Left that were not necessarily sympathetic to specific U.S. foreign policy positions. He cites specifically the Congress of Cultural Freedom and such political journals as *Encounter* in England and *Der Monat* in West Germany.[37] This strategy was presumably dictated by the view that the major ideological battleground in Europe was on the Left and that the more conservative organizations would, in any case, have fewer problems in obtaining funding domestically. It points out, however, a typical ambiguity in covert action: It is often possible to work with people with whom one has major disagreements. The embarrassment the revelation of such an arrangement would cause becomes another reason for secrecy.

A more controversial U.S. program of this sort was conducted in Chile following the inauguration of the Marxist Salvador Allende as president in 1970. This program was designed to provide opposition political parties and media with the financial resources to survive the country's economic chaos and hostile regulatory action by the government. The controversy surrounding it focused on two issues (aside from the larger question of what the U.S. policy toward the Allende regime should have been).

First, the program was condemned as unnecessary, since, according to the Church Committee, CIA national intelligence estimates during the Allende period indicated that "despite attempts to harass and financially damage opposition media," the opposition press (and in particular *El Mercurio,* the nation's largest newspaper and the most important anti-Allende medium) remained free and that "the traditional political system in Chile continued to demonstrate remarkable resiliency."[38] However, the committee noted that those responsible for the estimates were unaware of the covert action program: "Thus, there was no estimate of whether those sectors would survive *absent* U.S. money."[39]

Another controversy concerned the purposes for which U.S. aid was given. A strong attempt was made to keep U.S. assistance away from those groups that were actively seeking to overturn the government (such as the truckers' union, whose long, damaging strikes provided the occasion for the military coup) and to limit it to opposition parties and media. According to Gregory Treverton, a critic of covert action who was a staff member of the Church Committee, "The pattern of deliberations within the U.S. government suggests a careful distinction between supporting opposition forces and funding groups trying to promote a military coup. The attempt to draw that distinction was, so far as I can tell, an honest one."[40] Nevertheless, as Treverton concludes, this distinction was fundamentally artificial, one that existed "in the minds of Americans, not Chileans."[41] The opposition groups chose their own strategy for achieving their objectives and picked their tactics and allies accordingly; if the various anti-Allende forces wished to cooperate with each other, then U.S. support for some groups helped their allies as well.

Influencing Political Events by Violent Means

In the public mind, covert action is most often associated with violent methods of influencing political events. As the discussion so far has shown, many nonviolent techniques can be covertly employed to influence political behavior, events, and circumstances in foreign countries. But in addition to these activities, which make up the vast majority of covert action operations, there are also techniques that involve the supporting or use of violence.

Support for Coups, "Wars of National Liberation," and "Freedom Fighters" Support for political groups need not be limited to the peaceful opponents of a foreign government but can be extended to groups that seek either to influence that government's policy through violent means or to overthrow it. This could involve the support of an existing group or the creation of a "puppet" group to carry out these activities.[42]

The precise type of support would depend in part on the group being supported and the strategy it was following. It could take the form of military aid for an insurgent fighting force; operational support for a coup d'état; external political and economic pressure, or internal subversion, directed against the target government; or training and economic support for the development of cadres for a long-term guerrilla struggle. The two large, basically overt, "covert" actions undertaken by the United States during the Jimmy Carter and Ronald Reagan administrations (support for the guerrilla struggle against the Soviet-supported Afghan regime and support for the Contra resistance in Nicaragua) exemplify this type of covert action.

A particular form of this sort of activity that has received a great deal of attention is patron-state support for international terrorism. The support governments provide to terrorist groups can vary greatly in magnitude and importance. At the low end of the spectrum, a patron state might provide training facilities or a haven where terrorists would be safe from arrest while planning their attacks or to which they could flee afterward. At the higher end, this support could include money, weapons, genuine or forged passports, or use of the diplomatic pouch to send weapons or explosives into the target country. The amount of control the patron state exercises over the terrorist group's activities can also vary; in some cases, it may be fairly detailed, while in others almost nonexistent, as long as the general nature of the activities is consistent with the patron's interests.

Paramilitary At the borderline between real covert action and military action are cases in which a government uses irregular (or volunteer) forces in a military conflict, either alone or in alliance with similar groups or indigenous forces. Because a relatively large-scale effort of this sort can hardly remain secret for long, we might argue that this type of activity should be excluded from the category of covert action. On the other hand, since intelligence services are likely to be tasked to carry it out, it is usually grouped with more covert types of action. In any case, since the activity would not be publicly acknowledged by the government carrying it out, it remains covert action in that sense, regardless of how transparent the pretense of noninvolvement becomes.

Specific Acts of Destruction or Violence, including Assassination Finally, covert action can take the form of specific acts of violence, directed against individuals (such as the assassination of foreign government officials, key political figures, or terrorists) or property.

"Wet affairs" (a euphemism for assassination and sabotage) were, at various times, a regular element in Soviet intelligence operations. Perhaps the most famous instance was the murder of Leon Trotsky in Mexico in 1940. In the United States, the CIA's bungled attempts to assassinate Fidel Castro, as well as its involvement with the political forces responsible for assassinating Patrice Lumumba of the Congo and Rafael Trujillo of the Dominican Republic, were among the main issues that surfaced during the investigations of the agency during the mid-1970s and were minutely studied by the Church Committee.[43] One result of these revelations was the inclusion in President Gerald Ford's executive order on intelligence of an explicit ban on "engag[ing] in, or conspir[ing] to engage in, political assassination."[44] This provision was retained in the executive orders on intelligence promulgated by Presidents Carter and Reagan.[45] This issue resurfaced in the late 1980s in connection with U.S. policy toward Panamanian strongman Manuel Noriega, when it was alleged that the provision prohibited the CIA from assisting anti-Noriega members of the Panamanian Defense Force in planning a coup (for fear that it might involve or, at any rate, result in Noriega's assassination).[46] From this point of view, the provision thereby contributed indirectly to the U.S. invasion of Panama in December 1989, which achieved Noriega's overthrow, but at a much higher price.

One of the better-known covert actions involving violence against property was the blowing up, by French intelligence agents, of the *Rainbow Warrior* in 1985. This ship, which was attacked while at harbor in New Zealand, was owned by the environmental organization Greenpeace, which intended to use the ship to protest and interfere with French atomic weapon tests in the South Pacific. A Portuguese photographer on board was inadvertently killed in the explosion.

A more destructive instance of this type of activity was the German covert campaign of sabotage that took place in the United States prior to its decision to enter World War I. Although officially neutral, the United States was nevertheless a key supplier of munitions and war material to Great Britain and its allies during the conflict's first three years. In order to disrupt this flow of material to its enemies—and do so without generating an American backlash against Germany—German intelligence carried out scores of covert operations in the United States. These included sabotaging ships carrying supplies to Britain and Russia, manufacturing anthrax viruses to be injected into horses and mules being sent to Europe, and bombing munition and powder plants along the East Coast. The most spectacular operation of all was the sabotage of the rail and sea terminal at Black Tom, New Jersey, in July 1916. Using incendiary devices and explosives, German agents completely destroyed the site and with it a massive amount of munitions destined for the war in Europe. The destruction of the terminal, which was situated across from the Statue of Liberty, rocked the Brooklyn Bridge, blew out windows throughout Manhattan, and could be heard as far south as Philadelphia.[47]

COVERT ACTION AND SECRECY

Although secrecy appears to be at the very heart of covert action, its actual importance and function, as noted at the beginning of this chapter, is not at all a simple matter; it depends very much on the type of covert action involved and the circumstances in which it is undertaken. The degree of secrecy required, and the motivation for it, can differ greatly from case to case.

In some instances, secrecy may be absolutely essential to the operation's success. For example, Adm. Stansfield Turner, President Carter's director of central intelligence, has described an operation that involved sending a CIA agent to Teheran to facilitate the escape of six Americans who had taken refuge in the Canadian embassy after the American embassy was seized in November 1979.[48] Any revelation of the operation (even if the identities of the CIA agent and the six in hiding were not revealed) would have endangered the safety of the seven people involved by heightening Iranian vigilance, inducing the Iranians to invade the Canadian embassy, or complicating the process of extracting the Americans from Iran using false passports.

Similarly, keeping certain details of an operation secret may be necessary to prevent interference with it, even though the broad outlines of the program are generally known. For example, consider the U.S. program to assist the *mujahedeen* resistance against the Soviet Union in Afghanistan in the 1980s. There were any number of countries and specific channels used to transfer supplies to the resistance; had these been public at the time, they would have been vulnerable to sabotage or diplomatic pressure by the Soviet or Afghan governments.[49] Thus, with respect to this detail of the covert action, secrecy would be needed, regardless of the publicity the operation as a whole received.

Cases such as this, where secrecy about either the entire operation or a specific part of it is crucial to carrying them out at all, are probably rare. In many other cases, however, secrecy is very important for an operation's effectiveness. In this category, we could consider the kinds of unattributed propaganda or support for political activity that have already been discussed.

These activities are carried out covertly on the grounds that public awareness of the foreign source of the propaganda or the funding for political activities would diminish the effect. The concept of "black" propaganda, for example, is that information that would be questioned or rejected were it known to come from an adversary or from some other foreign source with an obvious ulterior motive will be more acceptable if its origin can be hidden or falsely identified. (In many cases, secrecy would also be required because the funding of political organizations would violate the law of the target country.)

In addition, "black" propaganda can be used to sow dissension in the adversary's ranks by falsely attributing provocative words or actions. In this case, secrecy concerning the true source of the propaganda is necessary to support its credibility. Sefton Delmer, who ran British "black" propaganda operations in World War II, claimed that "the simplest and most effective 'black' operation is to spit in a man's soup and cry 'Heil Hitler.'"[50] Similarly, many of the forgeries produced by the former Soviet Union were fabricated U.S. government memorandums that evinced a hostile attitude toward a third country.

In other cases, secrecy may be necessary to secure the cooperation of a third party that is willing to help only if the activity is concealed, in order to avoid damaging its other foreign relationships. For that reason, even in a case in which the contours of a covert activity could be safely made known, keeping it secret might be important.

A final category deals with cases where public awareness is avoided less because it would endanger those carrying out the operation or harm its effectiveness than because diplomatic reasons make it desirable not to acknowledge governmental involvement.[51] For example, the lack of official acknowledgment of an operation may inhibit an adversary's response, even if the adversary is aware through intelligence information of the involvement. This is particularly true if the adversary is a democracy in which the government must obtain public approval or understanding for any response it might make; the adversary may be inhibited from trying to obtain public support by the fear that publicizing the incriminating evidence will jeopardize the means by which it was collected. Thus it makes sense for a state that supports international terrorism to disavow any connection with a specific terrorist event, even when its complicity otherwise becomes known.

For example, the U.S. government's ability to respond to the Libyan-supported terrorist bombing on April 5, 1986, of a discotheque in West Berlin, in which an American serviceman and another person were killed, ultimately depended on U.S. willingness to divulge sensitive intelligence information proving Libyan involvement. While the U.S. government finally did this, it paid a heavy price; the Libyans were made aware of the extent of U.S. intelligence capabilities directed against them and hence were able to reduce the effectiveness of those capabilities.[52]

More generally, although governments are understood to engage in covert action (as they are in espionage), covert action is frequently illegal under the laws of the country in which the covert action is taking place. It may also be said to be contrary to the norms of international law, of which nonintervention in the internal affairs of sovereign states is a basic premise, although this principle has been substantially weakened by international practice since the end of the Cold War.[53]

For these reasons, it is less provocative and less disruptive to diplomatic relations not to acknowledge an operation even if the country adversely affected by it is well aware of one's involvement. The target country, either in the interests of good relations or because it cannot effectively prevent it, may ignore the covert action; it is much harder for it to do so if the government conducting it publicly acknowledges what it is doing.

Plausible Denial

Closely related to this is the doctrine, long considered axiomatic, that even if a nation's involvement in covert action becomes known, the chief of state should be able to deny that he authorized or even knew of the action. He should be able to assert, with some plausibility, that it was carried out by subordinates who acted without his knowledge or authority.

In the post–World War II period, this doctrine came to public attention most forcefully when, as already described, President Eisenhower disregarded it and publicly admitted that he had authorized overflights of the Soviet Union by the U-2 reconnaissance plane. Eisenhower's action came in May 1960, after a U-2 plane, whose high-altitude flight had previously made it invulnerable to air defenses, was brought down by a Soviet surface-to-air missile while on a reconnaissance flight across that country. (Although not covert action, this incident, involving an apparent violation of international law, raised the same issue of plausible deniability.)

In his memoirs, the Soviet first secretary in those years, Nikita Khrushchev, would claim that it was Eisenhower's admission of responsibility rather than the flight itself that caused him to scuttle the Paris "Big Four" summit meeting scheduled for later that spring.[54] Eisenhower, however, felt that he could not deny knowledge without suggesting that he did not effectively control U.S. military forces, especially given the large infrastructure necessary to support the flights. While it is possible to disavow the actions of a small group of secret agents, who can be portrayed as renegades acting without or contrary to orders, it is another matter to disavow an operation that obviously required the cooperation of many people at various air bases around the world.

An example of plausible denial in recent years arose from the case of the French intelligence agents who blew up the *Rainbow Warrior*. Responsibility for this affair became evident when the French intelligence officers involved were arrested in New Zealand. The French government maintained that official involvement in the affair went no higher than Defense Minister Charles Hernu, who was responsible for the DGSE (Direction Générale de la Sécurité Extérieure, the French foreign intelligence service, subordinate to the Ministry of Defense) and who resigned three months after the attack. President François Mitterrand escaped essentially unscathed.[55]

In the United States, the doctrine of plausible denial was in effect abolished by Congress in connection with its investigations into intelligence matters in the mid-1970s. At the end of 1974, following revelations about a covert action program in Chile, Congress passed the Hughes-Ryan Amendment, which prohibited CIA covert actions

> unless and until the President finds that each such operation is important to the national security of the United States and reports, in a timely fashion, . . . to the appropriate committees of the Congress, including [the Senate Foreign Relations Committee and the House Foreign Affairs Committee].[56]

Congressional consideration of the amendment focused on the part that required the executive branch to inform Congress about covert actions. However, the amendment's requirement that the president find that proposed covert actions are important to the national security destroyed the president's ability plausibly to deny involvement in any covert action operation that became publicly known.[57]

In the course of the Iran-Contra investigation, Adm. John Poindexter's claim that he had not informed President Reagan about the diversion of the proceeds from the Iranian arms sales to the Nicaraguan resistance represented an attempt to revive the plausible-denial doctrine. In particular, Poindexter testified that he did not tell the president about the diversion in order to "provide some future deniability for [him] if it ever leaked out."[58]

The Abandonment of Secrecy

Because of the increased congressional role in controlling covert action, among other reasons, the United States has, in effect, abandoned secrecy in recent years with respect to some operations that would ordinarily be (and often still are) called covert action. For example, the question of aid to the Afghan and Nicaraguan insurgents was openly discussed and debated in Congress and in the press. The United States even asserted, in connection with the 1988 Geneva agreement on Soviet withdrawal from Afghanistan, a right to continue aiding the rebels as long as the Soviets provided aid to the Kabul government. Despite the fact that these activities were called covert action, they were overt in many respects. Indeed, in some cases Congress has openly taken the lead in proposing actions, such as providing aid to Iraqi forces opposing the rule of Saddam Hussein, that in the past would have been thought of as covert action.[59]

In other cases, the United States has abandoned secrecy altogether for activities that previously would have been considered to require it. In 1973, for example, after CIA funding of Radio Free Europe/Radio Liberty (RFE/RL) had been publicly confirmed, Congress replaced the covert funding mechanism with overt government funding via a newly created independent federal agency, the Board for International Broadcasting. While this change was not undertaken voluntarily, it may not have had much effect on RFE/RL's credibility in the target countries. Whether the extent to which the initial disguising of sponsorship enhanced RFE/RL's effectiveness, it would seem that by 1973 the radio stations already had long track records by which their audiences could judge them.

Similarly, following President Reagan's speech in London on June 8, 1982, in which he called for strengthening the infrastructure of democracy on a global basis, the National Endowment for Democracy, a federally funded private organization, was established in 1983. It provides overt support (directly and via affiliated institutes of the AFL-CIO, the U.S. Chamber of Commerce, and the Democratic and Republican parties) for institutions—trade unions, business associations, other civic organizations, media, and political parties—

that promote democratization or contribute to democratic life in foreign countries where democracy is weak, threatened, or nonexistent.[60]

This effort was to some extent modeled on the international activities of the political foundations associated with the West German political parties;[61] these foundations are funded by the German government and work through similarly minded political organizations in other countries to promote democracy. They are generally credited, for example, with providing vital support for the noncommunist parties in Portugal during the turbulent and dangerous period following the overthrow of the Caetano dictatorship in 1974. In certain respects, this type of overt support for democratic institutions partially replaced the covert support the United States provided to democratic forces in Western Europe right after World War II.

COVERT ACTION AND INTELLIGENCE

Having reviewed the wide range of activities that come under the heading of covert action, we now look at its relation to the rest of intelligence. Two questions suggest themselves. First, should covert action be conducted by the intelligence-gathering and analysis agencies, or should it be lodged in a separate bureaucratic structure? Second, should covert action, from a purely theoretical perspective, be considered part of intelligence?

Should Covert Action Be Separate?

Arguments against a Separate Covert Action Agency As noted in the first chapter, both the United States and Britain have discovered through experience that having two organizations involved in running clandestine operations—one for intelligence collection (espionage) and one for covert action—can create serious practical problems. During World War II, the British Special Operations Executive (SOE), charged by Prime Minister Winston Churchill with "setting Europe ablaze," was separate from the Secret Intelligence Service (SIS, or MI6) and reported to the minister for economic warfare. This gave rise to the inevitable interdepartmental rivalries as the two agencies competed for scarce resources.[62]

Similarly, in the United States, a special CIA component called the Office of Policy Coordination (OPC) was set up in 1948 to conduct covert action. Although administratively part of the CIA, it operated on the basis of policy guidance provided by the Departments of State and Defense, and its head was appointed by the secretary of state.[63] This office was separate from the CIA's Office of Special Operations (OSO), which collected intelligence via espionage. Eventually, this arrangement was found to be unworkable, and the two offices were consolidated in 1952 into the newly created Directorate for Plans.[64] According to the Church Committee, this step was due to (1) the anomalous position of the director of central intelligence in having an office (the OPC) for which he was administratively responsible (and that was funded through the CIA) that nevertheless took policy guidance directly from the Departments of State and Defense and (2) the competition between the OPC and the OSO for the services of the same agents and the difficulty, given that rivalry, of ensuring operational cooperation between them where necessary.[65]

Although conceptually different in function, covert action and human intelligence collection rely on similar means, especially the secret cooperation of agents able to operate effectively in the target country. In many cases, the agents who would be useful for one function can perform the other function as well; two separate offices could easily find themselves competing for the services of the same individuals. In addition, many of the support functions, such as ensuring communications between officers and agents or making clandestine payments, are similar or identical and require similar skills, contacts, and resources. Close coordination would be necessary to ensure that the operations of one office in a given country did not inadvertently interfere with those of the other; such coordination might be difficult to achieve, especially if it required that one office's interests be subordinated to those of the other. Thus, a strong case can be made for combining these functions in a single organization whose operations in a target country or region of the world would be controlled by a single chief.

Arguments for a Separate Covert Action Agency Despite the operational convenience of consolidating these functions, it has been argued that the different nature of the tasks involved makes consolidation inadvisable. In particular, the argument is made that giving the same organization responsibility for implementing policy (via covert action) with respect to a given country, on the one hand, and collecting and analyzing intelligence about that country (including assessing the results of the covert action), on the other, jeopardizes the objectivity of the analysis. In essence, this is the same argument that is made for the existence of a central intelligence agency—that is, one that is not a part of a policy-making and policy-implementing ministry or department of the government.

Is Covert Action a Part of Intelligence?

Aside from this organizational question, the more theoretical issue remains of whether covert action should be considered a part of intelligence. In including covert action among the elements of intelligence, I have noted that it is typically a function of intelligence agencies; this alone does not address the question of whether it makes sense to consider it a part of intelligence for theoretical purposes.[66]

To answer this question, one has to get a better sense of just what covert action is. As already noted, the term itself is taken from the U.S. intelligence lexicon and does not have clear counterparts in the usages of the intelligence services of other countries. Furthermore, the various U.S. definitions of covert action were developed in the context of attempts to regulate it by law or executive order; they are not necessarily useful for the present theoretical purpose.

In reviewing the types of covert action, some (such as secret support for a friendly regime) seem almost indistinguishable from diplomacy, and others (such as paramilitary activity) shade off into guerrilla or "low intensity" warfare. What seems to be uniquely covert action is a middle ground between diplomacy and war that involves the secret manipulation of the perceptions of others to induce them to take actions that one sees as in one's interest. As such, is covert action reasonably considered a part of intelligence?

On the one hand, it has been argued that covert action—a means of implementing policy—is so different from the rest of intelligence, which deals with obtaining the information on which policy should be based, that it is a mistake to consider it a part of intelligence. From this point of view, it is more reasonably categorized as one of many foreign policy tools—such as diplomacy, economic aid, "most favored nation" trade status, overt propaganda, exchange programs, Peace Corps–type programs, public diplomacy, military aid, and the threat or use of military force—that a nation uses to advance its interests.[67]

On the other hand, it may be countered that defining intelligence as the obtaining of information is too narrow: if obtaining information is so important, the denial of valuable information to one's adversary also must be an important part of intelligence. As becomes clear in the next chapter, an effective and particularly profitable way of preventing one's adversary from learning the truth is to deceive him into believing a falsehood. From this perspective, covert action and counterintelligence have important similarities. In particular, both may involve affecting the adversary's behavior by manipulating his perceptions.

The question of whether covert action is a part of intelligence is intimately tied up with the question of what intelligence is. This question will be discussed again in the concluding chapters of the book.

Chapter 5

Spy versus Spy: Counterintelligence

Of the elements of intelligence, counterintelligence is probably the hardest to define. In its most general terms, counterintelligence refers to information collected and analyzed, and activities undertaken, to protect a nation (including its own intelligence-related activities) against the actions of hostile intelligence services. Under this definition, the scope of counterintelligence is as broad as that of intelligence itself, since all manner of hostile intelligence activities must be defended against.[1] In a narrower sense, however, counterintelligence often refers specifically to preventing an adversary from gaining knowledge that would give him an advantage. We examine this notion of counterintelligence first.

In conceptualizing what is involved in such a defense against an adversary's intelligence collection, we can begin by distinguishing between passive and active measures. The most important passive measures, which seek to deny the adversary the information he is seeking simply by blocking his access to it—by, as it were, building a wall around it—are usually referred to as "security."[2] The nature of the wall—prohibiting access to sensitive information by individuals whose trustworthiness has not been ascertained, the protection of documents and communications in safes and by encryption, and so forth—is discussed later in the section on security. First, however, a government and its various departments and agencies must decide what information is important enough to protect—what information must be kept within the walls.

THE CLASSIFICATION OF INFORMATION

Levels of Classification

A classification system categorizes information according to its sensitivity, that is to say, the amount of damage its revelation to a hostile foreign power could cause and, hence, the importance of protecting it. In the United States, the first such system for protecting national security documents was promulgated by the War Department in 1912; the War and Navy Departments set up their own classification systems during World Wars I and II.[3] President Harry Truman established the first government-wide system of classifying information in 1951.[4] The current system is governed by an executive order promulgated by President Clinton in 1995 that sets out definitions, rules, and procedures.[5]

Sensitivity The U.S. classification system attempts to classify information according to the degree of harm to the national security its unauthorized release to an adversary would cause. The more sensitive the information, the more carefully it is to be protected and the fewer the people who are "cleared" for it (authorized to have access to it). Under the current system, the basic levels of classification are confidential, secret, and top secret, which are defined in terms of the damage to national security their unauthorized disclosure reasonably could be expected to cause:.

- Top secret: "exceptionally grave damage"
- Secret: "serious damage"
- Confidential: "damage."[6]

In addition, numerous other caveats are used to restrict access to information further. With respect to intelligence issues, these refer to information about technical intelligence collection techniques and capabilities; they are imposed by the director of central intelligence (DCI) pursuant to his responsibility, under the National Security Act of 1947, to "protect intelligence sources and methods from unauthorized disclosure."[7] The years have seen, however, a proliferation of these special classifications (or "compartments") as various entities within and outside the intelligence community have tried to protect information they see as particularly sensitive. Periodically, attempts are made to systematize and contain this process; the most recent executive order, for example, directs that the number of special access programs be kept "at an absolute minimum" and subjects them to an oversight process within the executive branch.[8] It seems, however, to be an unending struggle, and the repeated admonitions not to create new classifications testify to the strength of the incentives to do so.

Need to Know As noted above, the more sensitive the information (in terms of level of classification), the fewer are the number of people authorized to have access to it. In principle, however, mere clearance is not enough to obtain access to the information. People seeking access also must establish a "need to know" such information in order to perform their official responsibilities. This aspect of the information-control system is much less formal than that dealing with clearances; in general, anyone controlling classified information is responsible for ascertaining a requester's need to know before providing the information.[9]

It is questionable whether this requirement constitutes an effective barrier to the unnecessary dissemination of classified information. In 1985, a Department of Defense (DoD) Commission to Review DoD Security Policies and

Practices, headed by retired U.S. Army Gen. Richard Stilwell, observed that "the principle that a cleared individual is authorized access only to that information he 'needs-to-know' is generally not enforced."[10]

What Should Be Classified?

The basic answer to the question of what should be classified, at least as far as the U.S. government is concerned, is contained in the definitions of confidential, secret, and top secret given on the previous page. These may seem straightforward in principle, although the key terms "damage," "serious damage," and "exceptionally grave damage" are vague, both in themselves and as applied to a concept as general as national security.

In fact, the real situation is quite complicated. The very way in which the problem has been posed—what information should be walled off from public access and discussion—presupposes a fundamentally liberal view of government and society in which the free flow of information is the rule, and its denial, by means of classification, the exception. This view is probably the exception rather than the rule, as far as history goes. Until recently, the more common tradition has been that of governmental secrecy, broken when the government itself sees some advantage in disclosing information.

Consider, for example, the fact that democratic countries routinely publish large amounts of data about their defense budgets. Although the notion of classifying a democratic country's entire defense budget is out of the question, nondemocratic governments often do so. For example, the Soviet government regarded, until 1989, the amount it spent on defense as a state secret; such governments as those of China and North Korea still exercise this type of secrecy.[11] U.S. intelligence devotes resources to determining the size of these secret defense budgets; if this information were not considered helpful to the U.S. government, these intelligence resources would have presumably been applied to other tasks. Similarly, if the United States did not disclose its defense budget, other intelligence services would have at the very least to redirect resources from other tasks to that of determining its size, and hostile nations would be less certain about U.S. military capabilities.

This example is meant to argue *not* that a democracy should classify its defense budget but that the reason it does not do so has more to do with internal political considerations (the democratic imperative that citizens be able to learn about the government so that they can exercise their political rights and duties) than with abstract criteria for classification. The key dilemma can be stated as follows: almost any organization—political party, business corporation, football team, or whatever—that is competing with other organizations wants, other things being equal, to keep secret most information about its strategy for carrying on that competition, the resources it has available, and so on. In general, any information that is released damages its competitive position.

The same is true of the government's national security activities. The question is *always* one of balancing the potential harm to national security against the requirements of the domestic political order. No natural harmony exists between these two standards, and no unambiguous line can be drawn.

The pressure for openness does not always come from the side of the citizenry. Despite the general tendency toward secrecy, any government, but especially a democratic one, often finds it useful or even necessary to release information to explain its actions and build public support for them. As noted earlier, the Reagan administration, to justify and secure public support for the 1986 bombing raid on Libya, released information derived from decrypted Libyan cable traffic implicating that nation in the terrorist bombing of a West Berlin discotheque. In alerting the Libyan government that its cable traffic was being read, the administration jeopardized an important intelligence capability.

Overclassification It has been a recurring complaint that the U.S. government classifies too much information and at too high a level. This criticism has been made not only by congressional committees and nongovernmental critics of the intelligence agencies or particular administrations but by "insiders" as well. For example, the 1985 DoD commission on security practices noted that

> too much information appears to be classified and much at higher levels than is warranted. Current policy specifies that the signer of a classified document is responsible for the classification assigned but frequently, out of ignorance or expedience, little scrutiny is given such determinations. Similarly, while challenges to improper classifications are permitted, few take the time to raise questionable classifications with the originator.[12]

To some extent, as already noted, secrecy is a natural characteristic of any government. Given the great and remarkable openness of the American political system, the practice seems particularly anomalous and has raised more objections in the United States than elsewhere. In recent years, the same issue has surfaced in other countries, particularly Great Britain, where the laws governing the release of governmental information are much stricter than in the United States.[13]

Aside from the primary harm—the unnecessary denial of information to the public, reducing its ability to understand and debate national security policy issues—overclassification also could have the drawback of reducing the credibility of the classification system, leading to a tendency to disregard its rules, carelessness, and "leaking."[14] If many innocuous documents are classified, the inhibitions against the unauthorized disclosure of classified information are bound to be weakened.

Whether such pervasive overclassification exists in the U.S. government is a difficult question to answer. While any system that deals with millions of documents each year is bound to produce some dubious results, the major source of disagreement is the existence of different views of what standards should be applied to the classification decision. A common claim of those who believe that overclassification is rampant is that documents are often classified to save government officials from embarrassment or censure. These people claim, in other words, that classification serves to shield officials from public accountability for their actions. While this is an unacceptable motive for classification, the situation is often more complicated; the embarrassment is often not simply to an official who may have done something improper vis-à-vis the public but to the government itself vis-à-vis foreign powers.[15]

As was discussed in the treatment of covert action, secrecy is sometimes desired more for diplomatic reasons than because it is operationally necessary. The same is true with respect to foreign policy activities generally. As in the case of covert action, however, governments have generally tended in recent years to be more open about many facets of foreign policy and less concerned about diplomatic niceties. Governments are more likely now than previously to admit that they conduct espionage and other intelligence activities. Thus, there is less room for invoking the excuse of governmental embarrassment. Nevertheless, valid diplomatic reasons may exist. For example, in 1977 the *Washington Post* asserted that King Hussein of Jordan had received subsidies from the CIA, a claim that could only be harmful to him politically.[16] Keeping such a relationship secret to avoid embarrassing and weakening the political position of a friendly head of state is a legitimate motive for secrecy even though it is not, strictly speaking, operationally necessary.

Underclassification? Although it is often claimed that governments naturally tend to overclassify, it is worth considering whether the opposite is likely in certain areas. This might occur with information developed outside the government that is significant enough to national security to justify its being classified and controlled. The most obvious example of this is information relating to nuclear weapons technology. We would expect that information that could facilitate nuclear proliferation would be carefully controlled, regardless of whether it originated inside or outside government.

In the United States, this issue was addressed in the Atomic Energy Act of 1954, which defined restricted data as "all data concerning (1) design, manufacture, or utilization of atomic weapons; (2) the production of special nuclear material; or (3) the use of special nuclear material in the production of energy."[17] Under the act, this type of information is subject to controls regardless of whether it was developed inside or outside the government. (The same act also prohibits the dissemination of unclassified information relating to the design of, and security measures for, various facilities for the production or utilization of nuclear materials.)[18] Nevertheless, considerable amounts of information about nuclear materials and weapons exist in the public domain in the United States—hence the occasional report that a bright physics graduate student, working at a public library with unclassified sources, has drawn up plans for a nuclear bomb that unspecified experts have acknowledged as viable.

Other information that cannot be classified, but that might, under certain circumstances, deserve some protection include:

- Financial information that would enable one to earn illegitimate (insider) profits on financial or commodity markets
- Technological information a nation may wish to prevent adversaries from obtaining
- Personal information that might enable a hostile intelligence service to recruit government officials either by offering money to those with financial problems or by blackmailing them.

Protecting this sort of information has involved communications security, discussed below. However, it can, on occasion, involve other issues. For example, efforts have been made in the United States to apply the regulations concerning the export of technology to the dissemination of scientific papers dealing with these technologies; however, no feasible scheme for accomplishing this has been developed. In 1982 the deputy director of central intelligence, Adm. Bobby Ray Inman, noted the problem in a speech to the American Association for the Advancement of Science. Speaking of theoretical and applied cryptologic research, he expressed concern "that indiscriminate publication of the results of that research will come to the attention of foreign governments and entities and, thereby, could cause irreversible and unnecessary harm to U.S. national security interests." Among the areas where publication of technical information could harm national security Inman included "computer hardware and software, other electronic gear and techniques, lasers, crop projections, and manufacturing procedures."[19]

In the years following 1982, the mushrooming of public cryptography gave rise to a major controversy in the United States concerning the control of computer software incorporating sophisticated cryptologic algorithms. As noted in chapter 2, more and more cryptologic research is being done in the private sector, driven in particular by the increased use of computer-based communications for business purposes. While this has important benefits from a national security point of view (for instance, encrypted communications may thwart attempts to steal technological information by "hacking" into companies' e-mail or other communications systems), it has created the concern that terrorists, organized crime groups, money launderers, etc., may gain access to encryption capabilities that will thwart law enforcement efforts to keep tabs on them.

> Notwithstanding the accepted benefits of encryption, we have long argued that the proliferation of unbreakable encryption—because of its ability to completely prevent our Nation's law enforcement agencies from understanding seized computer files and intercepted criminal communications that have been encrypted and then being able to promptly act to combat dangerous criminal, terrorist, and espionage activities as well as successfully prosecute them—would seriously and fundamentally threaten these critical and central public safety interests.[20]

One proposed way to mitigate this danger was to control the export of cryptographic software involving encryption algorithms beyond a certain "strength" (as measured by the difficulty of solving the resulting ciphers).[21] In reply, U.S. software manufacturers argued that strong U.S. export controls of this sort merely allowed foreign competitors to gain market share at the expense of American firms. The latter argument eventually carried the day.[22]

SECURITY

Security measures are steps taken to obstruct a hostile intelligence service's ability to collect intelligence. Such measures are designed to prevent a hostile intelligence service from either gaining access or exploiting any access it may have to personnel, documents, communications, or operations to gain important information; they constitute the wall surrounding classified information. The more traditional aspects of security, which deal with protection against the adversary's human intelligence collection efforts, are discussed in this section; those that deal with his technical collection capabilities are discussed later under the heading of "multidisciplinary counterintelligence."

Personnel Security

Personnel security involves procedures for screening potential employees before hiring them for jobs that give access to information a hostile intelligence service might wish to collect, and for ensuring that current employees continue to meet the standards for access to such information. A screening procedure's primary function is to judge the potential employee's willingness and ability to keep classified information secret. The key elements of this judgment are the potential employee's character and loyalty.[23] Judgments about character must consider both the individual's mental stability and whether, for any reason, he or she would be vulnerable to blackmail by a hostile intelligence service.

Investigations In the United States, the screening investigation determines whether an individual is to be granted a security clearance—that is, authorized access to classified information. The investigation relies on information supplied on a security questionnaire by the individual, supplemented and verified by a national agency check (interrogation of the data banks of various law enforcement and other government agencies), and depending on the sensitivity of the information to which access is to be granted, interviews with friends and acquaintances, present and former neighbors, work associates and schoolmates, and so forth. In the case of particularly sensitive information, a periodic reinvestigation is required to maintain access. For a number of reasons, however, background investigations of this sort are probably not very effective in ascertaining the loyalty and character of personnel to be granted access to classified information.

Various legal prohibitions, discussed in the next chapter, prevent the FBI and other government agencies from collecting and maintaining membership lists of what used to be called subversive organizations, even if the organizations openly advocate the violent overthrow of the U.S. government.[24] A member of such an organization who was prudent about discussing his membership with acquaintances and who did not disclose the membership on the security clearance forms could reasonably hope to remain undetected.

In addition, societal changes in the United States have made it considerably harder to get candid responses from acquaintances, colleagues, neighbors, and others. First of all, there is a typically American resentment at government snooping that makes respondents disinclined to pass on negative information. In addition, the increased geographic mobility of U.S. society makes past acquaintances and neighbors harder to locate and means that they may have only a superficial knowledge of the candidate. Through the 1990s, at least, the political climate meant that respondents were less likely to take questions of loyalty and subversion seriously. The same is true with respect to questions about character and lifestyle. For example, the vast increase in narcotics usage among the middle class (and in particular its young) during the past several decades makes it harder to distinguish the cases in which past drug usage indicates a real personality problem and potential vulnerability to blackmail from those in which it does not.

Finally, there is the question of whether informants can be assured that their candid remarks will remain confidential. Under the Privacy Act of 1974, individuals have extensive rights to access government files about themselves; while an exemption exists that allows an investigative agency to withhold the name of an informant who requests anonymity, this may not be entirely reassuring to potential informants who would be quite embarrassed, or worse, if their identities were revealed.

First, such potential informants may worry about the possibility that their names or identifying facts about them (such as phone numbers) will be released inadvertently. Second, they may be concerned that even if their identities are not explicitly revealed, the subjects of investigations will be able to deduce them from the substance of the information the government files contain. (In other words, the release of a seemingly insignificant detail—which, however, only the informant knew—could give away his identity. Since the officer reviewing the file before its release would not likely be aware that this detail provided a solid clue to the identity of the informant, he might well release it, unaware of the damage he was causing.) Finally, as a Department of Justice official told the Senate Judiciary Committee in 1978, "In theory, the [Privacy and Freedom of Information] acts provide an adequate basis for protecting our sources, but whether they in fact do so is largely irrelevant as long as our sources think they do not."[25]

One method of augmenting the background investigation as a protection against unsuitable personnel is the use of the polygraph machine, commonly known as the lie detector. This technique has been used primarily by U.S.

intelligence agencies; neither other Western intelligence services nor non-Western ones place as much faith in it. Within the United States, the CIA has placed the greatest emphasis on the polygraph. The agency requires that any candidate for employment take a polygraph test and that all personnel be subject to periodic retesting as a condition of continued employment. However, extension of polygraph use to the rest of the U.S. government has been strongly resisted over the years. On the other hand, following the arrest for espionage of Geoffrey Prime, an employee of the British Government Communications Headquarters (GCHQ, the British communications intelligence agency), American officials urged that the polygraph be adopted by GCHQ as well. (Prime is believed to have compromised various comint capabilities that involved close United Kingdom–United States cooperation.) The implicit threat was that the United States might be less willing to cooperate on communications intelligence matters if this were not done.

While use of the polygraph appears to have a strong deterrent effect and in many cases induces the revelation of information that was otherwise concealed, its overall accuracy remains controversial.[26] Aside from the question of the frequency with which innocent subjects fail the test and are unfairly rejected for employment or forced to resign as a result, foreign intelligence services apparently have developed methods for beating it.[27] Perhaps the strongest publicly available evidence of the inadequacy of the polygraph comes from the case of Aldrich Ames, the CIA officer who spied for the Soviet Union and Russia for almost nine years, from April 1985 to February 1994. On two occasions during this period (1986 and 1991), he passed polygraph examinations.[28]

The Changing Nature of the Threat Since the mid-1970s, a succession of espionage cases have involved employees of U.S. government agencies or contractors.[29] In these cases, the motivation has been primarily financial, occasionally compounded by emotional instability.[30] One of the more puzzling cases in this regard is that of Robert Philip Hanssen, an FBI agent who spied for the Soviet Union and Russia from at least 1985 until his arrest in 2001; his messages to his "handlers" suggest a loyalty to Soviet/Russian intelligence that had nothing to do with ideology.[31]

These cases differ markedly in this respect from the famous American and British espionage cases of the 1940s and 1950s (such as those of the Rosenbergs and Kim Philby), in which the motivation was primarily ideological. This pattern suggests additional steps that could be taken to improve personnel security, such as developing detailed psychological profiles and instituting a system for alerting security officials when individuals with access to classified information either run into financial difficulties or appear to be living beyond their means of support.

Physical Security

Physical security refers to the steps taken to prevent foreign intelligence agents from gaining physical access to classified information. It deals with such matters as the strength of safes in which classified information is kept, and the features of alarm systems to detect unauthorized intrusion into the areas in which officials deal with classified information and, increasingly, sophisticated systems involving passwords to protect classified data kept in computers.[32] For the most part, the requirements of physical security are not arcane and differ only in degree, if at all, from those a commercial enterprise might take to prevent thefts of merchandise, equipment, or sensitive corporate data and documents.

One major difference, however, is that physical security seeks to safeguard not only the material objects, such as documents, that contain information but also the information itself. This requires much stricter controls on access to the relevant areas and the equipment used there, since an intruder can quickly and unobtrusively implant a bugging device that would give a hostile intelligence service access to what was being said within the classified work area.[33] Therefore, it is important to control what is taken into the area as well as what is removed.

Similarly, it is important to have some means of "sweeping" an area to detect any bugging devices so they can be removed. This in turn leads to the development of less detectable systems for monitoring conversations. The high level of technical sophistication to which this spiral can lead came to public attention in a series of incidents involving the U.S. embassy in Moscow. In the 1970s, for example, a Soviet antenna was found in the chimney of the chancery (the embassy office building). Then, in the 1980s, a significant number of the embassy's electric typewriters were found to be bugged.[34] Later, it was revealed that the Soviets had compromised virtually the entire structure of the new chancery the U.S. had constructed there. The Soviets had been allowed, without any U.S. oversight, to manufacture the precast concrete columns and beams from which the chancery was constructed. The Soviets had taken advantage of this lapse in security to design a bugging system that used the entire structure as an antenna for picking up signals and relaying them. The system appeared to be quite sophisticated, and the United States does not yet understand how it was intended to operate.[35]

COUNTERESPIONAGE

The security measures discussed above are passive, in that they do not go after the hostile intelligence threat directly but seek to deny it access to information. More active measures that try to understand how a hostile intelligence service works in order to frustrate or disrupt its activities and ultimately to turn those activities to one's own advantage are usually referred to as *counterespionage.*

Surveillance Operations

An obvious way to learn about the activities of a hostile intelligence service is to mount surveillance operations against its officers (keep them under constant observation) wherever they operate. Such surveillance tries to determine where the officers go and with whom they communicate or are in contact; these contacts can then be used as leads for further investigation.

While simple in concept, this is in practice a complex task. The officer's tradecraft, which was discussed earlier in connection with human intelligence collection, is devoted primarily to frustrating this sort of activity. Not only will the officer be trained in evading surveillance, but techniques such as "brush passes" and dead drops may be used to conceal the identity of persons with whom he is in communication. In addition, if the surveillance is observed, it may prompt the officer to cancel any planned meeting to avoid endangering his contact. Thus, it is important to hide the surveillance. To do this is difficult and requires a great deal of manpower, since an officer trained in countersurveillance techniques will notice if the same person is trailing him for any length of time.

Because this sort of surveillance is cumbersome and expensive, it is important to target it against actual intelligence officers. One place to look, of course, is at the kinds of official cover positions available to the hostile intelligence service: diplomats, consular officials, trade representatives, journalists working for government-owned media, and employees of international organizations such as the UN, when the employees are selected by their own governments. The problem is to determine which individuals holding these sorts of positions are really intelligence officers.

This problem can be attacked in several ways. In general, the more knowledge an officer has about the operation of, for example, a given foreign embassy, the more likely he can tell which officials seem engaged in actual diplomatic or consular activity. If an official does not seem to be engaged in such activity, he may be involved in intelligence work instead.

Similarly, it may be possible, by observing patterns of rotation and replacement of personnel, to determine who is replacing whom; if X has been identified as an intelligence officer, X's replacement is likely to be one as well. Also, the same techniques used to collect intelligence in general may be targeted on the hostile intelligence service and its presence in the agent's own country. The more learned about that service and the way it operates, the more effectively surveillance can be targeted. Finally, double agents, as discussed later in this chapter, may be able to determine the identities of hostile intelligence officers.

Intelligence Collection

The most direct way to achieve counterespionage's goals is to collect intelligence directly from the hostile service, either by human or technical means. For example, in the years immediately following World War II, Soviet agent Kim Philby, working within MI6 (the British foreign intelligence service), was able to provide his KGB handlers timely information on U.S. and British covert operations in the Baltic states, the Ukraine, Russia, and Albania. By 1951, when Philby was forced out of MI6, he had, according to his own count, compromised hundreds of British and American agents. In similar fashion, British intelligence counted among its assets in the early 1980s the KGB deputy resident in London, Oleg Gordievsky. Gordievsky was able to reassure the British that the KGB had no source inside either MI5 (British security service) or MI6 and to warn them immediately in 1983 that a disaffected MI5 officer had offered to spy for the KGB.[36]

As these examples suggest, counterintelligence does not in this respect differ much from intelligence collection in general; its target, however, would be the adversary's intelligence service rather than the governmental leadership, armed forces, or other institutions.

Defectors and Double Agents

As is true with other types of humint collection targeted on a closed society like the former Soviet Union, recruiting and running an agent within a country's intelligence service is extremely difficult. Thus, in the past, the United States and other Western countries relied heavily on defectors from Soviet intelligence services for counterespionage information. A prominent example was Vitaliy Yurchenko, the deputy chief of the KGB department responsible for espionage against the United States and Canada. After defecting in the summer of 1985, he provided information about Soviet espionage successes against the United States. For example, although he did not know their real names, personal and operational details he provided led to the arrest of Ronald Pelton, a former employee of the National Security Agency, and the indictment of Edward Lee Howard, a former CIA employee.[37]

The other major method of conducting counterespionage is through double agents. They are agents who, while pretending to spy for a hostile service, are actually under the control of the country on which they are supposed to be spying. Such agents may have originally been real spies who upon being detected were "turned," or converted into agents of the country that caught them. Or they may be "dangles," agents who pretend to volunteer to spy for the hostile intelligence service but in fact remain loyal to their country. In between would be individuals who, having been approached by a hostile intelligence service, report the recruitment attempt to their own countries' authorities and are encouraged by them to play along.

These types of double agent operations all serve the same counterintelligence purposes. At the simplest level, they allow the counterintelligence organization to penetrate the adversary's cover mechanisms and identify officers of the hostile intelligence service engaged in running agents. As a result surveillance can be concentrated on the actual intelligence officers, while less attention need be paid to the other officials who really are the diplomats, trade officials, and so on, that they appear to be.

In addition to identifying the hostile intelligence officers, these operations also enable counterintelligence officers to learn their adversaries' operational methods. Using double agents, one can learn how their handlers pass instructions to sources and receive information from them, when and where they prefer to meet them, what precautions they take against being detected, and so forth. In short, by knowing how and when the adversary communicates with his sources, counterintelligence learns about its adversary's tradecraft and can better counter it. In addition, knowledge about the adversary's tradecraft and the general pattern of his intelligence officers' activities contributes to counterintelligence's ability to identify them. Finally, if a double agent is provided with some special piece of equipment, such as a radio transmitter specifically designed for use by agents, his intelligence service gets a chance to examine it. This might lead to, for example, the interception of radio traffic between the intelligence officers of the hostile service and their real sources.

From the instructions handlers give the double agents, an intelligence service might also be able to learn about the hostile service's collection priorities. This could provide valuable clues to the adversary's thinking about major issues.

One of intelligence history's more intriguing questions, for example, revolves around the collection instructions given a British double agent (code-named "Tricycle") by German intelligence just prior to the entry of the United States into World War II. The agent, sent to the United States in mid-1941, carried with him a questionnaire that, among other items, requested detailed information about American military installations in Hawaii. Passed on to the FBI by the double agent, the list of questions and their possible import was essentially ignored.[38] Could a more alert U.S. intelligence system have exploited this information to help predict the Japanese attack on Pearl Harbor?

Alternatively, lack of interest in an area that would seem very important might indicate that the adversary already had good sources of information about it; this could provide an important clue for counterintelligence investigation.

In addition to obtaining information about the hostile intelligence service, its modus operandi, and its collection priorities, double agents can exert some control over the service's actions. The mere existence of a double agent achieves this purpose to some extent; if the hostile service believes it has an agent with access to specific information, it may not bother to recruit another one. By deflecting the service's activities, the double agent can protect an important area of information. In any case, the handling of the double agent absorbs the hostile intelligence officer's time and effort, thereby reducing the resources available for recruiting and running real agents.

Furthermore, the window that one double agent provides into the operations of the hostile service may allow counterintelligence to dangle successfully another double agent, perhaps one who has or appears to have access to information the hostile service is particularly anxious to obtain. The first double agent might also be able to support the bona fides (credibility) of the second; for example, the first agent could confirm the supposed fact that the second had just received a promotion that gave him expanded access to sensitive data or that he was having financial difficulties and desperately needed an additional source of income.

Double agents obviously must provide *some* information to their handlers to remain credible. Frequently, this problem is solved with "chicken feed"—ostensibly classified, sensitive information that is in fact not very important. Alternatively, the double agent can provide true and important information that the adversary is thought to have already obtained through some other channel. In these cases, counterintelligence must balance the advantage of keeping the double agent credible against the damage done by releasing the information, however trivial or duplicative, by which this credibility is maintained. The goal is to provide as little useful information as possible without raising the suspicions of the hostile intelligence service.

A more ambitious use of double agents involves having them provide a judicious blend of information and misinformation designed to mislead the adversary. This to some extent controls not only the adversary's intelligence collection but also his analytic capabilities. The payoff from doing this can be enormous, although the difficulties involved are huge as well.[39]

Deception is discussed more fully later. This section discusses two examples of large-scale, very successful, double agent operations, one conducted during a war and one in time of peace.

Wartime Double Agents: The Double-Cross System One of the best-known examples of a large-scale double agent operation is the Double-Cross System, by which the British, during almost all of World War II, "*actively ran and controlled the German espionage system in [their] country.*"[40] Starting with a single German agent who was detained on his return to Britain from Germany at the beginning of the war,[41] the British were able to build up, under their control, a large network of supposed German agents and keep the Germans believing in them until the end of the war.

Among other things, the original agent sent back information the Germans used to produce false identification papers for additional agents to be sent in by parachute or boat, thus facilitating their capture by the British. In other cases, new agents were told to contact ones already in place (and already controlled by the British) for money or other aid. For the rest of the war, helped by some lucky breaks, the British kept control of the entire German espionage network by intercepting new spies on their arrival.

John Masterman, the MI5 officer who ran the system, listed seven objectives for it:

- To control the enemy espionage system
- To catch fresh spies being infiltrated into the country
- To gain knowledge of the personalities and methods of the German secret service
- To obtain information about the codes and ciphers of the German service
- To get evidence of enemy plans and intentions from the questions asked by them
- To influence enemy plans by the answers sent to the enemy
- To deceive the enemy about Britain's plans and intentions.

The advantages for the British were enormous. For example, in 1940, the original agent was given by Berlin a code for communicating with Germany.

Since this code turned out to be "the basis of a number of codes used by the Abwehr [German military intelligence]," possession of it led to Britain's "early and complete mastery of the [Abwehr code] system." Later in the war, when the British became more confident of the Double-Cross System, they achieved the last two objectives, which involved deceiving the Germans. The climax came in 1944, when double agents were used to bolster the deception campaign that induced the Germans to expect the main D-day landing at Calais rather than in Normandy.[42]

Because of its cryptologic success (Ultra), British intelligence was in a position to observe the German reaction to the information and misinformation reported by the double agents. Among other things, it could tell which reports were forwarded to the top leadership in Berlin and whether they were believed. This feedback was crucial for achieving the deception objectives, because it allowed the British to emphasize points the Germans had missed or to modify messages to relieve any German doubts.

Controlling the enemy's espionage network had its price: the network had to produce enough intelligence to keep the Germans satisfied with it. Furthermore, the information it produced could not be easily contradicted by information available to the Germans through other intelligence channels, including any uncaptured spies. (It turned out there were not any, but of course, the British could only become aware of that over time; at first, they had to assume there might be other agents of whom they were unaware.) However, this seemed a reasonable price to pay; since the Germans were likely to have an espionage network in Britain in any case, it made sense for the British to run it.

In retrospect, the manager of the Double-Cross System believed that he and his colleagues were probably too cautious, in the sense that the British probably surrendered more true information than they had to and did not make full use of the deception potential. Not only did the Germans possess fewer other intelligence channels than the British thought against which the Double-Cross information could be checked (as noted above, they had no loyal agents), but they also proved to be remarkably trusting of the agents they thought they had. This high degree of trust is illustrated by the failure of the following ploy:

> On one occasion an agent was deliberately run [ordered to behave in a given manner] in order to show the Germans that he was under control, the object being to give them a false idea of our methods of running such an agent and thus to convince them that the other agents were genuine. The theory was sound and the gaffes committed were crass and blatant, but the object was not achieved. . . . [T]he Germans continued to think of the agent as being genuine and reliable!

Peacetime Double Agents: Cuban Operations against the United States On August 12, 1987, the *Washington Post* reported that a defector from the Cuban foreign intelligence service, the DGI, had told CIA debriefers that "an undetermined number of Cuban government officials, once believed by the

United States to be secretly working for the CIA, were feeding the agency misleading or useless information prepared by the Cuban DGI."[43] Following this revelation, Cuban media published detailed accounts of the operations of many of these double agents, including photographs of them engaged in supposedly clandestine activities. That their activities were known to the Cubans in such great detail tends to confirm they were double agents for part, if not all, of the time they were purportedly spying on Cuba. According to Cuban sources, some of the agents, apparently aware that the United States now knew their true allegiance, sent farewell messages to their U.S. handlers.

Without a careful analysis of the information provided by these double agents, it cannot be determined whether Cuba was attempting systematically to mislead the United States to take steps contrary to its interests. Even without such an ambitious plan, the operation would have paid its way from the Cuban point of view, by absorbing large amounts of CIA time and effort that otherwise might have obtained useful information; by revealing CIA operational methods, thereby helping to counter its real agents, if any; and by feeding U.S. intelligence analysis random pieces of information and misinformation that confused it and prevented it from forming any coherent picture of events in Cuba.[44]

MULTIDISCIPLINARY COUNTERINTELLIGENCE (MDCI)

What Is MDCI?

Just as the hostile intelligence threat posed by a technically up-to-date adversary is not limited to human intelligence collection, active counterintelligence cannot be limited to counterespionage. Rather, it must take into account the full range of the adversary's technical intelligence collection capabilities, including overhead photographic reconnaissance and communications and signals intelligence.

Thus, the first task of MDCI is to assess the effectiveness of the adversary's technical intelligence collection capabilities. This knowledge, in turn, indicates where one's own information, communications, or activities are vulnerable and how best to protect them. The actual measures that can be taken may be labeled "security" or "technical countermeasures," and they vary from technology to technology. The multidisciplinary perspective, however, is important because it encourages one to look at the problem from the adversary's point of view—that is, taking into consideration the full range of collection capabilities available to him.

Communications Security

Just as the interception of messages, both those in written and electronic form, is a major method of collecting intelligence, protecting the contents of messages has long been a major counterintelligence task. Since the beginning of the twentieth century, this has focused on protecting electronic telecommunications transmitted either by wire or radio.

Messages transmitted by wire can be safeguarded by preventing the line from being tapped (reading the message either by drawing a small amount of current from the line or by sensing the fluctuations of the magnetic field around the line caused by the current flowing through it). Fiber-optic cable is even more secure, since intercepting messages being transmitted on it has proved to be a daunting problem.[45] Radio signals, on the other hand, cannot, in general, be protected; any receiver within range can pick them up. Some signals, such as microwave transmissions (which are used to carry long-distance telephone calls, among other things), are highly directional (not dispersed in all directions but concentrated in a beam pointed at the intended receiver), but even they can be intercepted if a receiver is properly placed in line-of-sight contact with the emitter.

The contents of radio messages have been protected primarily through encryption. Written messages can be encrypted in the ordinary fashion before transmission. In the past, when analog signals were used to transmit voice messages, "secure phones," or "scramblers," were used; they distorted the voice signals in a complex manner. Anyone intercepting such a signal receives a meaningless jumble of sounds analogous to the jumble of letters of a ciphertext. Restoring the original voice message was, in principle, comparably difficult. Currently, when voice is transmitted in digital form, more sophisticated methods of encryption are more readily applicable.

Secure phones are relatively expensive, and they are used primarily to discuss classified information. Outside the government, they are not common. Thus, most long-distance telephone communication, which uses microwave transmission either across a network of microwave towers (terrestrial microwave) or between ground stations and satellites, is vulnerable to interception.

In the mid-1980s, in the United States, this situation came to the public's attention because of the controversy surrounding the location of the new Soviet (now Russian) embassy in Washington. Built in the Mount Alto neighborhood several hundred feet above the center of the city, the chancery and associated buildings look out over downtown Washington and northern Virginia, including the White House, State Department, Pentagon, and most other government buildings. From this and other official Russian buildings in the United States (consulates and trade representatives in New York, Washington, and San Francisco; the UN mission in New York; and residential and recreational facilities in New York City, on Long Island, New York, and on Maryland's Eastern Shore), large volumes of long-distance telephone calls can be intercepted.

In addition to government officials using ordinary nonsecure phones, potential targets for collection of this sort probably include high-technology corporations, commodity traders dealing in products a nation might buy or sell in large amounts (grain, oil, and gold), and financial institutions. An intelligence service might also target individuals with access to classified information to try to learn compromising personal details that can be used to blackmail them.

Various countermeasures have been suggested to reduce this vulnerability. For example, one could redesign the microwave network to eliminate links passing near known or potential intercept facilities, replacing them with underground cables. Alternatively, one could encrypt all signals transmitted by microwave by scrambling the signal when it first goes on the air and decrypting it when it has finished the microwave portion of its journey. Both solutions have technical weaknesses and are expensive to implement. The situation may be eased by the widespread use of fiber-optic transmission, which is being adopted by communications companies for economic reasons. Fiber-optic cables are not only less vulnerable to being tapped but, because of their great capacity (ability to transmit many signals simultaneously), they tend to be cheaper than conventional copper cables or terrestrial microwave.

Emanations Security

Any piece of electrical equipment radiates electromagnetic waves; by intercepting these waves, it is possible in theory to deduce the characteristics of the electrical signals that caused them. Thus, from these waves, called "emanations," the text of a document being typed on an electric typewriter or being transmitted from a computer to a printer could be reconstructed. This can be guarded against, for example, by shielding the electrical equipment to reduce the intensity of the emanations, making them harder to intercept.

Other Technical Countermeasures

Countermeasures can be devised to guard against other technical intelligence collection means as well. With respect to satellite photographic reconnaissance, for instance, it is possible, assuming one can identify which of the adversary's satellites are for photographic reconnaissance, to predict their orbits and to warn military or other sensitive installations to stop activities and move sensitive equipment under cover when the satellites are able to photograph them. Of course, the more one knows about the satellites' capabilities, the easier it is to prescribe the necessary countermeasures. For example, after determining the points on the earth's surface directly beneath the satellite's orbit, one must still know at what distance on either side objects are still within the cameras' range. Similarly, electronic or telemetry intelligence collectors may be beatable by encryption, jamming, shifting to frequency ranges the collector cannot pick up, or ceasing emissions when collectors are within range.

DECEPTION AND COUNTERDECEPTION

So far, the discussion of counterintelligence has examined ways in which an adversary's intelligence collection capabilities may be countered. If done successfully, the adversary will presumably lack the information needed to analyze the situation in which he finds himself, and his actions, being blind, will be less likely to serve his purposes. As the treatment of double agent operations has indicated, however, one can try to counter the adversary's intelligence operations more ambitiously by targeting his intelligence analysis capability—that is, by taking steps to mislead him.

What Is Deception?

Deception is the attempt to mislead an adversary's intelligence analysis concerning the political, military, or economic situation he faces, with the result that, having formed a false picture of the situation, he is led to act in a way that advances one's interests rather than his own. It is considered a form of counterintelligence because it attempts to thwart the fundamental purpose of the adversary's intelligence operations; in addition, it often involves counterintelligence methods, such as double agent operations.

Deception and intelligence failure are related concepts. Indeed, one side's successful deception implies the other side's intelligence failure. The reverse, of course, need not be true; a side may make important mistakes in its intelligence analysis even without any deception by the other side. Nevertheless, it is often possible, in cases of intelligence failure, to identify some effort at deception by the other side. To what extent that effort is responsible for the failure is a more complicated question.

Deception can be attempted in wartime or in time of peace, although, for various reasons, one would expect deception to be much more common in wartime.[46] Deception ranges from tactical to strategic. Any battle that begins with a feint in one sector while the main weight of the attack falls on another exemplifies tactical deception. Examples of strategic deception are less common but often very important, such as the Allies' World War II deception operation that misled the Germans about the location of the Normandy D-day landings.[47]

Peacetime deception operations are not common, tend to be less well known, and are sometimes harder to identify as such. Among the more spectacular was one known as the "Trust," a Soviet organization that pretended to be hostile to the new communist regime but that was in fact established and run from 1921 to 1927 by the forerunner of the Soviet KGB, known as the Cheka.[48] Using this fake opposition group, the Soviets made contact with anticommunist emigré organizations and Western intelligence services, thereby channeling and neutralizing any hostile activities either might undertake; induced potential opponents within the Soviet Union to make contact with it, thereby allowing the Cheka to learn their identities; and disseminated abroad false information about the internal state of the Soviet Union.[49]

During the 1950s and early 1960s, the Soviet Union engaged in deception operations to convince the United States that the USSR possessed larger offensive strategic nuclear forces than it actually did. As noted earlier, at a ceremonial flyover in July 1955, for example, the Soviets "displayed" twenty-eight Bison bombers—probably more than they had in their entire inventory—by having the first group of planes circle around out of view of the spectators (including the U.S. air attaché) and return for a second pass.[50] Similarly, in the late 1950s, Soviet leaders, drawing on the prestige derived from the initial successes of their space program, made a series of exaggerated claims concerning their ICBM program.[51] In this way, the Soviets contributed to the bomber-gap and missile-gap fears in the United States (that held that the Soviets were about to surpass the United States in these measures of strategic nuclear capability). The Soviet deception appeared aimed at inducing the West to make political concessions (for instance, with respect to the status of Berlin) that it would otherwise be insufficiently motivated to make.[52]

The content of the deception—the false view one wishes one's adversary to adopt—obviously depends on the situation and on how one wishes one's adversary to react. In wartime, for example, one might wish to launch a surprise attack on the enemy, in which case the deception would be devoted to convincing him that no attack is on the way. Sometimes, as in the case of the Normandy D-day landings, the enemy fully expects to be attacked, and it is unlikely one could convince him otherwise. In such a case, the deception tries to convince him that the attack is coming at a time, in a place, or in a manner other than what is actually planned.

In time of peace, on the other hand, it is less obvious what goal the deception should pursue. One might wish to convince an adversary that one is stronger than one really is, to induce him to make political concessions that he would not otherwise feel compelled to make. Alternatively, one might wish to conceal one's actual military strength to lull one's adversary into complacency and failure to increase his own military forces. If one's forces are limited by an arms control treaty, one could have the goal of concealing a treaty violation, thereby leading the other party to continue to limit his own forces.

The Prerequisites of Successful Deception

Blocking True Signals and Manufacturing False Ones If we visualize the intelligence process as the reception and interpretation of signals emitted by the activities of the side under observation, then implementing a deception operation involves blocking, to the extent possible, the true signals (those that reflect actual activities) and substituting misleading ones. To use a simple example: the actual tank at point X is camouflaged, but a dummy plywood tank is placed out in the open at point Y. If an enemy reconnaissance plane flies over the area, it may miss the tank at X (the visual signal having been blocked by the camouflage) and report one at Y (assuming that the false signal emanating from the plywood dummy is similar enough to a true one). In the case of double agent operations, the real documents, for example, remain in government safes, while false ones, produced as part of the deception operation, are passed on by the double agents to their handlers.

The first half of the task is the problem of security. If too many true signals get through, the adversary is unlikely to be deceived, although he may be so confused by the mixture of true and false signals that he cannot form a coherent picture of the actual situation. Thus, the first prerequisite of successful deception is the ability to block most, if not all, of the channels by which the adversary collects intelligence information about one's activities. In general, this is easier to do in wartime than in peace, which is one reason (among several) that successful deceptions are more likely to occur in the former than in the latter.

Blocking intelligence-gathering channels requires, among other things, comprehensive knowledge of the intelligence channels by which the adversary receives signals. A good counterespionage capability is necessary, since one well-placed human source could reveal the actual situation or, for that matter, the deception plan itself. Beyond that, one must know about the adversary's technical intelligence-collection capabilities in order to thwart them. Thus, ships and planes can adopt radio silence (more properly "emission control," or "emcon," since radar and other electronic emissions could give away the vehicle's position as quickly as would radio transmissions) to avoid detection by enemy comint or elint. If ground forces can rely on landlines (communication via telephone or telegraph wires, fiber-optic cables, etc.) rather than radio, as did the German forces before the December 1944 Ardennes offensive (the "Battle of the Bulge"), the same effect may be achieved. Similarly, if the orbits of the adversary's photographic reconnaissance satellites are known, activities can be halted and equipment moved indoors or camouflaged when the satellites are overhead and able to photograph them.

The second half of the task, manufacturing false signals, is also planned with the adversary's human and technical intelligence-collection capabilities in mind. Double agents can pass whatever fake documents or reports one wishes, as long as they can produce plausible explanations for their access to them. Deceiving technical collection systems is more complicated but possible. To achieve surprise at Pearl Harbor, the Japanese did not merely impose radio silence on their attack fleet on its trip across the Pacific. In addition, other naval radio operators were kept busy passing bogus messages to each other using fleet call signs but transmitters in Japan. Thus, if the radio signals had been intercepted (it does not appear that they were) and the transmitters' locations determined, the United States would have concluded that the Japanese aircraft carriers were engaged in exercises in home waters.[53] Similarly, photographic reconnaissance can be fooled by dummy weapons or vehicles; to know how accurate the dummies must be to be indistinguishable from the real thing, one needs to know how good the adversary's photographic reconnaissance capabilities are.[54]

The importance of understanding enemy collection capabilities (the channels by which information flows to him) is illustrated by the failure of a British ploy in World War II. During the war's early months, the British navy outfitted three merchant ships with dummy guns and false superstructures to make them look like battleships and an aircraft carrier. The hope was to draw German air attacks away from the main fleet in port at Scapa

Flow and, more generally, confuse the Germans about the overall strength of the Royal Navy. However, as the official history of British deception during the war notes:

> At this stage of the war unfortunately no channels had been developed for informing the Germans of [the ships'] existence except their physical display for reconnaissance aircraft; and the German Air Force does not appear to have picked them up. The need for harmonization of multiple channels for deception had not yet been fully appreciated.[55]

Feedback In conducting a deception operation, one faces major uncertainties:

- Were all the real signals blocked?
- Did the manufactured signals reach the adversary?
- Did he draw the desired conclusions from them?

To answer these questions, successful deception typically employs some method of finding out how the adversary is assessing the situation. If he is not alert enough to have noticed the false signals, or if he has not interpreted them as the deceiver wished him to, more can be manufactured to get his attention and lead him to the desired interpretation. If he begins to sense anomalies in the (false) picture of the situation the deceiver has planted in his mind, new signals can be created to explain them away. If enough true signals have reached the adversary to enable him to understand the situation correctly, one may wish to abandon the deception and change plans.

Feedback can be obtained in many forms. In some cases (such as wartime deception, or deception in support of a surprise attack), the adversary's actions (or lack of them) may be sufficient indication of whether he has been deceived. Thus, the absence of any signs of heightened military activity (which would have been easily observable) by the Hawaiian-based U.S. fleet in the first week of December 1941 would have told the Japanese what they needed to know. In other cases, adequate feedback may require good intelligence about the other side's views of the situation; in the case of the British World War II Double-Cross System, this feedback was provided by the Ultra intercepts, which gave the British good access to the internal deliberations of the German high command.

The more long-term and strategic the deception, the more important good intelligence feedback becomes. The deceived party's responses to such deception take longer to become manifest; thus, one needs some other way of knowing whether the bait has been taken. In general, peacetime deception operations require better intelligence feedback than those conducted in wartime. In wartime, the adversary is more likely to have to act quickly based on his understanding of the situation, thus perhaps revealing whether he has been deceived. During peace, the adversary is under less pressure to take actions that reveal his understanding of the general situation.

This is an important reason why deception is likely to be rarer in peacetime than in wartime. In addition, in wartime, the victim of a deception operation is likely to be under more pressure to react quickly; thus he has less time to analyze the situation and compare the signals being received through the various channels; thus, he is more likely to be successfully deceived.

Deception and Self-Deception The false view of the situation one wishes an adversary to adopt must be determined by the action one wishes the adversary to take. Nevertheless, the view must be plausible to the adversary; in fact, success is more likely if the deception scenario is based on what the adversary thinks is the case anyway. For example, the D-day deception worked so brilliantly in part because Hitler was already convinced that the Allied landing would take place at Calais, where the English Channel is narrowest. Thus, the manufactured signals only had to reinforce this view and prevent it from being undermined by any true signals that managed to get through; this is an easier task than having to induce the adversary to adopt the deception scenario in the first place. Thus, it is not accidental that most impressive deception successes involve large elements of self-deception.

Counterdeception

Experience shows that defeating every attempt an adversary might make at deception is very difficult. Even as they were running Double-Cross, the British were being similarly tricked by the Germans with respect to their intelligence and guerrilla-type operations in the Netherlands. Starting in the late summer of 1941, with the arrest of a Dutch intelligence agent working for MI6, the Germans managed to catch all subsequent British agents sent to the Netherlands by the Special Operations Executive (SOE, whose mission included sabotage and support for anti-German resistance groups).

Having broken the cipher system used by these agents, the Germans sent to Britain messages that purported to come from the agents, who had in fact been arrested. Some arrested agents cooperated in preparing and transmitting the messages; in other cases, German radio operators impersonated them. Among other things, these messages made the arrangements for additional airdrops of agents and supplies, which were in turn captured immediately. The operation, which the Germans called *Nordpol* (North Pole) and *Englandspiel* (the match against England), continued in 1944 until two of the captured agents escaped from the camp in which they were being held. At this point, concluding that the game would be given away in any case, the German military counterintelligence officer in charge of the operation chose to end it with a plaintext message to London on, appropriately enough, April 1.[56]

One incident from this operation shows how strong is the psychological resistance to the idea that one is being deceived. When British agents in Holland enciphered their messages for transmission back to London, they were supposed to include a "security check"—a specified deviation (which would appear as a simple, random error) from the cipher system. It would indicate to those receiving the message that they really were who they were supposed to be and that they were operating freely and not under German compulsion. For example, an agent might be instructed to make a "mistake" in the fiftieth letter of each outgoing message. If the Germans obtained the ciphering system but did not understand the principle of the security check, any message they sent would be treated as bogus, since it would not contain the required "error."

In this particular incident, a German radio operator transmitted messages in the cipher system obtained from a captured British agent. Since a radio operator can often be identified by the manner in which he hammers out the dots and dashes of Morse code (his "handwriting," or "fist"), the first message explained that a new operator had been recruited in Holland because the original agent had sprained his wrist. This message contained no security check at all and should have been recognized as bogus by SOE headquarters in London; this was, after all, the very situation for which the security check had been devised. Instead, the staff officer in London, disturbed by the failure to follow proper procedure and seemingly oblivious of the reason the procedure had been instituted, replied with an order to "instruct [the new radio operator] in the use of his security check."[57]

In any case, understanding deception is the first step toward figuring out how to avoid being deceived; by understanding the factors that facilitate deception, one can at least be alert to the possibility of deception and recognize some warning signs. One is particularly vulnerable to deception when one is dependent on a small number of channels of information and when the adversary is aware, at least in general terms, of the nature of these channels and their mode of operation.

For example, a heavy dependence on photographic reconnaissance satellites, whose identities and orbits most likely will become known to those whom they are photographing, may make one vulnerable to being deceived. The adversary, knowing when his facilities can be photographed, may make sure certain things are not seen; the items may be moved into garages or sheds or covered with camouflage or tarpaulins whenever a photographic reconnaissance satellite passes overhead. Similarly, the adversary knows when to display dummy equipment to increase the chance of its being noticed and mistaken for the real thing.

The situation is obviously worse (from the point of the potential deception victim) if the adversary can find out ahead of time not only which sites can be photographed but which *will* be photographed. Similarly, it is also worse if the adversary knows the satellite's precise capabilities. If he knows the satellite's ground resolution distance, for instance, he knows how similar to the real thing the fake pieces of equipment have to be to appear identical to the satellite. For this reason, it was an important intelligence coup for the Soviets to obtain the manual for the U.S. KH-11 photographic reconnaissance satellite. They bought it for a mere three thousand dollars from William Kampiles, after he resigned his position as a junior CIA officer in November 1977.[58] It is also for this reason that satellite photos (which might indicate the degree of detail that can be detected) are classified. (If satellite photos must be released publicly, they may be degraded in quality—made fuzzier—in order to obscure the system's precise capabilities.)

Once one understands the risk of being deceived that comes from heavy reliance on a single known channel, one can decide what to do about it. The best corrective is to maximize what might be called "unexpected collection," such as taking photographs at times and places the adversary does not anticipate. Given the predictability of orbits, this is hard to do in the case of satellite reconnaissance; along the borders or coasts of the adversary's territory, where aerial photography is possible, this is easier to achieve.

Nevertheless, certain steps are possible even with respect to satellites. Although the adversary may be able to determine (by studying their orbits, for example) which satellites conduct photographic reconnaissance, it will take him some time to do this and to warn his military facilities accordingly. During the satellite's first few hours of flight, it is likely that the pictures it takes will be unexpected. Hence, it makes sense to consider carefully which facilities should be photographed on a satellite's first few orbits. Similarly, thought could be given to ways to prolong the period of unexpected collection, perhaps by varying the launch and orbit characteristics of satellites, so that it takes the adversary more time to determine their functions.[59] Finally, if it were feasible to have several photographic satellites in orbit at the same time (including, if possible, dummies the adversary could not easily distinguish from operating satellites), the adversary might find it impossible to protect sensitive military equipment and operations against all of them without impeding his activities to an unacceptable degree.

Conversely, many proponents of signals intelligence (and, in particular, communications intelligence) prefer it to other types of intelligence collection, because several factors ensure the reliability of the information it collects. Comint may be collected in vast quantities, which implies that the true signals are more likely to get through. By the same token, it would take a larger effort to deceive comint by means of a fake radio network (which would require the use of real resources and personnel to create the signals) than that involved in displaying dummies or turning an agent and running him as a double.[60]

Even more important is the fact that the adversary will ordinarily be unable to tell which of his many communications channels others may be reading; he may well transmit fake messages that are never intercepted, while some of the real ones are. However, even this is not foolproof; through espionage (as with the cases of Geoffrey Prime, who worked for General Communications Headquarters [GCHQ], the British equivalent of the U.S. National Security Agency [NSA], and Ronald Pelton, who worked for NSA) or by some technical means, an adversary may learn on which frequencies or communications lines others are eavesdropping.[61] If so, these communication channels might be used in a deception effort.

A complicated situation of this sort, one that illustrates the difficulty of assessing potential deception operations, took place in 1953–56. The United

States and Britain dug a tunnel from the American into the Soviet zone of Berlin to tap a set of telephone and telegraph cables that linked the Soviet air force headquarters at Karlshorst with the city. The tunnel was built jointly by MI6 and the CIA. Unfortunately, George Blake, a senior MI6 officer in Berlin, was a Soviet spy. (He was finally tracked down, arrested, and convicted in 1961.) Blake attended an early planning session regarding the tunnel and informed the Soviets.[62]

However, the most sensitive Soviet telegraphic communications being transmitted on the tapped lines were encrypted. According to John Ranelagh, whose history of the CIA seems to have benefited from a considerable amount of information from its former officers, the real secret of the affair was the existence of a technique that enabled the CIA to recover the clear text of the encrypted messages.[63] This technique was not shared with the British; hence Blake should not have been able to betray it. Thus, even knowing of the tap, the Soviets might have continued to use the telegraph line for sensitive messages in the belief that their encryption rendered them secure.

On the other hand, the British shared in the intelligence collected from the Berlin tunnel operation. According to Ranelagh, "The British were to carry out the analysis of half the material" produced by the intercept.[64] If so, then it should have become evident that the United States had some method of interpreting the intercepted messages; if Blake were aware of this, the Soviets would have learned that the tunnel posed a real threat to them.

The tunnel operation ended on April 21, 1956, about a year after the first message was intercepted, when it was ostensibly discovered by Soviets in the course of repairing one of the tapped cables that had been damaged by heavy rainfall. At the time, the CIA, not knowing of the existence of a Soviet spy in the MI6 Berlin office, regarded the Soviet discovery as accidental. In retrospect, of course, one would have to consider the possibility that the Soviets contrived to make the discovery appear so to protect Blake.

The interesting question is to what extent the "take" from the operation should be regarded as potentially deceptive. On the one hand, it seems likely that the Soviets, via Blake, would have learned about the operation quickly; that they let it go on so long could suggest that they were using it to deceive the United States and Britain. On the other hand, the Soviets had to be concerned about protecting their source; if they had taken action right away to shut down the tunnel or to reroute communications, they would have risked alerting the United States and Britain to the possibility that they had a traitor in their midst. Similarly, had they warned large numbers of officers that the communication links in question were not secure, they ran the risk that the United States and Britain would learn of this and deduce that the Soviets had been told about the tunnel.

In any case, one would have to look at the actual information the operation produced; valuable information would mean it was less likely that the Soviets realized that the line was insecure (Ranelagh claims that the first indications that the Soviets had an agent in MI6 in Berlin were acquired by the tunnel operation).[65] The intelligence take would have to be studied as a function of time to determine if the Soviets became aware of the operation before their supposedly accidental discovery of it, and if so, when.[66]

Even without the knowledge that the adversary is listening to a particular communications link, a deception operation could create an entire net of radio transmitters whose sole purpose is to send messages the adversary might intercept; if the net is big enough, the adversary is bound to stumble across it. This would be an expensive and elaborate measure; in wartime, however, it is clearly possible. Before the D-day landings, the United States and Britain created such a radio net to help deceive the Germans into believing that there existed a large First U.S. Army Group, based in southeastern England, which was poised to conduct the "real" invasion against the Calais area. In fact, the army group contained very few real soldiers, as well as a "commander," George S. Patton Jr.; most of its divisions and other components existed only on paper and in the radio chatter among the station operators of the false network.

This was a key part of the D-day deception operation; it not only supported the prelanding deception but helped prevent the Germans from moving reserves into Normandy in the crucial days following the landings there. It allowed the Germans to interpret the Normandy action as a diversion, a means of distracting their attention from the invasion that was to come. According to a study of deception in World War II,

> The networks which were set up to carry the fake radio traffic were extensive and complicated. At the peak there were 22 fake formations [that is, the supposed headquarters of the army group and its constituent armies and divisions]. . . .
>
> There is little doubt that the simulated radio traffic, most of which was carried on within a very short distance of the enemy and was therefore easy to monitor, was—after the contribution of the double agents—the most important factor in the overall deception.[67]

The same factors help one determine the risk of being deceived by humint collection capabilities. In particular, heavy dependence of human intelligence collection capabilities on defectors increases vulnerability to being deceived. First, unlike the case in which one has an agent in place, the adversary knows the defector's identity and can determine, more or less, what information he had access to. The adversary cannot prevent the defector from telling what he knows but can take account of that information in any deception planning. In this respect, information that comes from a defector is similar to "expected collection."

Second, the adversary can relatively easily plant a defector with false (deceptive) information designed to mislead. If one relies heavily on defectors, the adversary may provide several of them, whose reports, although false, will nevertheless support each other. Suspicions that the Soviet Union had done just that to the United States since the early 1960s led in the early 1970s to some of the most severe internal conflicts in the history of the CIA, between those who took this possibility seriously and those who found it overblown. The latter group finally triumphed when the CIA's counterintelligence chief, James Angleton, the major proponent of the former view, was fired by DCI William Colby in December 1974.[68]

COUNTERINTELLIGENCE ANALYSIS

As the discussion of double agents and deception indicates, protecting the integrity of intelligence operations can become very complicated, involving much more than catching the occasional spy. In fact, cases may be linked to each other in various ways; the overall task of guarding an intelligence apparatus against penetration and deception requires a special counterintelligence analysis office to serve as an institutional memory and analyze these connections.

The best way to determine whether one's intelligence apparatus has been penetrated is to acquire a high-level source in the hostile service (either an agent in place or a defector). Even then, however, it would be a rare stroke of luck if the source could identify by name the spies in one's ranks. This would be the case only if the source were directly involved in handling them or were a very high-ranking officer of the hostile service. In the much more likely scenario, the source will be able to provide only clues to the spies' identities. Analytic work will be necessary to make those clues yield results.

For example, one may discover that the adversary has had access to several classified documents on a subject. Assuming they all came from the same agent, one could review the distribution lists for the compromised documents and note which officials had access to all of them. Alternatively, the source may know that the spy held a meeting with his handler in a certain foreign city on a specific date. Reviewing travel records would indicate which officials with access to relevant information were in that city then.

In addition, other clues may be available that suggest penetrations of some sort. Thus, if one's operation fails (an agent is discovered or a technical collection system is thwarted) in a way that suggests the adversary had been aware of the operation before it took place, it is necessary to investigate how he may have learned of it. There will no doubt be many avenues (individuals with access to the information, as well as security vulnerabilities or lapses) by which the information could have reached the adversary. If there is a series of such failures, however, it may be possible to narrow the options; for example, maybe only one particular individual had been authorized access to all of the information. On the other hand, a series of failures may also indicate that a communication channel or system has been compromised. For instance, from the late 1960s through the early 1980s, U.S. Navy officials were routinely surprised to find Soviet ships waiting for American warships in areas that had been secretly designated for exercises. One admiral was quoted as saying, "It is as if they had a copy of the OpPlans." But it was not until the espionage ring of John Walker was discovered in 1985 that the United States learned that naval cipher materials were being regularly given to the Soviets and hence that large amounts of enciphered naval message traffic were possibly being read by them.[69] In any event, such a series of events should alert an intelligence service to the possibility that its adversary has effective human or technical intelligence collection capabilities that must be discovered and neutralized.

Similarly, when the treachery of Aldridge Ames led to the loss of a number of intelligence sources in the Soviet Union in 1985–86, the CIA was alerted to the existence of a serious problem.[70] At first, the CIA's suspicions focused on the possibility that the KGB had penetrated CIA communications or that the cases had been poorly run (i.e., the tradecraft had been bad, providing opportunities for Soviet surveillance to detect them) and that "each case might have held 'the seeds of its own destruction.'"[71]

Subsequent CIA steps to determine the cause of these losses were hampered by a variety of factors: KGB deception operations, the Lonetree case, and suspicions that the Soviets had been able to bug the U.S. embassy in Moscow.[72] Ultimately, the CIA came to focus on Ames not as a result of a counterintelligence analysis of the losses suffered but because a fellow employee noticed and reported that Ames was living beyond his means.[73]

Chapter 6

Guarding the Guardians: The Management of Intelligence

The preceding four chapters have discussed the types of intelligence activities and some issues that arise with respect to them. We now turn from the intelligence activities themselves to the relationship between intelligence and the government of which it is a part and to questions concerning the management of intelligence by its nonintelligence superiors, or "political masters."

From a management (or public administration) point of view, intelligence presents two major sets of issues. The first set arises from the secrecy in which intelligence activities are necessarily conducted; it centers on the special difficulties that secrecy creates for the political superiors whose job it is to oversee and control intelligence activities. The second set arises from the uneasy relationship between expertise and policy making. It deals with the problems of determining the appropriate weight that the views of the experts (who claim special knowledge) should be given in governing the actions of the policy makers (who have the actual authority to make decisions) and of ensuring that the experts' views receive the attention they deserve.

SECRECY AND CONTROL

In a modern government, with its many thousands of employees arranged in complicated bureaucratic structures, the problem of controlling their myriad activities and ensuring that they are in accordance with the law and the policies of their superiors is bound to be difficult. With respect to intelligence agencies, this basic problem is compounded by secrecy, however legitimate the need to keep knowledge of certain intelligence sources, methods, and activities secret from the public and restricted to the smallest possible number of officials within the government.

In principle, of course, control of government activities is organized in a hierarchical fashion, so that every official is ultimately responsible, through a chain of command, to the head of the government. Thus, the minimum condition for control is that each superior have the right to know all the information to which his subordinates have access. In general, this condition is probably met, although the notion of plausible denial raises some important questions in this regard.

Having theoretical access to information about an activity is not, however, the same as knowing enough to control it effectively. In other areas of governmental activity, the direct top-down control exercised by superiors is supplemented by other mechanisms, both formal and informal: examinations by auditors or inspectors general, challenges and complaints by competing parts of the bureaucracy, investigations by law enforcement agencies, legislative oversight, press coverage, and complaints or other feedback from the public.

Applying these mechanisms to intelligence activities requires spreading knowledge about them beyond the narrowest possible circle of officials whose need to know derives from their actual involvement in them. How far the knowledge would have to be spread depends on the mechanism in question, since one such mechanism might involve informing only a few additional executive branch officials; another, members of the legislature and their staffs; and a third, the public at large. In each case, a balance must be struck between the risk inherent in widening the circle of those with access to the information, on the one hand, and the benefit derived from the increased capability of the intelligence agencies' political superiors to control their work, on the other.

Plausible Denial

Because these control mechanisms all involve more dissemination of information, one could say that in general a tension exists between secrecy and effective control. With intelligence activities, however, achieving effective control may further be complicated by the doctrine of plausible denial, which suggests that even fundamental top-down control by superiors may be placed in doubt. According to this doctrine, as discussed above, intelligence activities that might cause embarrassment (because they violate international law, or for some other reason) should be planned and executed in such a way that the head of government can credibly deny that he or she had anything to do with them or even knew they were occurring. As noted, this doctrine is usually associated with covert action, although it is also applicable to other intelligence activities as well, such as espionage or aerial photographic reconnaissance violating the target's airspace.

Plausible denial can complicate control of the intelligence activities to which it is applied. To be effective, it requires not only that knowledge of the activity be restricted to the smallest possible number of officials but also that there be no formal procedure by which it is approved and no document in which the approval is recorded. The activity itself should be conducted with a minimal amount of record keeping, and any files created would probably be destroyed once the activity is completed. Obviously, this creates preconditions for misunderstanding and uncertainty as to whether a specific action had ever been authorized. In particular, without a written record (or "paper trail"), it could easily prove impossible to determine whether an activity had been approved by the head of government or other senior nonintelligence officials.

All this does not mean that any intelligence agency in particular is, in the phrase attributed to Senator Frank Church, a "rogue elephant,"[1] let alone all of them. It does suggest, however, that other things being equal, an intelligence agency may more easily "jump the rails" than other governmental organizations. Against this inference, on the other hand, one should note that intelligence agencies investigate the character of potential employees more carefully than do other government offices and that the opportunity for illicit personal enrichment in an intelligence agency is less than in many other government offices, such as those that deal with economic statistics or regulations, or that conduct business on behalf of the government—by, for example, awarding contracts or leasing government lands for private exploitation.

Perhaps the most intriguing example of how plausible denial operates in practice was provided by the congressional investigation of U.S. intelligence activities in 1975–76. A Senate committee, headed by Senator Church (and formally known as the Senate Select Committee to Study Governmental Operations with Respect to Intelligence Activities) examined the CIA's attempts in the early 1960s to assassinate Cuban leader Fidel Castro. According to the committee's report on the CIA's involvement in assassination plots, "there was insufficient evidence from which the Committee could conclude that Presidents Eisenhower, Kennedy, or Johnson, their close advisors, or the Special Group [the interagency group that reviewed covert action proposals] authorized the assassination of Castro."[2]

In fact, the record the committee found was bewilderingly vague about authorization. The key CIA officials said they had felt fully authorized to do what they had done but that this authorization had not been conveyed in so many words, either orally or in writing. In short, the committee confronted precisely the sort of documentation, or rather lack it, that one would expect in a situation in which the doctrine of plausible denial held sway. Nothing in the available record would have kept President John F. Kennedy or his brother, Attorney General Robert F. Kennedy (who played a major role in formulating policy toward Cuba), from plausibly denying any involvement or contemporaneous knowledge of the assassination attempts.[3]

Thus, despite the a priori argument that control of intelligence agencies by their political superiors may be problematic, the Church Committee report does not actually show that this was the case regarding attempts to assassinate Castro. Rather, it demonstrates how the plausible-denial doctrine would work to shield the president from blame. This, of necessity, leaves open the possibility that the CIA was out of control, but it seems unlikely that it actually was.[4]

For Whom Does Intelligence Work?

In any case, it is a peculiar control by a head of government that can be consistent with the plausible-denial doctrine. It is unlike the ordinary control the head of government exerts over departments or ministries through an official chain of command and written orders, cabinet decisions, policy statements, memorandums, and so forth. Its basis is a direct, or personal, loyalty of the intelligence service to the head of government, rather than bureaucratic subordination.

In past ages, intelligence services commonly worked for a monarch, chief minister, or commander-in-chief in a personal capacity, outside the ordinary governmental structures. For example, Sir Francis Walsingham, the powerful secretary of state to Queen Elizabeth I of England, supported a very effective intelligence service largely out of his own funds (and nearly went bankrupt in the process).[5] Similarly, the duke of Marlborough, the British commander-in-chief during the War of the Spanish Succession, used a traditional 2.5 percent commission on the British-paid salaries of his army's foreign troops, as well as other perquisites (or tradition-sanctioned kickbacks, to use less elegant language) on various procurement contracts, to finance an apparently successful secret service. He regarded these funds as properly expended by him for "procuring intelligence and other secret service," but he was later prosecuted by his political opponents for embezzlement.[6] In both instances, the distinction between public and private funds or activities was cloudy. Clearly, this sort of arrangement cannot easily accommodate itself to a modern bureaucratic state, in which the separation between officials' public duties and their private interests is supposed to be absolute.[7]

But the issue goes beyond ensuring accountability for public funds. There is the more fundamental question of who can authorize anyone to engage in such activities at all. This is particularly important in a constitutional government like that of the United States, in which the powers of government are divided among the branches of government and political officials are responsible to the electorate. The president claims the power to engage in intelligence operations on the basis of his foreign policy and military responsibilities under the Constitution. At the same time, as discussed in chapter 4 on covert action, Congress has insisted on a complete paper trail leading back from intelligence activities to those who authorized them. Thus an important effect of congressional involvement in this area has been to subject intelligence activities to formal bureaucratic control within the executive branch.

But congressional involvement has gone beyond the question of how intelligence activities should be authorized and controlled within the executive branch. The House and Senate intelligence committees have successfully asserted a right to be kept "fully and currently informed of all intelligence activities" and to receive "any information . . . concerning intelligence activities which is in the possession" of any intelligence agency.[8] Taken together with a reinvigorated "power of the purse" (the power of Congress to appropriate or withhold funds for intelligence, as for all other governmental, activities), Congress could use, and to some extent has used, these levers to establish a joint authority with the president over intelligence.

The result, in the words of a former director of central intelligence, Robert M. Gates,

> is that the CIA today finds itself in a remarkable position, involuntarily poised nearly equidistant between the executive and legislative branches. The administration knows that the CIA is in no position to withhold much information from Congress and is extremely sensitive to congressional demands; the Congress has enormous influence and information yet remains suspicious and mistrustful.[9]

This discussion of congressional involvement in intelligence matters helps to explain a further problem of control: However adequate a head of government may find informal direction for the control of an intelligence service, such controls will not let a legislative body feel it is exercising its authority over the service effectively. For that, more formal means of control are necessary, such as those already noted (formal right of access to information, notification of certain types of activities, and the requirement that funds for intelligence activities be appropriated by law). Thus, in the United States, the result of congressional involvement has been to subject the CIA, as well as other intelligence organizations, to full executive branch control and to the same system of legislative oversight as any other part of the government. The question of legislative oversight itself is dealt with later in this chapter, in connection with the discussion of the relationship of intelligence and democracy.

EXPERTISE AND POLICY

The previous section concerned the relationship between the need to conduct activities secretly and the management of intelligence activities. Another set of problems involves the difficult relationship between expertise and policy—that is, between those who possess specialized knowledge about an issue and those who are authorized to determine and implement government policy concerning it. This relationship is a problem in other parts of the government, regardless of the policy areas with which they deal, and is thus a recurrent theme in public administration theory.

Many issues and conflicts typically arise between expertise and policy. At the center is the question of what role expertise ought to play in the policymaking process. Where should one draw the line between the functions and responsibilities of the experts, on the one hand, and those of the policy makers, on the other? Clearly, we want policy to be guided by the best information available; we would be very critical of a policy maker who ignored the available facts and based his actions on his unsupported views of what the world was like. At the same time, we want policy to be made by those to whom the political system (via election or appointment) has given leadership authority; in any case, they must take ultimate responsibility for their policies, regardless of the information on which those policies were based.

Contemporary social science resolves this problem theoretically by means of the "fact-value" distinction: social science can provide the facts (including contingent predictions, such as "if the government follows policy X_1 it will obtain result Y_1"), but policy makers have a monopoly on choosing the values to be pursued (whether to prefer result Y_1 to result Y_2, or vice versa).

This theoretical solution provides, however, very little useful guidance in practice. First of all, the social sciences are far from being able to make contingent predictions with any confidence in most areas; certainly, with respect to the national security issues with which intelligence deals, this type of predictive ability is not available. Second, debates in the national security arena deal much more frequently with differing assessments of the factual consequences of policies than with disagreements concerning which values should be sought. Everyone can easily agree on peace, liberty, and prosperity as goals, but the means to achieve them are debated endlessly. Conversely, if it could be asserted with any certainty that a given policy would attain these goals, the policy-making role would diminish to the point of extinction.

Since intelligence analysis can provide the policy maker with only the roughest approximation of what will happen if a given policy is adopted, the theoretical fact-value distinction does little to illuminate the appropriate roles of intelligence and policy. In practice, policy makers' choices depend more on their views about the consequences of policies than on their choices of goals. (Indeed, the choice of ultimate goals is considered so self-evident that the issue is rarely addressed at all.) Thus, what policy makers do is not so clearly separated from what the experts (in this case, the intelligence analysts and estimators) do as it might seem; hence, it is not surprising that the intelligence-policy relationship holds a certain amount of tension. Each side often views the other side's actions as infringing on its territory.[10]

"Killing the Messenger"

From the typical perspective of intelligence officers, the difficulties between intelligence and policy look like the latter's fault. The difficulties stem, in their view, from policy makers' tendency to disregard intelligence reports that do not support the policies they wish to adopt, or have already adopted and to which they are committed. Intelligence officers often think policy makers are interested in the intelligence product only insofar as it can be used to support their policies, which they have adopted for completely different reasons. When the intelligence product does not support their policies, they either ignore it or try to "cook" it by using political pressure to change its contents.

This perspective has led to the view, which tends to predominate in both academic and political discussions of intelligence, that the most important characteristic of any intelligence-producing organization is its independence from policy makers. Only an independent intelligence agency, in this view, can resist the political pressures that policy makers would otherwise bring to bear on it to conform its analyses to their policy preferences.

In the American context, this has provided the most important argument for the existence of a *central*—that is, not associated with any cabinet department, such as State or Defense—intelligence agency, with its own collection and analysis capability. Such an organization, the argument runs, will be free of the biases that would distort the output of an intelligence service that is part of the Department of State or Defense and is forced to take account of its parent organization's policy preferences or budgetary interests.[11]

This independence is intended to permit the intelligence agency to be guided entirely by the data, without having to worry about how its product will affect the policy process. As one former senior American intelligence officer recounts,

> I remember when, at one point as the national intelligence officer for the Middle East, I was taken down to Congress to testify on the issue of American policy (and Marines) in Lebanon, along with a senior State Department official—a political appointee. On our way he pointedly warned me that when answering questions on the course of events in Lebanon I must limit myself to discussion of only very current data and the prospects for the next few days. No long range views for him. Mercifully our system enabled me to tell him to shove off.[12]

In short, independence is supposed to help negate what may be called the "killing the messenger" syndrome, the tendency to blame (or at least ignore) messengers—intelligence analysts—who bring unwelcome news, analyses that do not support favored policies.

The common understanding of this syndrome is that it reflects some irrationality on the part of the policy maker; it may perhaps best be illustrated by a passage from Shakespeare's *Antony and Cleopatra.* After threatening the messenger who has informed her that Antony has married Octavia, Cleopatra explains her behavior as follows:

> Though it be honest, it is never good
> To bring bad news: give to a gracious tiding
> A host of tongues; but let ill tidings tell
> Themselves when they be felt.[13]

The idea that one should not be forewarned of unpleasant developments until they come up and bite is one that obviously cannot guide an intelligence agency. Any policy maker who adopted such a position would indeed be acting irrationally.

However, a policy maker need not be influenced by this irrational motive to wish to prevent an intelligence agency from reporting unwelcome news. In a modern bureaucratic state, no official—even the head of government—receives intelligence information or assessments bearing on a given policy that other high officials do not receive as well. Some of these other officials may have been enemies of the policy and can be expected to use any negative intelligence information or assessment to question or try to overturn it.

This difficulty is only exacerbated when intelligence is routinely shared not only with the official's colleagues and bureaucratic rivals but also with his political opponents (for example, the opposition party in Congress). From this perspective, it is not at all irrational for a policy maker to wish to ensure that intelligence provides the "right" answer.

Of course, what is in the interest of any one policy maker need not be in the nation's interest. From the national point of view, we should seek whatever will bring about the best implementation of the best policies. Unfortunately, these two goals may have conflicting requirements. In general, formation of the best policy requires that all relevant intelligence product be available to everyone involved. Intelligence information and analyses will most likely support arguments both for and against any proposed policy; all these arguments should be weighed in reaching a final decision. Suppressing pieces of information or lines of argument, or keeping them from certain participants in the policy-making process, will in principle bias the process and reduce the likelihood of its yielding the best result.

Implementation, however, poses a different problem; once a policy is chosen, the arguments against it must be largely ignored. Attempts to reargue the basic policy question whenever a tactical decision must be made or to reorient the policy in response to each new piece of intelligence can only lead to a weak, confused, vacillating, and ultimately ineffective policy.[14]

The wide dissemination of an intelligence product, parts of which are bound to contradict the assumptions on which a policy was based, or reflect poorly on its progress, can look like a needless evil to the official in charge of implementing the policy. In the earthy language of President Lyndon Johnson, the problem is as follows: "Policy making is like milking a fat cow. You see the milk coming out, you press more and the milk bubbles and flows, and just as the bucket is full, the cow with its tail whips the bucket and all is spilled. That's what the CIA does to policy making."[15]

"Imperial Intelligence"

While the intelligence analyst may often feel that the policy maker's attachment to a policy leads him or her to ignore or to try to distort or suppress relevant information, policy makers may feel that although intelligence often offers only tenuous judgments, they are expected to treat those judgments as gospel and make decisions accordingly. In many cases it is not clear why the intelligence judgment should be treated as more authoritative or objective than anyone else's, including the policy maker's.

For example, often an intelligence judgment dealing with major political issues is based not on a sensitive nugget of hard data (for example, the report of an agent inside the adversary's cabinet or general staff) but on data available to the policy maker (or to a journalist, for that matter) as well. In this case, the policy maker may feel justified in deciding to trust his own judgment rather than that of an anonymous (to the policy maker) analyst; his critics, however, are likely to assert that he is behaving as irrationally and illegitimately as Cleopatra. What may increase the tension is the typical failure of the intelligence product to make clear the kind of evidence on which it is based. (Except for the highest officials, policy makers may not learn very much about the sources underlying the written materials they receive.) The policy maker may come to believe that this lack of information about sources implies that the main intelligence judgments are just speculative judgments, not based on hard data.

In any case, the probability that the policy maker is right—that his judgment will be superior to that of the intelligence analyst—is not necessarily small. It is true that in the United States, at least, the policy-making community is sometimes characterized by a high turnover rate among top officials, giving rise to a certain amateurism. It may well be that, as a U.S. intelligence official put it, "after a few months on the job [new intelligence analysts] are among the most knowledgeable people in the government on a particular issue. . . . [F]or the first time in their lives, they are writing for an audience that knows less than they do."[16]

However, this is not necessarily the case, and policy makers who do have expertise in an area would likely dismiss an intelligence report that reflects this view of their abilities. Furthermore, the "policymaker may have direct access to information unavailable to the analyst (confidential conversations with foreign officials, for example) and, in any case, knows U.S. policy—often a key piece of the puzzle—far better than the analyst."[17] Thus, in the absence of a particular piece of secret information, or of a specialized method of analysis, the intelligence analyst's judgment often does not have any special entitlement to be accepted over the judgment of anyone else. As Charles Fairbanks has pointed out with respect to a controversy over Soviet intentions toward Iran in 1985 (whether there was a Soviet threat to Iran was a major question affecting U.S. policy toward that country),

> As for the means of analysis the Intelligence Community uses, these are not anything arcane: the means is ***thinking,*** of the same kind that an official outside the Intelligence Community or a reporter or a citizen would use in trying to interpret similar facts. The composition of a Special National Intelligence Estimate on [such] an issue . . . is essentially the same exercise as the one the members of the [National Security Council] staff engaged in, well or badly, when they decided to sell arms to Iran. It is an exercise in policy reasoning.[18]

It is only when the result of such a reasoning process receives the label of "intelligence" (and a classification stamp) that it becomes possible to pretend that what is involved "is some hard nugget of fact that transcends the dubious or self-interested policy arguments of other agencies and will serve as a neutral test to evaluate them."[19]

This same situation may arise even when there are "hard facts" available to the intelligence analyst, because very rarely will these facts speak for themselves. They must be interpreted in some context, and this context is supplied, first of all, by the analyst. Yet this context rests on speculative judgments in which the intelligence analyst may have no particular advantage over the policy maker. As Graham Fuller, a former national intelligence officer for the Middle East, has pointed out,

> As intelligence grows broader, more strategic in nature, its susceptibility to interpretation . . . grows. . . . [For example, questions such as h]ow long will the geriatric tyrants in Beijing retain power? Will Iraq split apart if Saddam's power is destroyed? Will Europe maintain NATO? . . . [are] the stuff of strategic intelligence. Facts are important for the analyst to have, but in the end, judgment is required to attempt answers[,] . . . [and such judgment will] draw upon an individual's general sense of 'the way the world works' . . . a coherent view of international politics. . . . This kind of understanding is inherently ideological . . . because it imposes an order . . . on a highly diffuse body of data and events. . . . Nothing else can overcome the modern curse of information glut. . . . Yet to lack this construct is to bring an immense shallowness of understanding to human affairs.[20]

These arguments go against the mainstream of current opinion on this topic, which emphasizes the importance of maintaining the independence of intelligence from policy and of forcing policy to listen to it. The consonance of a policy with the intelligence view is often taken as a measure of its reasonableness. What is lost is any sense of the solidity of the intelligence view itself—is it based on incontrovertible fact or on quite controvertible speculation?

This point may be seen with respect to the circumstances surrounding the Fairbanks article quoted from the previous page. The conclusion of the SNIE to which he refers—that the likelihood of a Soviet invasion of Iran was relatively small—had been leaked to the press, evidently to criticize "the secret sale of U.S. arms to Iran, which President Reagan ordered in January 1986 partly to assist Iran against 'intervention by the Soviet Union.'" The article in which the leak appeared claimed that the "analysis appears to have called into question a primary White House rationale."[21] In other words, the intelligence judgment was used as the touchstone of the reasonableness of a policy, regardless of the "hardness" of the evidence on which it was based.

This type of controversy occurs because of the importance placed on intelligence "independence" in the American system. By contrast, the intelligence systems of other countries (such as the United Kingdom) are less concerned with protecting the "purity" of intelligence judgments and more interested in making sure that the policy makers' own expertise can be brought into the estimative process. As Loch Johnson notes,

> The American end product is an *intelligence* estimate, while the British end product is a much broader assessment that blends the judgments of policy *and* intelligence officers. . . . [T]he British culture actually encourages commingling [of intelligence and policy], in the belief that the best policy decisions are likely to result from a pooling of knowledge from among the country's international affairs experts.[22]

The Independence of Intelligence

Given these potential sources of friction in the intelligence-policy relation, the question of how independent of policy intelligence should be is bound to be a complicated one. In a military command, for instance, the chief intelligence officer is as much a part of the commander's staff (and hence as much under his command) as any other aide; there is no question of any independence. Indeed, the very meaning of the demand that an intelligence agency be "independent" is not clear. In principle, nobody would advocate that an intelligence service be independent from the head of government. Nevertheless, as the above discussion indicates, people often want to use intelligence as a neutral arbiter of policy fights—not only among government officials but between government officials and their legislative and extragovernmental critics. This implies independence from all government officials, and a corresponding direct responsibility to some other group, either a legislative body (as a representative of the public) or the public itself.

As previously discussed, the main argument for independence derives from the "killing the messenger" syndrome: intelligence must be independent if analysts are to be able to tell the truth as they see it. In this context, independence means the ability to shield individual analysts from pressures or threats that might induce them to make their conclusions more palatable to the product's consumer. To some extent, this sort of independence can be achieved by the creation of a *central* intelligence agency, one that is subordinate to the head of government but not to the major intelligence consumers such as the foreign affairs or defense ministries or departments. However, heads of government are themselves intelligence consumers who may have invested a great deal of personal prestige in a policy. In this case, the problem reappears at a higher level. Ultimately, as long as the intelligence service is a part of the government, the only safeguards are the backbones of the chiefs of the intelligence services—their willingness and ability to protect analysts from outside pressure.

Independence is particularly important when it is necessary to abandon policies that are not working or that changed circumstances have rendered obsolete or counterproductive. For this to take place, some mechanism must ensure that all relevant information, positive and negative, is available for reviewing the policy. As the Johnson quote suggests, policy makers must devote most of their energy to implementing policies with some consistency in the face of constant crosscurrents, doubts, political attacks—not necessarily motivated by sincere belief in the superiority of some other policy—and so forth. Under these conditions, it is particularly difficult for such officials to change gears and conduct a fully open-minded policy review.

In this situation, intelligence takes on an adversarial posture, since its most important function becomes pointing out areas in which the policy is not working or has become inappropriate. It must counteract, in other words, the political pressure on bureaucrats to be good team players and cheerleaders for current policies. Therefore, the intelligence service presenting information that suggests the policy is obsolete or wrongheaded must have enough independence to withstand the pressures such a situation generates.

In the past, one such situation that attracted public attention was the intelligence community's role in verifying compliance with arms control agreements. An accusation that a party to an arms control agreement had violated it would call into question the wisdom of having made the agreement in the first place, or at any rate, of continuing to adhere to it. The desire to maintain the agreement (or to maintain or improve relations generally with the party in question) provided a strong incentive to ignore or hide the disturbing evidence. In any case, the difficulty of forcing the party to comply with the agreement or doing anything else about a violation was, and remains, a strong inducement for denying that one exists.

In addition, an intelligence service must be sufficiently independent to take the initiative in looking at issues or areas of the world without being told to do so by the policy community. An intelligence service should scan the horizon, as it were, for potential issues and problems in areas that are not attracting the policy makers' attention. This warning function inevitably involves giving the policy makers information that they have not requested and do not particularly want, because they do not know its value.

Independence carries some disadvantages as well. Perhaps the greatest is the risk that the intelligence work will become, or will be perceived as, irrelevant to the policy process. This can occur because the intelligence analyst does not know what problems appear most important to the policy makers or what options are being considered for dealing with them.

More than mere organizational or physical distance from the policy makers can cause this problem. Intelligence analysts occasionally refuse to cooperate in implementing policies they do not support. Former Director of Central Intelligence Robert Gates provides an example of this problem:

> When Secretary of State Alexander Haig asserted that the Soviets were behind international terrorism, intelligence analysts initially set out, not to address the issue in all its aspects, but rather to prove the secretary wrong—to prove simply that the Soviets do not orchestrate all international terrorism. But in so doing they went too far themselves and failed in early drafts to describe extensive and well-documented indirect Soviet support for terrorist groups and their sponsors.[23]

In other words, a policy to address the problem of international terrorism that would have pressured the Soviet Union to reduce its support (whether direct or indirect) of terrorist groups was thwarted by the unwillingness of the intelligence analysts to cooperate, based on their view that such Soviet involvement was a relatively small part of the terrorism problem. Their view may have been true, but that does not imply that the policy was incorrect; it might be, for example, that the major psychological, sociological, or even political causes of terrorism simply could not be addressed by U.S. policy, or that addressing them would have conflicted with other foreign policy goals.

If intelligence concentrates too much on its (admittedly necessary) adversarial role (such as would be involved in reviewing ongoing policies), it becomes all the more difficult for it to support the actual implementation of policy. In a supportive role, intelligence must concentrate its efforts on finding and analyzing information relevant to implementing the policy. In the above example, it might have meant discovering the mechanisms by which an international terrorist group received financial and logistic support from its patrons. In supporting policy implementation, an intelligence agency should be willing not to insist on its view—that patron-state support is not a major cause of international terrorism—of why the policy is misguided or wrong.

INTELLIGENCE AND THE "INFORMATION AGE"

The rapid progress in technologies related to telecommunications and data processing—the key technologies of what has been called the "information age"—has led to widespread changes in the ways in which organizations deal with information.[24] Even more important has been the explosion of open source information. In addition to the widespread use of the Internet, the collapse of Soviet communism was perhaps the most important single cause of the increased availability of open-source information: from Vladivostok to the Elbe River (marking the border between the former East and West Germanys) an entire apparatus designed to keep secret even the most mundane of facts had disappeared.

More generally, the process known as "globalization" has increased the flow of information across borders and has created many new information channels. Globalization is a vague concept; probably its most important manifestation is the increase in international trade and division of labor, which has penetrated all but a handful of the world's nations. With that have come increased travel and increased penetration of the developed countries' news media into all parts of the world (for example, the availability of CNN and other news services in hotels around the world).

Even before the advent of the information age, a great deal of information reached policy makers outside traditional intelligence channels. However, changes in the international political environment and those associated with the "information revolution" suggest that more information generated outside of intelligence circles will be available in the future.

Although the existence and increasing availability of sources of information outside traditional intelligence channels presents important opportunities for the policy maker, it also creates problems:

- How to locate these sources
- How to evaluate their reliability
- How to analyze the information they provide and fuse it with information available via intelligence channels
- How to preserve confidentiality with respect to the issues in which the policy maker is interested.

While these issues are hardly new, the question arises as to whether the changes brought about by the information age are of such magnitude as to require that they be addressed more systematically than has been the case in the past. In particular, do policy makers need "information specialists" to help them sort through the welter of sources that the information age makes available to them? Currently, this information function is performed in three ways:

- By the policy makers themselves
- By their staffs
- By intelligence analysts.

Each of these has certain advantages and disadvantages. Policy makers are, of course, ultimately responsible for their actions and so must have confidence that the relevant information has been received and properly understood. Thus, at least some of the analysis has to be their own. Furthermore, as already noted, they may have access to information sources that others do not: high-level communications with other governments, and the thoughts and plans of high-level officials of their own government and certain key nongovernmental actors (such as business leaders, "graybeards," etc.) In addition, some policy makers have more extensive experience in the given policy area than intelligence analysts or their staffs.

On the other hand, policy makers are simply too busy to do much information gathering and analysis, other than reading newspapers, highly sensitive cables (which cannot be handled by subordinates because their circulation is restricted), and materials that have been selected and highlighted by their staffs. Inevitably, most of their information will reach them in excerpted or analyzed form, either in briefings or written summaries.

Unlike their bosses, staff members can have the time to gather and analyze much of the necessary information. Since they are also involved in the policymaking process, they should know what issues are relevant, what kinds of objectives are being sought, and so forth. Except for the most sensitive items, they will be cognizant of interactions with other governments or other parts of their own government. In general, they will enjoy the trust of their bosses;

however, there may be cases in which superiors wish to explore issues without their staffs' becoming aware of the fact.

Nevertheless, staff members are likely to be focused more on policy formation than on information gathering and analysis. Accordingly, they may not develop the necessary expertise in the information area. In any case, these information-related responsibilities will have a lower priority than those related to policy formation; staffers do not in general have the time to develop substantive knowledge beyond the "intellectual capital" they possessed when they entered into their positions. Furthermore, they typically have neither access nor expertise relevant to specialized intelligence sources and methods; thus, they may not be able to fuse the information that reaches them from intelligence agencies with other information. Also, they may be subject to pressure from their superiors to ensure that any analyses they produce support policy preferences or decisions already taken.

Finally, intelligence analysts are fully focused on the information tasks and are free from direct responsibility for policy choices. Their career paths remain within the information arena, although it is often the case that analysts must become managers of analysts in order to advance professionally. Not being part of the policy process, it may be easier for policy makers to ask them questions that hint at policy choices too controversial to discuss more widely within the policy bureaucracies. Analysts have access to and familiarity with specialized intelligence sources and methods, and so they are better able to fuse information from these channels with other information. Finally, they are—or at least should be—trained to evaluate the possibility that what appears to be valid information is in fact the product of an adversary's deception effort.

However, intelligence analysts possess certain drawbacks as well. Lack of awareness of their own governments' policy options may make their products less useful than they might otherwise be, both because it reduces their relevance and timeliness, and because it can lead to an underestimation of the extent to which others take actions in anticipation of, or in response to, one's own. In particular, the "taboo" on analyzing one's own capabilities or strategies may make it difficult to provide an accurate and useful picture of the state of the "balance of forces" between oneself and another party. In addition, intelligence analysts may tend to ignore sources of information outside the usual intelligence channels, because the reliability of such sources may be more difficult to determine, and because providers of information who are outside the government (such as academics or businessmen) may be less willing to cooperate with an intelligence organization than with another government agency.

It is probable that no single resolution of this issue will be suitable in all cases. Nevertheless, it might pay civilian policy makers to look at the standard military practice in this area. Typically, a commander has an intelligence officer on his staff (the "G-2," in U.S. Army parlance.) This officer is trained in intelligence matters, but he works for the commander rather than for an intelligence agency. He is charged with collating, analyzing, and explaining the significance of *all* relevant information, whether it comes from intelligence, other governmental, or open sources. In addition, because of his training and ties to the intelligence world, he need not be a passive recipient of information; he can scour the intelligence agencies for information his commander needs and represent the commander's priorities with respect to the collection and dissemination of intelligence.

INTELLIGENCE AND DEMOCRACY

Democracy and Secrecy

Secrecy, as already noted, raises a potential problem for the control of intelligence agencies by their nonintelligence superiors. The legitimate need to restrict knowledge of many details of operations to the smallest possible circles may facilitate a cover-up of unauthorized actions, thereby preventing higher, nonintelligence authorities from finding out about them.

In a democracy, however, secrecy poses an additional problem: the potential to call into question the political legitimacy, as opposed to the actual control, of an intelligence service. If democracy is government not only for the people but of and by them as well, it is not surprising that institutions that rely so heavily on secrecy can easily become objects of popular mistrust. This suspicion is not limited to intelligence services. President Woodrow Wilson's promise that the international issues of the post–World War I period would be resolved by "open covenants, openly arrived at" reflected public suspicion of prewar secret diplomacy, as well as of secrecy generally.

Legislative and Public Oversight

This skepticism concerning governmental secrecy, which is probably endemic in democratic societies, has led in the United States, and to a lesser extent in other democratic countries, to calls for oversight of intelligence agencies by a part of the government that enjoys some degree of independence from the head of state. In the United States, a system of congressional oversight by means of two committees created for that purpose (the House of Representatives Permanent Select Committee on Intelligence and the Senate Select Committee on Intelligence) was established in the mid-1970s.

The cornerstone of this oversight system is the president's statutory obligation to keep the committees "fully and currently informed of the intelligence activities" of the government.[25] The two committees' right to be informed is particularly significant in light of the congressional power of the purse. The result, according to Robert Gates, has been that at least under some circumstances,

> the oversight process has . . . given Congress—especially the two intelligence committees—far greater knowledge of and influence over the way the CIA

> and other intelligence agencies spend their money than anyone in the executive branch would dream of exercising, from expenditures in the billions of dollars to line items in the thousands. . . . Congress may actually have more influence today over the CIA's priorities and its allocation of resources than the executive branch.[26]

The congressional oversight system may be viewed as a compromise between the requirement for secrecy and the desire to bring public opinion to bear on the intelligence agencies to make sure that their secret activities neither use means nor seek ends that public opinion would condemn. Congressional oversight allows the intelligence committees to serve as sounding boards, surrogates for the much wider debate (intra-executive branch, congressional, and public) that might otherwise accompany a governmental policy or initiative.

The ambiguities created by using the intelligence committees as surrogates for public opinion are most readily seen regarding covert action, concerns about which led to the current system of congressional oversight in the first place. The legal basis of the committees' role is the requirement that they be notified each time the president orders a covert action. While in principle the notification requirement does not imply a veto power, strong objections from committee members can cause revision or even cancellation of a covert-action proposal, if the political cost looks as if it will be greater than the expected results.[27] Thus, one purpose of prior notification might be described as testing a proposal against a (somewhat restricted) cross-section of political opinion, represented by individuals independent of the president, to see if it is out of line with fundamental beliefs or values.

Beyond this sounding-board function, spreading the knowledge of covert action to members of Congress creates the opportunity for bringing into play the congressional power of the purse. This power can be exercised by the intelligence committees themselves, or it can involve full-scale debate on the floor of the Senate and House of Representatives, as in the case of the various "Boland amendments" restricting or prohibiting aid to the Nicaraguan resistance in the 1980s.[28]

The fundamental claim on behalf of congressional oversight of covert action is that it combines the advantages of checks and balances on the one hand with those of secrecy on the other. Committee consideration serves as a surrogate for full-scale public debate and the ordinary democratic decision-making process—which are, of course, incompatible with secrecy.

The validity of this claim, however, has been attacked in both practical and theoretical terms. Practically, the issue is whether congressional oversight does not inevitably lead to public revelation of the information, regardless of what the rules say. In fact, there is little hard information about the source of the numerous leaks that occur with respect to covert action, and investigations of particular leaks almost never produce results. Given the importance journalists place on not revealing their sources, this is not surprising.[29]

In any case, there is no doubt that congressional oversight broadens the number of people who are given access to information about covert action. In general, the risk of a leak varies with the number of people with access to the information. Furthermore, congressmen and their staff aides typically are less used to dealing with classified information, and they work in a more political setting than the average intelligence official. The requirement to brief Congress probably draws in people within the executive branch itself, since some of those who handle congressional relations for the administration have to be informed as well. In most cases, enough executive branch employees have access that the expansion due to congressional oversight probably does not significantly increase the risk of a leak; in special cases, where access is strictly limited within the executive branch, the increase would be relatively greater, as would the additional risk of a leak.

While much of the public debate about congressional oversight at the time it was established concerned leaks, the more theoretical challenge to congressional oversight of covert action deals with the propriety and effectiveness of Congress's adopting secret procedures as a routine matter.

Thus, a former American Civil Liberties Union official, Morton Halperin, testified before the Church Committee against the concept:

> [Better forms of control] cannot succeed in curing the evils inherent in having a covert capability. The only weapon opponents of a Presidential policy, inside or outside the executive branch, have is public debate. If a policy can be debated openly, then Congress may be persuaded to constrain the President and public pressure may force a change in policy. But if secrecy is accepted as the norm and as legitimate, then the checks put on covert operations can easily be ignored.[30]

While this prediction has proved excessively dismissive of what congressional committees can achieve in quiet negotiation with the executive branch (the threat to "go public" remaining in the background), it does contain a kernel of truth: In cases of major disagreement, such as the "covert" aid to the Nicaraguan resistance in the 1980s, the norm of secrecy has been abandoned, and issues have received full-scale and public congressional debate.

Thus, the notion of congressional oversight conducted secretly contains a self-contradiction: One wants to obtain the benefits of legislative deliberation on intelligence matters, but one rules out from the start the major method of such deliberation—full and open public debate.

These issues of intelligence secrecy and oversight often become confused with what is properly a separate issue: To what extent does the fact that a nation is a democracy affect the kind of foreign policy it ought to adopt? This is particularly true with respect to covert action, which is the element of intelligence that in the United States has attracted the most criticism as being antidemocratic. However, much of the criticism directed against the CIA for its covert action programs would have been more properly directed against the foreign policy those programs served.

In the United States, the main complaint against covert action in the 1970s and 1980s was that it interfered in other countries' internal affairs. It seems that it should have been a secondary question whether that interference was secret or overt. The argument was sometimes made that such activity was undemocratic, in the sense that it was carried on covertly precisely because domestic public opposition to it would be overwhelming if it were known. This situation, however, is not so clearly the case as those who make this argument claim. For example, the various covert actions directed against Fidel Castro, including the assassination attempts, might have received public support at the time they were under way. When the Church Committee complained that these actions went counter to American public opinion, it was judging the CIA's past covert actions not by the public opinion of the late 1950s and early 1960s (when the attempts were carried out) but by the post-Vietnam public opinion of the mid-1970s.[31] By the 1990s, public opinion had changed again; it easily accepted U.S. intervention in the internal affairs of Haiti and Yugoslavia (with respect to Kosovo).

Since the mid-1970s, when the congressional intelligence oversight committees were created in the United States, other democratic countries have considered establishing some form of independent oversight of intelligence activities. For example, in 1984, the Canadian Parliament created the Security Intelligence Review Committee (SIRC) to exercise oversight of the country's domestic intelligence apparatus, which was at the same time separated from the Royal Canadian Mounted Police and made into a new civilian agency, the Canadian Security Intelligence Service.

Unlike the American oversight committees, the SIRC is not a committee of Parliament but is composed of privy councilors appointed by the prime minister after consultation with the opposition party leaders. (The Privy Council is a group whose members, usually former cabinet members, have been officially recognized by the Canadian government as senior advisers.) The SIRC reports to Parliament annually but has no legislative or budgetary powers. The differences between the Canadian and U.S. oversight mechanisms reflect the differences in the two political systems; the main tension within the U.S. system is between the executive and legislative branches of the government, which is not the case in Canada's parliamentary system, with its strong party discipline. (In such systems, the prime minister is the leader of the party, or coalition of parties, holding the majority of seats in Parliament and is in fact technically a member of Parliament him- or herself.) Instead, in Canada, the necessary independence from the executive branch is obtained by relying on eminent senior statesmen.[32]

Other countries, including the United Kingdom, Australia,[33] New Zealand, and Germany, have created parliamentary committees with oversight responsibilities, although they differ in various ways from the U.S. model.[34] The main difference, as noted above, is that these parliamentary systems do not afford the inherent legislative independence found in the U.S. presidential system, with its built-in separation of powers between the executive and legislative branches. Thus, in the United Kingdom, the members of the Intelligence and Security Committee are "appointed by the Prime Minister after consultation with the Leader of the Opposition" (the "opposition" being the minority party or coalition in Parliament).[35] In addition, it reports to the prime minister, who "may—after consultation with the Committee—exclude material which he considers to be 'prejudicial to the continued discharge of the functions' of the Agencies, before laying it before Parliament."[36]

In addition, the scope of responsibility of these committees varies. Thus, according to its founding legislation, the inquiry powers of the Parliamentary Joint Committee on the Australian Security Intelligence Agency (ASIO) do not extend to "matters that relate to the obtaining or communicating by ASIO of foreign intelligence" or to "an aspect of the activities of ASIO that does not affect any person who is an Australian citizen or permanent resident."[37]

Democracy, Counterintelligence, and Domestic Intelligence

In fact, however, counterintelligence, not covert action, is the element of intelligence most fundamentally affected by the democratic nature of the regime it serves; most difficulties in the relationship between democracy and intelligence concern counterintelligence. In particular, these difficulties involve defining the circumstances under which a government agency may legitimately conduct surveillance of its citizens, and determining the limits, if any, on the amount and kind of such surveillance.

In the United States, this discussion tends to be conducted in terms of constitutional law. For example, questions arise as to how the prohibition, contained in the Fourth Amendment to the U.S. Constitution,[38] against unreasonable searches and seizures should be interpreted with respect to national security cases. One such question involved the legitimacy of wiretaps (which are considered a form of search) for such cases: Should the requirement that a judicial warrant be obtained before conducting a wiretap operation for law enforcement purposes be extended to national security cases as well? This question was resolved by the Foreign Intelligence Surveillance Act of 1978, which required that a judicial warrant be obtained for wiretaps in national security cases but created a special court to grant such warrants, operating under procedures designed to protect the secrecy of the entire process.[39] In 1994, physical searches for national security purposes were subjected to a similar procedure.[40]

This focus on the admissibility or inadmissibility of various *means* of counterintelligence (means that will not be discussed in detail here) has been accompanied by a neglect of the more fundamental questions concerning the proper *ends* of counterintelligence or domestic intelligence in a democracy.[41] What kind of information, in other words, is needed? What purpose is such information supposed to serve? What kinds of threats give rise to domestic intelligence requirements?

These questions are very difficult to answer with respect to a democratic state, as opposed to a totalitarian or authoritarian one. In the latter kinds of states, any opposition to the current leadership of the state is, in principle, of intelligence interest. By constantly monitoring dissent, the government strives to be in a position to take whatever steps are necessary, either through the ordinary law enforcement system or outside of it, to maintain its power.

In a democratic state, on the other hand, mere opposition to the government of the day is not, and should not be treated as, a threat to the country or its system of government. The country's national security interests (as opposed to the government's political interests) are not threatened by opposition as such, and domestic intelligence collection about it is not needed. The question is, then, what forms of activities *are* so potentially threatening to national security that intelligence should be collected about them?

In particular, where is the line to be drawn between activities that are legitimately of intelligence interest and those that are not? Should intelligence ever be interested in someone's opinions, in and of themselves, or only when they are accompanied by actions? Should the criterion be the legality or illegality of the activity? Are there activities, although legal, about which the government has a legitimate need to know and hence may keep under some form of surveillance?

The Criminal Standard Because of the focus on the *means* used in domestic intelligence collection (especially in terms of their constitutionality or lack of it) rather than its *ends,* these questions have not been addressed explicitly in public debates on intelligence. However, an answer of sorts was suggested in the mid-1970s in the United States (at the time of the congressional intelligence investigations), when an attempt was made to apply what was called the "criminal standard" to domestic intelligence. In other words, domestic intelligence investigations would be strictly limited to situations where a violation of the law has occurred or was about to occur. The implication was that the proper scope of domestic intelligence would be delimited by the law; an illegal action may be a proper subject of domestic intelligence, but a legal one cannot be.[42] While this principle was never promulgated in so many words, it set the tone for guidelines issued by the attorney general in 1976. Its impact also can be seen in the Foreign Intelligence Surveillance Act of 1978, the sole piece of congressional legislation enacted in this area in that period.[43]

The guidelines were established by Edward Levi, then the attorney general, to specify the circumstances under which the FBI could use various surveillance and investigatory techniques. For the purposes of these guidelines, domestic intelligence was divided into two parts—domestic security on the one hand, foreign intelligence and counterintelligence on the other; separate guidelines were established for investigations in each category.

The guidelines governing foreign intelligence and counterintelligence investigations are classified and have never been made public in their totality.[44]

It is therefore difficult to know to what extent they embody the criminal standard with respect to the investigations they govern. The vast majority of the investigations conducted under these guidelines would deal with detecting and preventing espionage. Thus, they would focus on potential criminal activity. The same holds for the detection and prevention of terrorist activities carried out under foreign direction, which is probably the FBI's other high-priority task to be accomplished in accordance with these guidelines.

It is not clear to what extent the guidelines envisage the investigation of legal political activities carried out on behalf of a foreign government—that is, cooperation with covert action or active measures conducted by a foreign government and targeted against the United States. It is true that, according to the guidelines,

> the FBI is, *under standards and procedures authorized in these guidelines,* authorized to detect and prevent espionage, sabotage and *other clandestine intelligence activities,* by or pursuant to the direction of foreign powers through such lawful foreign counterintelligence operations within the United States and its territories, including electronic surveillance, as are necessary or useful for such purposes.[45]

This implies that such generally legal activities as political propaganda, organizational work, and fund-raising are subject to surveillance when carried out pursuant to the direction of a foreign power. Furthermore, theoretically at least, anyone engaged in such activity on behalf of a foreign government is obliged to register as a foreign agent under the Foreign Agent Registration Act (FARA), and failure to register itself constitutes a crime.[46]

On the other hand, failure to register is rarely used as the sole basis for a foreign counterintelligence investigation or prosecution.[47] Perhaps the only such investigation involved the Committee in Solidarity with the People of El Salvador (CISPES), which was the subject of a three-month FBI probe in 1981. The investigation was conducted at the request of the Criminal Division of the Department of Justice "to determine whether CISPES is required to register under" FARA as an agent of the Salvadoran Frente Democrático Revolucionario, the political arm of the Salvadoran guerrilla movement.[48] However, given that this was an exceptionally rare case, it is unclear (at least on the basis of publicly available information) to what extent the standards and procedures authorized in these guidelines would permit any effective investigation of clandestine intelligence activities that did not involve violence or the violation of any law (other than FARA).

In contrast to the foreign counterintelligence guidelines, the domestic security ones (called the "Levi Guidelines") have been made public.[49] They deal primarily with investigations of groups once called "subversive" or "un-American." While these are vague terms, they generally include groups (1) that are hostile not merely to the government of the day and its policies but to the constitutional structure and its fundamental principles, (2) that seek to deprive some class of persons (such as a racial, ethnic, or religious group) of their civil rights, or (3) more generally, that seek to bring about political change by violent means.

The key point in the Levi Guidelines is that investigation of such groups is permitted only when a group (or an individual) is or may be engaged in activities "which involve or will involve the use of force or violence and which involve or will involve the violation of federal law."[50] This is the essence of the criminal standard that effectively defines the government's interest in the domestic security area.

The most important motive for adopting this standard has been to ensure that no surveillance takes place just because an individual or group exercises its rights of freedom of speech, of the press, or of association, as protected by the First Amendment to the U.S. Constitution.[51] Two general lines of argument support this goal. First, there is the view that government investigation of an individual or a group is itself a kind of punishment, from which those who have done nothing illegal should be exempt. The second argument holds that this type of investigation, either because of its intrinsic unpleasantness for the target or because it seems to threaten future punishment, inevitably "chills" the activity (the exercise of the right) that forms the basis of the surveillance. These reasons have some plausibility but are not as compelling as is sometimes claimed. In constitutional terms, the questions would be whether surveillance under these conditions would amount to an abridgement of the freedoms of the First Amendment.

This issue cannot be dealt with here at length. A few points, however, illustrate the arguments for and against the criminal standard. On the one hand, the violation of privacy involved in the government's keeping tabs on an individual is indeed distasteful. However, this is true of all law enforcement investigations that target individuals who are not suspected of having committed specific crimes: income tax audits, customs inspections, and any number of other law enforcement actions are invasions of privacy, which the government may and does undertake without cause to believe that the target has committed a crime.

Similarly, the possibility of government surveillance might indeed scare people away from controversial political activity, because they fear the inclusion of their names in a file might lead to unpleasant consequences in the future. Nevertheless, the chilling effect of a secret investigation that leads to no government activity can only be minimal, if it amounts to anything at all. The effect seems more equivalent to the social obloquy one might earn by espousing unpopular opinions than to an abridgement of First Amendment freedoms. As a matter of constitutional law, the Supreme Court has rejected the contention that an individual suffers harm from "the mere existence, without more, of a governmental investigative and data-gathering activity." It has ruled that as far as achieving the legal status ("standing") to contest a governmental investigation in court is concerned, "allegations of a subjective 'chill' [resulting from the secret government investigation] are not an adequate substitute for a claim of specific present objective harm or a threat of specific future harm."[52]

As has been noted by Kenneth Robertson, this issue is typically discussed in terms of constitutional-law prohibitions against certain types of governmental activity. The question also must be faced of whether these standards allow the government to meet its legitimate needs for information about what is going on in its own society.[53] In at least two areas of interest an argument can be made that theoretically at least, these standards do not allow the government enough leeway.

The Criminal Standard and Personnel Security The first area has to do with the government's personnel security program for screening potential or current government employees before giving them access to classified information. For such purposes, it is legitimate for the government to want to know if the applicants have any affiliations or loyalties that might lead them to disclose classified information to representatives of foreign powers or otherwise act against the country's interests. In general, it is difficult to determine this information during the screening, for all the reasons noted in chapter 5. The only way the government can have some confidence that the applicant is disclosing any such affiliation is if the government possesses other sources of information, derived from surveillance of the organizations in question.

In this regard, it is important to understand how far the First Amendment's protection extends. According to the Supreme Court's decision in the case of *Brandenburg v. Ohio*, "abstract advocacy" of the overthrow of the U.S. government is protected. Advocacy can be forbidden only when "such advocacy is directed to inciting or producing *imminent* lawless action and is likely to incite or produce such action."[54] Thus, under a strict criminal standard, an organization that openly called for the violent overthrow of the U.S. government could not be subject to surveillance unless and until its advocacy passed from the abstract to the concrete, as defined above.

Furthermore, membership in an organization involved in "nonabstract" advocacy can be considered criminal only if it is active, rather than nominal, membership and involves "knowledge of the [organization's] illegal advocacy and a specific intent to bring about violent overthrow [of the U.S. government] 'as speedily as circumstances would permit.'"[55] This implies that under a criminal standard, it would be impossible to conduct surveillance of such an organization for the purpose of compiling a complete list of its members, since there would not be evidence that each member met the standard for criminal membership, even if the organization as a whole met the *Brandenburg* test.

To some extent, this inability to compile membership lists of "subversive" organizations (that is, organizations whose goals were such that membership in them might raise questions about an individual's suitability for access to classified information) was an intended result of the adoption of the criminal standard. As John Elliff has noted, in describing the initial policy decisions taken by Attorney General Edward Levi:

> Levi rejected the federal employee security program as a basis for FBI intelligence investigations. As Levi saw it, the Executive Order [on the personnel security program] authorized the Bureau only to investigate Executive Branch employees and applicants. It could not supply a basis for the FBI's authority to conduct domestic intelligence investigations in general.[56]

In other words, investigations cannot start with a group's public words or actions. They have to start with the application for government employment by an individual whose affiliation with the group might be well hidden.

Without surveillance of such groups for the purpose of compiling a list of their members, the federal government cannot, in general, guard against granting access to confidential information to, or placing in sensitive positions, individuals who are members of political parties loyal to a hostile foreign power, of various cult groups fanatically devoted to leaders whose ultimate aims may not be compatible with constitutional government, or of hate groups that want to expel parts of the American people from the body politic. This may or may not pose a problem at any given time, depending on whether such groups exist and whether one of them is sophisticated enough to develop a strategy of concealing its members' connection to the group while placing them in sensitive government positions ("penetrating" the government).[57]

The Criminal Standard and Counterterrorism A somewhat different issue arises in the case of terrorist groups. While an active terrorist group would meet any conceivable criminal standard for surveillance, it can be extremely difficult to establish such surveillance if the group is as sophisticated as the major terrorist groups of the past decades in the Middle East and Western Europe. Given the rarity of known fixed facilities and means of communication, which might be covered by technical collection means, the most fruitful investigative technique, and often the only useful one, is to penetrate a group with agents. However, a sophisticated group will be suspicious of outsiders and will take into its confidence only individuals with whom current members have had long personal associations or who have proved their loyalty to the group by committing serious crimes. Absent a lucky break, it is difficult or even impossible for an intelligence service, starting from scratch, to penetrate a terrorist group once it is organized and in operation.

Intelligence agencies have to fall back on other strategies to deal with this problem. First, they must be able to collect information about support groups, which are groups of sympathizers who provide various kinds of backing—financial, logistical, political, and legal—but do not take part in the actual terrorist activities.

Penetrating a support group, while much easier to accomplish, is not as valuable as penetrating the terrorist group itself. Nevertheless, it can be very useful; the kind of aid provided may make it possible to deduce the timing and nature of future terrorist acts. Furthermore, a support-group member, through personal ties or actual recruitment by the terrorist group, may work his way into a position to provide much more precise information. Finally, an agent within a support group might be able to foil a terrorist act, either by providing the police with a key piece of information (such as the description of the rental car to be used in a terrorist act) or by directly sabotaging a bomb (perhaps by replacing the gunpowder with sawdust) or other equipment. As explained by Shlomo Gazit, former director of Israeli intelligence,

> Very few [terrorist] organizations can operate in a complete or full compartmentalization and do not depend on networks of local supporters. Such supporters help the terrorist organization, either because of ideological motivation or through fear and blackmail, without being directly involved in terrorist operations. The importance of penetrating the sympathizers' or supporters' system lies in the fact that it is easier to penetrate it than the more highly closed terrorist organizations. By penetrating this supportive system it may be possible to penetrate the organization itself or obtain indirect information about it.[58]

The criminal standard inhibits the penetration of support groups, since they typically present themselves to the public as political or charitable groups, which they may actually be in part. One group may describe itself as being engaged in political propaganda in favor of various causes, which just happen to be the same as those espoused by the terrorist group. Similarly, another will characterize its activity as the charitable support of the wives and children of alleged terrorists who have been imprisoned or killed. A third group may claim to limit its activities to providing lawyers and funds for the accused terrorists' legal defense.

Without getting an informer into the support group, it may not be possible to establish the exact nature of the group's additional (and not so innocent) efforts on behalf of the terrorist group. But the use of this or other intrusive techniques is permitted only if evidence is already available that the group is involved in violent, criminal activities.[59] In this respect, the criminal standard is something of a Catch-22: One cannot know about the support group's additional activities because one may not look, and one may not look as long as one does not know.

A second way of overcoming the difficulty of conducting surveillance against terrorist groups relies on the fact that terrorist groups are typically offshoots of politically extremist, nationalist, or separatist groups; they are usually composed of members of such groups who become frustrated with the failure of less violent means to accomplish their goals. By having informers in the groups from which terrorist groups are likely to form, one would know about a new terrorist group as soon as it exists and possibly have a penetration agent in it from the beginning. A criminal standard, on the other hand, makes it impossible to maintain the initial surveillance that could provide the first indication of a new terrorist group.

A particular circumstance that comes under the rubric of counterterrorism involves the responsibility of the U.S. Secret Service to protect the president, other senior government officials, and foreign dignitaries. As with counterterrorism in general, the goal here is to prevent a criminal act from taking place, rather than reacting to one by punishing the perpetrators to deter future attacks. The Secret Service's responsibility requires advance intelligence on assassination attempts against its protectees. A criminal standard for investigating groups that might engage in assassination may mean the Secret Service will not receive warnings about assassination attempts until after the group has engaged in illegal violence, which might be too late. In 1982, the Treasury Department official responsible for the service explained the problem this way: "Today, the [Secret S]ervice has to be . . . concerned about the terrorist. . . . The Secret Service needs to know . . . about the intentions and activities of terrorists or other extremist groups. Further we need to know about this kind of threat before it materializes, not after."[60]

This official also noted that a reasonable allocation of the service's resources would require that it "know, for example, that an organization using extreme rhetoric is either disinclined to put words into action or incapable of launching dangerous activities." In his view, the current

> problem is that the FBI is not . . . able to collect enough intelligence. This partly because [of] . . . Attorney General Levi's Domestic Security Guidelines. . . . Prior to the Levi Guidelines, the Secret Service received from the FBI a vast amount of intelligence information on individuals and potentially violent groups. . . . Although it has been claimed that this resulted in the Secret Service being overinformed—the service obviously had to sift through an awful lot of information and sort out the wheat from the chaff[,] . . . the situation was ideal as far as the Secret Service was concerned.
>
> The problem now is that investigations in important areas are simply not being pursued. The result is a lack of information about the location, structure, plans, and activities of groups that may not be labeled terrorist as such, but that certainly are radical, . . . that support terrorist causes and are potentially terroristic or violent.

Of course, this general point would apply to all law enforcement; in general, very little law enforcement activity is devoted to preventing crime (except by deterrence) as opposed to detecting it afterward and apprehending the perpetrators. Certainly, it would be impossible for ordinary law enforcement organizations to set themselves the goal of preventing crime by establishing an intelligence network that would warn them of planned criminal activity. In counterterrorism and executive protection, however, because of the potential seriousness of a single incident, there is a strong desire to prevent crime and not merely to punish it; this implies a requirement to collect intelligence about individuals or groups who, although they have not yet done so, are likely either to engage in such activities or to maintain close ties with those that do.

The question of whether the guidelines, as they apply to domestic counterterrorism situations, provide adequate powers to the FBI arose again in 1995, following the bombing of a federal building in Oklahoma City that resulted in a large number of fatalities. Attorney General Janet Reno and FBI Director Louis Freeh, however, decided that revisions to the guidelines were unnecessary; instead, they announced that the existing guidelines (the Levy guidelines having been revised by Attorney General William French Smith in 1983)—which permitted a counterterrorism investigation to begin when "facts and circumstances reasonably indicate that two or more persons are engaged in an enterprise [to further] political or social goals . . . through activities that involve force or violence and a violation of the criminal laws of the United States"[61]—would be interpreted in a more expansive manner. According to Freeh, this reinterpretation would "allow the FBI to begin an investigation of a group advocating violence to achieve social or political objectives somewhere short of an imminent violation of federal law, if it was apparent the group had the ability to carry out its objectives."[62]

While the standard of "reasonable indication" is certainly vague enough to accommodate Freeh's interpretation (that is, an imminent violation is not required), it presumably requires more than (constitutionally protected) "abstract" advocacy of violence; indeed the Smith Guidelines go on to explain that this standard requires a consideration of the magnitude, likelihood and immediacy of the threat (which is to be balanced against "the danger to privacy and free expression posed by an investigation").[63] Thus, this reinterpretation, while relaxing the requirement for evidence of an "imminent" violation, nevertheless remains within the spirit of the "criminal standard."

The Case for the Criminal Standard Asserting the theoretical argument against the criminal standard for domestic security investigations is much easier than determining what could replace it. The criminal standard was adopted after the Church Committee documented many cases in which the FBI had conducted investigations that represented both a waste of resources and unwarranted intrusion into political activities that posed no domestic security threat. This "overbreadth," as the Church Committee termed it, argued for a relatively clear-cut standard that would limit investigations to those undeniably necessary. Necessary investigations were defined as being targeted against specific acts of criminal violence that had already occurred or were about to occur.

The examples of this overbreadth in domestic security investigations fall under various headings. Perhaps the most glaring were those cases in which, at White House direction, the FBI undertook investigations against the president's partisan opponents, apparently for purely political purposes. Judge and former Deputy Attorney General Laurence Silberman testified in 1978 that "of all the abuses of various agencies of Government over the last 20 years, I think the single most egregious abuse was President Johnson's direction to the FBI to see if they could find any dirt on [Senator Barry Goldwater's] staff 2 weeks before the [1964 presidential] election."[64] There are other similar examples of the use of the FBI against political opponents in Congress, the media, or elsewhere.

In many other cases, investigations were directed against activist political groups targeted under vague labels, such as

- "Rightist" or "extremist" groups in the "anticommunist field"
- "Anarchistic or revolutionary beliefs"
- "Black nationalists" and "extremists"
- "White supremacists"
- "Agitators."[65]

In these cases, while there might have been some nexus between the organization being investigated and potential violence or links to foreign intelligence services, clearly the investigations were indeed overbroad in terms of the individuals and groups involved, the extraneous information collected about them, and the length of time unpromising investigations were allowed to continue. The extraneous information that was collected was not only retained in investigatory files but freely disseminated within the government; thus, information about legitimate political activities was made available for the administration's partisan use.[66]

From the history the Church Committee compiled, it seems clear that excesses were facilitated by the absence of clear standards for domestic intelligence investigations. Thus, it is easy to see how a criminal standard would be an attractive, clear-cut option. If that limitation is too narrow, then one must search for a broader one that still would protect against the sorts of abuses that have occurred.

This task cannot be accomplished quickly. To approach it in a responsible manner, one would have to start by considering what domestic political or other activities a democratic government legitimately needs to know about to protect against threats to the country. In the United States, the legislation, executive orders, and guidelines dealing with domestic intelligence have been cast in terms of the conditions that must be met before various investigative techniques may be employed. There is, on the other hand, no formal statement of what the purpose of domestic intelligence is or of what type of information it is supposed to provide. Such a statement would have to be elaborated before one could develop guidelines that focus on the goal (what sorts of information are necessary) rather than on the means (which investigative technique may be used).

By contrast, Canadian law defines the threats with which the agency responsible for domestic intelligence, the Canadian Security Intelligence Service

(CSIS), should be concerned. The CSIS is authorized to collect information regarding activities "that may on reasonable grounds be suspected of constituting threats to the security of Canada." These are defined as:

- Espionage or sabotage, or activities directed toward or in support of espionage or sabotage
- Foreign-influenced activities that are detrimental to Canadian interests and are clandestine or deceptive or involve a threat to any person
- Activities directed toward or in support of the threat or use of serious violence to achieve a political purpose
- Activities directed toward or intended ultimately to lead to the destruction or violent overthrow of the Canadian government.[67]

Even with an adequate definition of the scope of domestic intelligence, questions will arise as to whether a given group constitutes a threat or is simply engaging in hyperbolic rhetoric, and as to the amount and type of evidence required for a group to be considered a threat that should be investigated. But without an understanding of what domestic security information is required, it is impossible to judge whether specific restrictions on investigative means are reasonable.

Chapter 7

Two Views of Intelligence

In the five preceding chapters, we have discussed the four elements of intelligence—the four general headings under which intelligence activities may be categorized—as well as some of the issues concerning the relationship between intelligence and the rest of the government and society of which it is a part. We now return to the more general issue of the nature of intelligence as a whole, starting with a comparison of what may be called the "traditional" view of intelligence (which emphasizes obtaining, protecting, and exploiting secret information relevant to the struggle among nations) with a newer, characteristically American view of intelligence that has evolved since World War II.

To some extent, the "traditional" view as developed here is our invention—hence the quotation marks. While it reflects traditional concepts of intelligence, those concepts were not typically articulated in this manner. (It should be remembered that public writings about intelligence were rare in the past.) It is used here primarily as a foil to highlight the distinctive aspects of the American view of intelligence that arose after World War II.

The "traditional" view can be traced back to one of the oldest known thematic discussions of intelligence, which is found in a Chinese classic entitled *The Art of War,* attributed to a sixth century B.C. general and military thinker named Sun Tzu. He explains the importance of intelligence as follows:

> Now the reason the enlightened prince and the wise general conquer the enemy whenever they move and their achievements surpass those of ordinary men is foreknowledge.
>
> What is called "foreknowledge" cannot be elicited from spirits, nor from the gods, nor by analogy with past events, nor from calculations. It must be obtained from men who know the enemy situation [directly—that is, men with access to the enemy camp].[1]

Espionage is at the center of this understanding of intelligence. Given the close connection between learning the enemy's secrets and achieving victory over him, it would follow that the protection of one's own secrets (counterintelligence) must be as important as the obtaining of the adversary's. Sun Tzu mentions two methods of achieving this:

- Doubling enemy agents, presumably by making them a better offer
- Sending into the enemy camp spies who have been deceived as to one's own situation, so that, once captured by the enemy and forced to talk, they will unwittingly deceive him.[2]

The ultimate goal of this espionage is to understand the adversary's strategy so well that one can devise means of circumventing and defeating it, at the lowest possible cost. Indeed, from the point of view of Sun Tzu, for whom defeating an enemy's strategy is more important than defeating his army, the intelligence component of international struggle is as vital as the armed component:

> Thus, what is of supreme importance in war is to attack the enemy's strategy; Next best is to disrupt his alliances; The next best is to attack his army.[3]

Intelligence is as much a struggle with an enemy as is armed combat; the difference lies in the means employed.

In an article that calls for the "growth of a truly American intelligence system," former Director of Central Intelligence William Colby distinguishes such a system from traditional intelligence systems, which he describes and dismisses, as follows:

> For centuries, intelligence was the small, private preserve of monarchs and generals. Governmental and military espionage ferreted out the secrets of other powers in order to provide its sponsors with advantage in their dealings. Secret agents intrigued and subverted in order to discredit an opponent or support their [sic] adversaries within his own camp. The spy was the prototype of this traditional "intelligence" discipline.[4]

Elsewhere, Colby defines the "traditional concept of intelligence" as a "secret service which ferrets out an enemy's secret plan and shares it with a monarch so that he can win a battle."[5] He claims that the American experience during World War II saw the rise of a new view of intelligence that challenged the "traditional" one in major respects. In the postwar period, this view had continued to develop both within U.S. intelligence and among some academic students of the subject. This chapter discusses that new view and compares it with the "traditional" one.

HISTORICAL DEVELOPMENT OF THE AMERICAN VIEW

The unsettled conditions brought about by the beginning of World War II and America's subsequent entry into it led to massive increases in resources the United States devoted to intelligence. It also led to a new bureaucratic development, the creation of a central intelligence service (known first as the

Office of the Coordinator of Information and then as the Office of Strategic Services, or OSS), whose purposes included the collection, analysis, and correlation of national security information and data.[6] Despite President Franklin Roosevelt's decision in July 1941 to create a central capability to correlate information, none was in place by December 1941, when the failure to foresee the Japanese attack on Pearl Harbor highlighted the lack of intelligence correlation and analysis, since many relevant bits and pieces of information had been available.

The Centrality of Analysis

The OSS set up a research and analysis branch that was to analyze "all the relevant information, that was overtly available as well as that secretly obtained."[7] Although this goal was not fulfilled during World War II, it remained the ideal situation, and it was essentially realized with the creation of the Central Intelligence Agency in 1947.[8]

This emphasis on intelligence analysis, the intellectual work of piecing together disparate bits of information to develop an accurate picture, suggests a view of intelligence different from the "traditional" one. This newer view pays less attention to secrecy and the means of overcoming it and more attention to the analytic function, broadly conceived.

This view was most influentially put forward immediately after World War II by Sherman Kent, former OSS officer and future head of the Office of National Estimates, the Central Intelligence Agency office then in charge of producing overall assessments of the world situation. His well-known book *Strategic Intelligence for American World Policy* argued the case for understanding intelligence as the scientific method (in its social science variant) applied to strategic matters:

> Research is the only process which we of the liberal tradition are willing to admit is capable of giving us the truth, or a closer approximation to truth, than we now enjoy. . . . [W]e insist, and have insisted for generations, that truth is to be approached, if not attained through research guided by a systematic method. In the social sciences which very largely constitute the subject matter of strategic intelligence, there is such a method. It is much like the method of physical sciences. It is not the same method but it is a method nonetheless.[9]

Of course, this social science method cannot be the whole of intelligence, even if it is its heart. There must, after all, be data upon which it can work. While recognizing that some of the data must be gathered by clandestine means, Kent insists that the popular view of intelligence as dealing primarily with secrets is a myth. Instead, in his view, intelligence analysis can rely on nonsecret, openly available information, with only a small number of clandestinely gathered secrets added as seasoning. Referring to the knowledge necessary to conduct foreign policy—the content of the strategic intelligence about which he is writing—he says, "Some of this knowledge may be acquired through clandestine means, but *the bulk of it must be had through unromantic open-and-above-board observation and research.*"[10]

In its most extreme form, this new view equates intelligence with a sort of universal, predictive social science. This hoped-for social science was described by former DCI Colby in 1981 as follows:

> A new discipline specifically designed for intelligence analysis must be refined, and the process of research and development has already begun. It will step beyond academic analysis through new techniques to project future probabilities rather than explain the past. Experiments in this new discipline are by no means limited to the official intelligence community, as they also take place in information science research centers, among political risk analysts, and in the projections of the Club of Rome, the Global 2000 study, and others.[11]

The central importance of analysis is a major distinguishing characteristic of the new view of intelligence. To understand this view better, we examine the argument that a proponent might use to convince a "traditionalist" of its truth. The starting point is the observation that whatever one's view of intelligence, one must recognize an important role for at least some kinds of analysis.

First of all, collection activity immediately generates the need for analysis, either technical (such as decoding coded messages) or more general (such as comparing reports from two different sources to determine whether they support or contradict one another). Some evaluation of the information received is needed to determine, for example, whether it should be accepted as genuine or whether it should be regarded as a deliberate attempt by the adversary to mislead.[12]

More significantly, it often may be too difficult to ferret out the relevant secret information directly. As a result, the only alternative is to try to deduce it from whatever data are available. This could include information that the adversary does not consider, in itself, to be sensitive and so does not keep secret.

For example, the most direct and reliable warning of imminent attack would probably come from an agent within the enemy's general staff. Failing this, one would have to attempt to deduce the enemy's intention from various pieces of information concerning the deployment of his armed forces, their readiness, the status of his reserves, and so forth. In addition, public information might be useful as well; before Pearl Harbor, for example, the United States paid attention to the locations and planned itineraries of Japanese merchant ships on the grounds that were Japan planning to go to war, it would make sure that its merchant fleet had been recalled to relatively safe waters.

Thus far, those holding the "traditional" view would not argue with the necessity of such activities, despite their view that intelligence deals primarily with secrets. The questions come as the sphere of intelligence concerns expands to the dimensions of Colby's "new discipline . . . [of] intelligence analysis," a universal, predictive social science covering all aspects of society.

Obviously, to manage military affairs and to conduct foreign policy, a country's governmental officials must know more about its potential adversaries than merely their military or diplomatic secrets. Other factors, such as the potential adversary's economic activity and potential, its demographic trends, and its internal political forces and concerns, also must be considered. With respect to these factors, the difficulty is likely to lie not so much in gathering the raw data (although in the case of a closed society with an idiosyncratic political system, this may present many challenges) as in evaluating the information correctly.

For example, despite the openness of the American political process, an observer, whether American or not, has difficulty understanding, let alone predicting, the course of a major political event, such as a congressional vote or a presidential campaign. Yet, clearly, to conduct its policy toward the United States, another country would find that a good understanding of such matters could be as important as obtaining U.S. national security secrets. As Eliot Cohen has pointed out, the openness of American political life in the 1930s did not by itself enable its future opponents to understand it:

> Although the United States . . . was nothing if not accessible to foreign agents, both legal and covert, it was in another sense impenetrable to the Axis powers because of their own failure to comprehend the workings of democratic states. Both the Germans and the Japanese repeatedly underestimated the American polity—its tenacity and ingenuity, as well as its ability to organize, improvise, and produce. And these colossal failures of intelligence helped doom both states to ruinous defeat.[13]

In other cases, the bit of information most important for a nation to have cannot be considered a secret because, when the information is most needed, it does not even yet exist. Sherman Kent gives as an example of this the intelligence problem the Soviet Union faced when it sought to determine whether the United States would resist the 1950 North Korean invasion of the South. Had Soviet agents been looking in U.S. files for documents containing the American decision whether to fight, they could not have found any, since the decision was made by President Truman only after the invasion began: "Thus, if knowledge of the other man's intentions is to be divined through the reading of his intimate papers and one's own policy is to be set on the basis of what one discovers, here is a case where policy was on the rocks almost by definition."[14] Kent argues that such information can be had only through research and analysis:

> I have urged that if you have knowledge of Great Frusina's [Kent's hypothetical great power] strategic stature [Kent's term for the totality of a nation's capabilities—military, political and economic—to act on the international scene], knowledge of her specific vulnerabilities, and how she may view these, and knowledge of the stature and vulnerabilities of other states party to the situation, you are in a fair way to be able to predict her *probable courses of action.*

> To strengthen the reliability of your prediction you should possess two additional packages of knowledge. First, you should know about the courses of action which Great Frusina has followed in the past. . . . Second, you should know, as closely as such things may be known, how Great Frusinans are estimating their own stature in the situation.[15]

There can be no doubt that such information, and the thought processes that lead to it, is a vital part of strategic thinking in general and high-level foreign policy making in particular. No policies can be adopted or implemented without some view of the potential actions of other countries. Nevertheless, it is not clear why it should be considered "intelligence" and why it should be located in the intelligence agencies.[16] This issue, which involves important questions concerning the relationship between intelligence and the policy makers it serves, has already been discussed in the previous chapter.

For present purposes, it is sufficient to observe two connected consequences of the nontraditional view of intelligence and its emphasis on the centrality of analysis. The first consequence is that a good deal of the thinking that goes into policy analysis can be, and ought to be, carried out within the intelligence agencies themselves. In intelligence agencies this work can be done according to some kind of scientific method. In other words, the social sciences can, or should be able to, provide for approaching these problems methods that deserve some of the respect and authority routinely granted to science. As a result, in this view, a superior wisdom may be attributed to intelligence results, even when these conclusions reflect not covertly obtained and jealously guarded hard data but speculation based on facts generally available to the policy community. In this view, it becomes possible to use intelligence to "grade," or judge the correctness of, policy.[17]

A second consequence is that intelligence analysis can be divorced from the policy process and, indeed, be apolitical in nature.[18] As a result, one can even talk about creating within an intelligence community an analytic arm along the lines of "a world-class 'think tank.'"[19] From this perspective, intelligence is less a specific aid to policy making than it is a kind of living encyclopedia or reference service whose information should be made available not only to the policy makers' political opponents in the legislature, but also to the domestic public and the world at large.[20] For example, Colby foresees an era of free trade in intelligence, in which nations recognize the "mutual benefit from the free flow and exchange of information, in the fashion that the strategic arms control agreements recognize that both sides can benefit from pledges against concealment and interference with the other's national technical means of verification."[21]

However fantastic this may sound, it illustrates the power of the view that intelligence is, at bottom, an endeavor similar to social science, if not equivalent to it.

Espionage versus Technical Intelligence Collection

No matter how central to intelligence the analytic process is considered to be, the raw data to be analyzed must come from somewhere. While some of it can be found in open sources (publications, radio and television broadcasts, and so forth), the fact remains that some nations do not make public even basic facts about their military forces or the economic resources that support them. Thus, even if Kent's view of the relative importance of open and secret sources were true for more ordinary states, it is clearly not true of a state that conceals almost all the details of the composition of its military forces.

The particularly strong security measures taken by the former Soviet Union made it very difficult, in the post–World War II period, for the United States and other Western countries to use espionage to obtain the missing basic data about Soviet military forces. As already discussed, the problem was solved primarily by the development of technical intelligence collection platforms that could overfly Soviet territory—first the U-2 plane, then reconnaissance satellites.

These technical means not only leapfrogged over Soviet security precautions but appeared to be free of espionage's other problems as well. The whole problem of determining whether a human source was trustworthy seemed to have been avoided by relying instead on machines, which could not lie or be suborned. At the same time, access to a particular location could be assured (although the ability to photograph it required the absence of cloud cover). In this way, too, technical intelligence seemed more reliable than humint.

The result was an exaggeration of the importance of techint at the expense of humint, a tendency that has been characteristic of the post–World War II American view of intelligence. This made intelligence seem a more scientific undertaking, not only because it required the latest and most sophisticated technology but also because it appeared that the uncertainty associated with human agents could be largely overcome by technical collectors that provided broad coverage of the adversary's territory and enabled one to see what was there for oneself. It remains a question whether this peculiarly American reliance on techint will continue in the absence of the overriding collection requirement that gave rise to it at the start.[22]

The Depreciation of Counterintelligence

Another characteristic of the new view of intelligence is its tendency to depreciate the importance of counterintelligence in general, and deception and counterdeception in particular. This is closely related to the notion that intelligence is a variety of social science, one dealing with foreign countries. Even though intelligence work obviously differs in some respects from social science, the two endeavors, according to this view, remain similar.

For example, Kent notes that strategic intelligence is, in his terminology, an "extension," in several senses, of the search for knowledge in general. One of these senses is that "difficult barriers," which "are put there on purpose by other nations," often stand in the way. Nevertheless,

> important as they are, these extensions, as I have called them, are *external* to the heart of the matter: intelligence work remains the simple, natural endeavor to get the sort of knowledge upon which a successful course of action can be rested. And strategic intelligence, we might call the knowledge upon which our nation's foreign relations, in war and peace, must rest.[23]

For the "traditional" view, on the other hand, the fact that an adversary is trying to keep vital information secret is the very essence of the matter; if an adversary were not trying to hide his intentions, there would be no need for complicated analyses of the situation in the first place.

These different stances toward the importance of secrecy reflect basic differences with respect to what intelligence is.[24] If, according to the "traditional" view, intelligence is part of the real struggle with human adversaries, we might say that in the new view, intelligence, like science in general, is a process of discovering truths about the world (or nature) that can be called a struggle only metaphorically. In other words, while there are secrets of nature, they are not pieces of information being jealously guarded from our view; they are simply truths we have not yet discovered. The paradigmatic intelligence problem is not so much ferreting out the adversary's secret intention (as the Korean War example shows, the adversary himself may not know how he will react to future events) as it is of predicting his behavior through social science methodology. This is particularly true the more the emphasis in intelligence analysis shifts to research on long-term trends, often societal and economic in nature. With respect to future social or economic conditions, no real secrets can be obtained, because the adversary himself is uncertain what will happen or, accordingly, what choices he will have and what circumstances he will face.

The same tendency to say that counterintelligence occupies a marginal place in intelligence also affects the importance accorded to deception and counterdeception. By categorizing intelligence as akin to a social science endeavor, the new view ignores, or at least minimizes, the possibility of deception. Nature, while it may hide its secrets from scientific investigators, does not actively try to deceive them.

The Audience for Intelligence

The two views of intelligence differ also regarding who the recipients of intelligence information, its consumers, are. In Colby's formulation the "traditional" view sees the head of state as the prime, and perhaps the only, recipient of intelligence. This view was also reflected in the National Security Act of 1947, which, having established the Central Intelligence Agency, placed it under the authority of the National Security Council and the president rather than under the Department of State or Defense. The implication of this bureaucratic arrangement seems to be that the CIA would remain close to high-level policy makers and would monitor and coordinate the work of the other, departmental, intelligence agencies on their behalf.

Since the new view, as advocated by former DCIs Colby and Turner, tends to depreciate secrecy, it is not surprising that it also seeks to widen the audience for intelligence as far as possible. For example, Turner envisages the creation of an international satellite agency to conduct technical intelligence collection on behalf of the United Nations, with the information being made available to the whole world.[25] Similarly, Colby argues that we are, or should be, entering a period of "free trade" with respect to intelligence, in which the large volume of information available because of modern technology "can be seen to provide mutual rather than one-sided benefits."[26] A philosophy to guide this new era is needed; such a philosophy "must insist on the recognition of mutual benefit from the free flow and exchange of information."

INTELLIGENCE AND MORAL ISSUES

It may seem strange, when writing on a topic in the usually hardheaded field of national security studies, to discuss moral issues explicitly. Certainly, one risks being accused of naivete for doing so. Yet, those who reflect on the subject of intelligence have often had to deal with the question of its morality or, more precisely, the difficult relationship between, for example, the seeming immorality of inducing people to commit treason, on the one hand, and the great usefulness and even necessity of doing so, on the other.[27] In Sun Tzu's view, the key to success in intelligence lies in one's ability to suborn officials in the enemy's camp. Sun Tzu realizes that this is a questionable business, especially for someone who regards loyalty as an important virtue. He regards "moral influence"—by which he means "that which causes the people to be in harmony with their leaders"—as the first fundamental factor determining success or failure in war.[28] He certainly seems aware that the necessity of corrupting officials and subjects of other states can hardly be squared with the ideal of harmony between subjects and rulers.

Even so, in a manner we might anachronistically call Machiavellian, he exhorts his reader to employ espionage. He argues that the opposite course—which he expects his readers would regard as more "honorable"—is in fact inhumane. Noting the great burden that war places on the people and the disruption it causes to their lives, he admonishes, in strident tones:

> One who confronts his enemy for many years in order to struggle for victory in a decisive battle yet who, because he begrudges rank, honors and a few hundred pieces of gold, remains ignorant of his enemy's situation, is completely devoid of humanity. Such a man is no general; no support to his sovereign; no master of victory.[29]

The fact that Sun Tzu makes a moral, and not only a practical, argument for espionage indicates that he feels it necessary to overcome moral qualms against it among his readers.

Despite the antiquity of this illustration, the moral question should not be regarded as a mere curiosity. It has practical effects in modern times. For example, in 1929, Secretary of State Henry L. Stimson, newly appointed by President Hoover, closed down the "Black Chamber," the State Department's cryptographic bureau, which had been reading foreign diplomatic and other coded messages for more than a decade. He is said to have acted on the grounds that "gentlemen do not read each other's mail."[30] From the point of view of U.S. success in World War II, it was fortunate that a cryptographic capability was maintained in the army and navy, paving the way for the major successes of the war in breaking the Japanese diplomatic and naval codes.

The moral issue concerning intelligence resides in the fact that it is a devious or underhanded form of struggle between nations, as compared with armed combat, which is traditionally seen as more open (and hence more honorable). In its very essence, intelligence involves deception and depends heavily on inducing the adversary's citizens to commit treason. As the Stimson example illustrates, this type of activity was hardly congenial to the characteristic (and recurring) American optimism about placing international relations on a higher moral plane. (That communications intelligence is now often regarded as "clean," compared to the "messy" business of espionage, may only demonstrate the extent to which our standards of international morality have been diluted.)[31]

Needless to say, Stimson's view did not survive the unsettled international conditions of the 1930s, let alone World War II itself. However, the new view of intelligence, as sketched out above, has many characteristics that make it seem more moral than the "traditional" one in the eyes of its proponents:

- The centrality of analysis (understood as a variant of science, and thus partaking of its prestige) as opposed to espionage
- The primacy of "clean" technical intelligence over "messy" espionage
- The depreciation of counterintelligence and deception, diminishing the unpleasant awareness that intelligence involves a struggle between nations
- The expansion of intelligence to include areas (societal changes, demography, narcotics trafficking, and so on) more remote from the political and military core of the struggle among nations
- The widening of the intelligence audience, tending to convert a handmaiden of policy (which is used to enhance national interests, often at the expense of others) into a morally neutral provider of information for the government, its opponents, and eventually the domestic and world public.

Thus, this new view of intelligence can be understood as a reassertion of America's optimistic outlook after the harsh realities of international relations during World War II and the earliest, harshest years of the Cold War.

Chapter 8

Toward a Theory of Intelligence

This concluding chapter returns to the original question: What is intelligence? On the basis of discussion of the elements of intelligence, we are now better able to evaluate the various current views of intelligence, particularly that presented in the preceding chapter as the "new American view," and to attempt a more general definition.

The word "intelligence" is used to refer to a certain kind of knowledge, to the activity of obtaining knowledge of this kind (and thwarting the similar activity of others), and to the organizations whose function is to obtain (or deny) it.[1] Of these three categories (knowledge, activity, and organization), the first is the most basic, since the other two are defined in its terms. Thus, the first problem in defining intelligence is to determine the scope of the knowledge with which it is concerned.

Sherman Kent provides a definition of what he calls "high-level foreign positive intelligence": the adjectives are meant to exclude intelligence that is operational or tactical intelligence (not "high-level"), domestic intelligence (not "foreign"), or counterintelligence (not "positive"). According to Kent, "What is left is the knowledge indispensable to our welfare and security. It is both the constructive knowledge with which we can work toward peace and freedom throughout the world, and the knowledge necessary to the defense of our country and its ideals."[2]

Thus, the knowledge involved is that necessary for conducting foreign policy and making the major decisions concerning the development and deployment of military forces in peacetime. It is the knowledge, according to Kent, on which national security policy may be based.

The very title *(Strategic Intelligence for American World Policy)* of Kent's book makes clear that it is a discussion of U.S. intelligence rather than of intelligence generally. Accordingly, his definition of intelligence is couched in terms of the information the U.S. government requires. Nevertheless, there does not seem to be anything about the definition or about the book as a whole that would limit the applicability of its propositions to the United States alone. The basic principles are all general, and indeed, in considering what one wishes to know about a foreign country, Kent does not look at America's potential adversaries but rather invents the country of "Great Frusina" to serve as the generic intelligence target. In this discussion, I therefore take Kent's statements as applying to intelligence generally.

As Kent implies (by his use of the qualifiers "high-level," "foreign," and "positive"), his description is too narrow to define intelligence altogether. One would have to take account, somehow, of what he calls "operational/tactical intelligence," "domestic intelligence," and "counterintelligence." But the most important point is that Kent's description of "high-level foreign positive intelligence," as given above, implies that these other kinds of intelligence are not necessary for "our welfare and security."

It seems fair to assume that Kent's definition is focused only on peacetime intelligence requirements. In time of war, intelligence would have to support not only strategic military decisions but also the operations of military forces in the field. Thus, the operational/tactical level of intelligence ought to be included in any overall discussion of intelligence, and it is hard to believe that Kent would disagree.

The situation may be different with respect to the other two limitations. First, limiting intelligence to foreign subjects seems arbitrary, at least in theory. Threats to the country and its ideals may be domestic as well as foreign, or they may involve domestic groups with foreign ties. As we have seen, defining the scope of domestic intelligence is a very difficult task.

Although we typically speak of *national* security, a nation acts in these matters through its *government,* which generally regards the survival of its form of government as a vital interest. Note that in the definition above, Kent refers to "the defense of [the United States] and its *ideals.*" This recognizes that American democracy coul l be threatened by something that did not threaten the country in a physical sense. Be this as it may, domestic intelligence, in the sense of the information necessary for the regime to protect itself against violent or revolutionary change, also seems to be a necessary part of intelligence. Of course, what the proper subjects of that information are and how much of it is required depend heavily on the nature of the government (the regime).

In addition, the defense of the country may depend on thwarting an adversary's intelligence activities, as well as his military operations; counterintelligence as well as positive intelligence must be regarded as necessary for the "defense of [the] country." It is less clear than in the previous example (operational or tactical intelligence) that Kent would agree to our additions.

In any case, the scope of intelligence must be broadened to include these areas as well. If intelligence is to provide the knowledge needed to conduct national security policy, it must include the knowledge to support the actual use of military forces to pursue national goals, as well as the knowledge that enables one to frustrate other countries' intelligence activities. Thus, Kent's definition of intelligence must be significantly broadened if it is truly to be "the knowledge indispensable to [a country's] welfare and security."

However, though we have to broaden Kent's definition to include knowledge relevant to conducting national security policy, in other respects the definition is already too broad. A great deal of information (for example, technical knowledge in physics or engineering) may be needed to make informed decisions on some military development questions, but such information would not ordinarily be considered intelligence. Similarly, a general understanding of meteorological phenomena is necessary to plan military actions, but again this type of knowledge would not be considered intelligence.[3] In other words, the fact that some branch of natural science makes a major contribution to a nation's pursuit of its security interests does not automatically make it a part of intelligence.

The situation is less clear when it comes to the social sciences. The subject matter of an intelligence analysis (for example, the political situation of a foreign country and how it is likely to evolve) may be similar to the work done in the social sciences. Even so, the two kinds of analysis exhibit important differences that suggest that different approaches may be necessary even if the substantive content is similar.

To be useful, an intelligence analysis ought, in discussing the determinants of the political situation in a foreign country, to emphasize those factors that can be manipulated or changed; the consumer of the analysis is, after all, typically interested in affecting that political situation, not just knowing about it. An academic analysis, on the other hand, will be meant to discover the most fundamental causes of a given situation, even if, or especially if, they are immune to change. To the extent that social science can predict the future course of events (which is, according to Kent, why it is useful for intelligence), it must regard the future as already determined.[4]

Thus, the relationship between intelligence and social science is complex. The nature of this relationship can be better addressed in the context of another major difference between intelligence and science—the close connection between intelligence and secrecy, on the one hand, and science and the free exchange of ideas, on the other.

From the point of view of the traditional understanding of intelligence (to say nothing of the popular understanding), what seems to be most glaringly missing from the definition of intelligence as a kind of knowledge is the element of secrecy. For Kent, indeed, concern with secrets is not an inherent part of intelligence; although he notes that one's adversary may attempt to deny one access to the information one requires, he regards this as an incidental problem, akin to the organizational problems that derive from the large size of a modern state's intelligence establishment:

> Important as they are, these extensions, as I have called them, [that is, subtlety, expertise, *clandestinity*, and size] are external to the heart of the matter: intelligence work remains the simple, natural endeavor to get the sort of knowledge upon which a successful course of action can be rested.[5]

However, the connection between intelligence and secrecy is central to most of what distinguishes intelligence from other intellectual activities. By depreciating its importance, Kent can maintain the position that there is no fundamental difference between intelligence and social science; the Colby article discussed earlier only takes this view to its logical conclusion when it puts forward futurology of the "Club of Rome" variety as the model for intelligence to imitate.[6]

The connection between intelligence and secrecy in turn reflects the fundamental issue of the relationship between intelligence and science. Whatever similarities might emerge, there is a fundamental difference in the ultimate goals of the two enterprises. The goal of science is knowledge, either for its own sake or to further the conquest of nature—the ability to manipulate natural forces according to man's will in the interests of comfort, health, longevity, and so forth. However, the concept of a struggle with nature is only a metaphor. In fact, nature, although sometimes complicated and difficult to understand, is indifferent to human efforts and is not purposefully acting to obstruct them.

Intelligence, on the other hand, involves a real struggle with human opponents, carried on to gain some advantage over them. It is neither surprising nor incidental, therefore, that these opponents often try not only to obstruct one's efforts to learn about them but also to mislead and deceive. One side's intelligence failure is likely to be another side's counterintelligence success. Conversely, an intelligence coup by one country implies a counterintelligence or security failure on the part of its opponent.

Once we understand that intelligence is part of a struggle between two countries, we see why counterintelligence is not an afterthought but is rather an integral part of it. Not only is it important to limit or distort what one's adversary can learn about one, but one cannot even be sure of what one knows about an adversary without the counterintelligence capability to detect any deception effort he might have undertaken.

One objection often made to this approach is that it ignores the important role that open-source information can play in the intelligence process. This objection is, however, based on a misunderstanding. Open-source information is vital for both intelligence and social science; the important distinction is that for the traditional understanding of intelligence, open-source is primarily a means to get around the barriers that obstruct direct access to the information being sought.[7]

Fundamentally, intelligence seeks access to information some other party is trying to deny. Obtaining that information directly means breaching the security barriers that the other party has placed around the information—by intercepting communications, stealing documents, overflying restricted areas and taking photographs, suborning officials with authorized access to the information, or some other means. But in the absence of direct access to the information, it may be possible to deduce it from the analysis of other data—open-source as well as whatever secret data are available.

In the context of this discussion it may appear that the difference between Kent's view of intelligence and that emphasizing the importance of secrecy is mainly a matter of emphasis. The latter view stresses the fact that the adversary is keeping the desired information secret, while Kent stresses the usefulness of open-source information in finding out what one needs to know. To some extent, Kent's emphasis on open sources reflects his view that secret sources are often unreliable. Perhaps one's agent on the enemy's general staff is really a double agent who is providing deceptive information; perhaps he is an imaginative swindler (the operator of a "paper mill") who is clever enough to forge plausible war plans to sell at a high price; perhaps the agent is genuine but already known to the enemy, who will arrest him just as he is about to relay a critical message.

While this is true, open-source data also can be manipulated to deceive. Take, for example, the Arab deception measures designed to convince the Israelis that no attack was imminent in the fall of 1973. They "ranged from welcoming Dr. Kissinger's peace initiatives in September 1973 to planting news items in a Lebanese newspaper about the neglect and deterioration of the Soviet equipment in the Suez Canal zone."[8] The point is that any type of intelligence data is subject to distortion, and analysis of it must take this possibility into account. Indeed, this is a fundamental difference between intelligence analysis and social science: No one falsifies election returns for the purpose of confusing the social scientist who is analyzing them (someone might, of course, do so for other reasons). The intelligence analyst is not so fortunate. In the intelligence context, even open-source information is not always as innocent as it appears.

For this reason, the information age (in particular, the vast explosion in the amount of open-source information readily available to policy makers) does not affect the issue fundamentally. While it is necessary that policy makers be able to exploit these sources of information effectively, care must be taken that they do not become additional channels for the propagation of disinformation. Indeed, one could argue that as policy makers become accustomed to getting up-to-the-minute information from Internet sources whose reliability is unknown or untested, and to getting that information directly, unfiltered by analysts whose job it is to evaluate it in the context of other bits and pieces of the puzzle, the likelihood of being misled or deceived increases.

However, Kent's depreciation of secret sources has a deeper motive than his insistence on the importance of open source information. Espionage is obviously limited to obtaining information the adversary already has; it is incapable of predicting the enemy's behavior when he has not yet made a decision and hence does not know what he will do. Kent, on the other hand, believes that such prediction is a feasible intelligence task, provided that intelligence learns to use the methods being developed in the social sciences.[9]

This method is not only *useful* for statesmen but, Kent implies, almost *mandatory*—anyone rejecting it can be accused of relying on a crystal ball or, to put it more politely, intuition:

> When the findings of the intelligence arm are regularly ignored by the consumer, and this because of consumer intuition, he should recognize that he is turning his back on the two instruments by which Western man has, since Aristotle, steadily enlarged his horizon of knowledge—the instruments of reason and scientific method.[10]

Thus, whatever insight into the political situation a statesman may possess is treated as intuition, as opposed to the "reason and scientific method" of the "intelligence arm."

If intelligence could reliably make the predictions implied in Kent's discussion, policy makers would indeed be foolish to ignore them, and their jobs would be made much easier. Kent's optimism on this point reflects the general optimism of the social sciences in the 1940s and 1950s. This optimism held that adopting a scientific method (such as the various quantitative methods) and a scientific outlook (such as behaviorism) would enable the social sciences to understand social and political phenomena in much the same way (and ultimately with the same success) as physics understands the atom. In particular, this understanding would be precise enough to support the predictive capability Kent attributes to intelligence.

In general, these prospects for the social sciences have not been realized in recent decades, and the social sciences themselves seem to have little confidence in their chances of realization. The predictive abilities of intelligence are likely to remain much less than Kent envisages. This raises a much more difficult question about the proper relationship between intelligence and policy.

Everyone would agree that intelligence is subordinate to policy, in the sense that intelligence activities are directed toward serving the policy maker (although, as already noted, this subordination would be moot if the predictive capability of social science–based intelligence could be perfected). The range of this service can be quite broad. At one extreme, intelligence is sometimes used as a reference service, a source of answers to very specific questions.[11] At the other, it prepares extensive analyses, complete with predictions, of major issues. In either case, however, it supports policy makers who must make the actual decision.

The belief in the availability (if not in the present, then in the near future) of a social science method that would be as rigorous and fruitful as is the scientific method with respect to the physical world naturally suggests that those who are expert in it deserve to be heeded regarding subjects with which the method deals. Thus, policy should not only accept the facts provided by intelligence (if relevant facts are available, it would be madness to ignore them) but its assessments as well.

Unfortunately, such a social science method does not exist. In that case, intelligence assessments that attempt to make predictions (especially contingent predictions) do not differ from the conclusions that policy makers might draw about the same situations. Other factors would determine the relative status to be granted the two estimates.

The intelligence analyst probably has a greater background in the area and almost certainly can devote greater resources (such as time and access to data) to the effort. The policy maker is likely to know more about his government's own policies in the area and other countries' diplomatic reactions to them; is more likely to focus on the possible actions to influence the situation; and is, in any case, responsible for the outcome. The most comprehensive and policy-relevant assessment of the situation is likely to result from a joint effort between two groups.

Intelligence is concerned with that component of the struggle among nations that deals with information. As such, it has a dual nature, one part governed by the fact that it deals with information, the other part by the fact that it is part of the conflict among nations (or with other adversaries, such as transnational terrorist groups or criminal organization). The first part, taken to its logical extreme, gives rise to the notion of intelligence as a universal, predictive social science that completely meets the needs of policy makers for information about other countries, including their futures. Furthermore, like scientific information, intelligence of this sort would be intrinsically capable of being shared; it would not lose the characteristic of being intelligence by being disseminated widely.

The second part, that concerned with the struggle among nations, leads in another direction. Because intelligence is part of a struggle, the obstacles to understanding do not arise simply from the difficulties of the subject matter; the more important of them, and those that are potentially the most dangerous, are put there by one's adversary, in the form of either information denial or deliberate deception. Thus, whatever else one wishes to know, one has to pay attention to the adversary's intelligence services as well; indeed, those services become a prime intelligence target, since the reward for penetrating and, at best, being able to manipulate them is so high. In this respect, intelligence has an internal dynamic that tends to transform it into a counterintelligence duel, in which each nation's intelligence service seeks, most of all, to penetrate and manipulate the intelligence service of its adversary.

In his memoir, former DCI Colby makes the following complaint about the way that James J. Angleton, the longtime head of the CIA's counterintelligence staff, conducted the operations of his division: "Indeed, we seemed to be putting more emphasis on the KGB as the CIA's adversary than on the Soviet Union as the United States' adversary."[12] Obviously, an intelligence service exists to serve the interests of its nation with respect to the nation's adversaries. But to do this, it often must focus particularly on the adversary's intelligence service.

When an intelligence service focuses primarily on the activities of the adversary service (and the possibility that the adversary service is engaging in deception operations), it runs the risk of descending into a "wilderness of mirrors" in which nothing and nobody can be trusted, and everything may be the opposite of what it appears. If the service constantly doubts the validity of all available evidence, it cannot make much progress in understanding the outside world. Intelligence would be analogous to a physics that concentrated on questions of epistemology to the exclusion of experimentation.

If an intelligence service ignores its adversaries, however, it runs the risk of being deceived and of misinterpreting the world it is trying to understand. In intelligence matters, analysts can rarely be completely confident of the solidity of the foundations on which they are building; they must remain open to the possibility that their evidence is misleading.

Intelligence is thus caught in a dilemma that reflects its dual nature. Intelligence seeks to learn all it can about the world, and its goal may be characterized by the biblical verse that Allen Dulles, President Eisenhower's director of central intelligence, adopted as the CIA's motto: "And ye shall know the truth and the truth shall make you free."[13] But intelligence can never forget that the attainment of the truth involves a struggle with a human enemy who is fighting back—or that truth is not the goal, but only a means toward victory.

Notes

INTRODUCTION

1. The work of Sherman Kent, a former intelligence officer, foreshadowed this school of thought in the late 1940s, and he remains its best-known and most important representative. The argument was first expressed in his book *Strategic Intelligence for American World Policy* (Princeton, N.J.: Princeton University Press, 1949; reprint, 1966) and is discussed in detail in chapter 7 of this work. See also Bruce D. Berkowitz and Allan E. Goodman, *Strategic Intelligence for American National Security* (Princeton, N.J.: Princeton University Press, 1989), which, according to the authors, is intended to be a book "written in the same spirit" as Kent's (although not an "update" of it). They appear to share, at least in part, Kent's understanding of strategic intelligence, arguing that in contrast to operational intelligence, it has "a wider base and broader objective, integrating economics, politics, social studies, and the study of technology. Strategic intelligence is designed to provide officials with the 'big picture' and long-range forecasts they need in order to plan for the future" (4–5).

2. Senator David L. Boren, then chairman of the Select Committee on Intelligence, stated the goal of his proposed intelligence reforms of the early 1990s as the creation of a "world-class think tank"—indeed, the "best 'think tank' in the world." "The Intelligence Community: How Crucial?" *Foreign Affairs* 71, no. 3 (Summer 1992): 61.

3. One of the earliest and best-known books of this type begins with the assertion that "there exists in [the United States] today a powerful and dangerous cult—the cult of intelligence." Publicity is an essential weapon in the fight against "this secret fraternity of the American political aristocracy": "The aim of this book is to provide the American people with the inside information which they need—and which they without question have the right—to understand the significance of this issue and the importance of dealing with it." Victor Marchetti and John D. Marks, *The CIA and the Cult of Intelligence* (New York: Knopf, 1974), 4, 12.

4. Of particular interest in this regard is the British journal *Intelligence and National Security,* which has published a wealth of historical research on the intelligence "dimension" of diplomatic and military history.

5. An example of this turn in the literature may be found in the writings of David Wise. Compare, for example, two of his earlier works (written with Thomas B. Ross)—*The Invisible Government* (New York: Random House, 1964) and *The Espionage Establishment* (New York: Random House, 1967)—with two more recent volumes, *The Spy Who Got Away: The Inside Story of Edward Lee Howard* (New York: Random House, 1988) and *Molehunt: The Secret Search for Traitors That Shattered the CIA* (New York: Random House, 1992). The titles alone suggest the change in

emphasis. His latest book, *Cassidy's Run: The Secret Spy War over Nerve Gas* (New York: Random House, 2000), also focuses on an espionage case, in this case a double-agent operation that may have had grave, unexpected consequences.

6. This explains the prevalence of World War II and Cold War examples; more is publicly available about the intelligence aspects of these periods of history than of other periods. It should be stressed, however, that the points that these examples illustrate are meant to be of general interest; their relevance is not confined to the particular circumstances of those struggles.

7. A convenient way of staying abreast with what is publicly available is to visit the various Websites that compile data on intelligence. Among the most useful are the Websites of the Federation of American Scientists (fas.org/irp); Muskingum College in Ohio (intellit.muskingum.edu/intellsite/maintoc.html), and Loyola College in Maryland (www.loyola.edu/dept/politics/intel.html).

8. It should be noted for the record that this book was submitted prior to publication to the Central Intelligence Agency and the Select Committee on Intelligence of the U.S. Senate for security review. These organizations' agreement that *Silent Warfare* does not contain classified information does not, of course, constitute an endorsement of its contents in any way.

CHAPTER 1: WHAT IS INTELLIGENCE?

1. Following Sherman Kent, whose *Strategic Intelligence for American World Policy* (Princeton, N.J.: Princeton University Press, 1949; reprint, 1966) is organized according to this three-part description of intelligence.

2. Herbert E. Meyer, *Real-World Intelligence* (New York: Weidenfeld and Nicolson, 1987), 6. A brief annotated bibliography of the business intelligence literature can be found in Robert David Steele, *On Intelligence: Spies and Secrecy in an Open World* (Fairfax, Va.: Armed Forces Communications and Electronics Association, 2000), 375–78.

3. Consider, for example, the results of an effort by U.S. government departments in 1991–92 to compile a list of "intelligence requirements" through the year 2005. The effect of the end of the Cold War can be seen in the wide variety of topics included. In addition to traditional intelligence requirements (such as the military plans and diplomatic intentions of key countries), the list included requests for information on international terrorism, weapons proliferation, narcotics trafficking, and a wide array of trade and economic matters. The review also produced requirements from policy makers for intelligence in such nontraditional areas as new technology, demographics, population migrations, and global environmental and health issues. See Loch K. Johnson, "Smart Intelligence," *Foreign Policy*, no. 89 (Winter 1992–93): 60–61.

4. For an exposition of this point as it relates to the practice of intelligence, see Adda Bozeman, *Strategic Intelligence and Statecraft: Selected Essays* (Washington, D.C.: Brassey's [U.S.], 1992).

5. Revelations in the wake of the collapse of the communist regime of East Germany strikingly illustrated what this can mean in practice. At the time of its demise, the intelligence service of the German Democratic Republic employed more than

eighty-five thousand personnel, utilized five hundred thousand part-time agents and informants, and retained files on six million East German citizens. As Jefferson Adams points out, "For a state with a total population of approximately 17 million persons, that meant an internal web of extraordinary density." Werner Stiller with Jefferson Adams, "Preface to English Edition," in *Beyond the Wall: Memoirs of an East and West German Spy* (Washington, D.C.: Brassey's [U.S.], 1992), ix–x.

6. Citizens of a democracy regard this as obvious, but the recognition that one can be an opponent of the government of the day without being an enemy of the regime or the nation is a valuable achievement that should not be taken for granted. On the other hand, the concept of a "loyal opposition" implies the possibility of an opposition that is not. While this is relatively clear in theory, the difficulty for liberal democracies is deciding where the line should be drawn in practice. For an overview of past U.S. government efforts to monitor, and sometimes disrupt, what it thought were subversive groups and organizations, see Richard E. Morgan, *Domestic Intelligence: Monitoring Dissent in America* (Austin: University of Texas Press, 1980), 15–87.

7. "The Attorney General's Guidelines on General Crimes, Racketeering Enterprise and Domestic Security/Terrorism Investigations," 1983, part 3. The guidelines are reprinted in U.S. House of Representatives, Committee on the Judiciary, *FBI Domestic Security Guidelines: Oversight Hearing*, 98th Cong., 1st sess., 1983.

8. On Soviet acquisition programs, see Katherine A. S. Sibley, "Soviet Industrial Espionage against American Military Technology and the U.S. Response, 1930–45," *Intelligence and National* Security 14, no. 2 (Summer 1999): 94–123, and *Soviet Acquisition of Militarily Significant Western Technology: An Update* (Washington, D.C.: Government Printing Office, 1985). For a brief account of the Soviet program of the 1970s and the U.S. and allied response, see Gus W. Weiss, "The Farewell Dossier," *Studies in Intelligence* 39, no. 5 (1996): 121–26, available at www.odci.gov/csi/studies/96unclass/farewell.htm.

It appears that the Russian foreign intelligence service has continued to collect industrial and technical secrets from other countries. The U.S. National Counterintelligence Center (NACIC, an interagency organization operating under the auspices of the National Security Council) states, "According to media sources, Russian President Boris Yeltsin confirmed in Moscow on 7 February 1996 that Russia is involved in industrial espionage, but that the data being collected by Russian intelligence agencies are not being used effectively." NACIC, *Counterintelligence News and Developments*, March 1966, 1, available at www.nacic.gov/cind/1996/mar96.htm.

With respect to the Chinese program, see the "Cox Committee Report": *Report of the Select Committee on U.S. National Security and Military/Commercial Concerns with the People's Republic of China* (Washington, D.C.: Government Printing Office, 1999), chap. 1, available at www.house.gov/coxreport.

9. A separate phenomenon, not directly related to the issue of intelligence support to policy making, is a government's use of intelligence to make money. An intelligence service has many opportunities to do so, either to fund its own operations or to remit to its government. The clandestine operational capability of a service could be used to conduct such profitable activities as narcotics trafficking and other kinds of smuggling, and the clandestine collection capability could obtain insider-type information for financial speculation. It is not clear to what extent nations have used their intelligence services in this manner.

One instance that has become public concerns France. According to the former head of French foreign intelligence, that service learned in November of 1971 that the U.S. government had decided to go off the gold standard the following month, thus effectively devaluing the dollar. "By quietly selling dollars and buying francs in a number of markets around the world, the central bank [of France] was able to accumulate some enormous profits—by themselves, enough to have financed all the operations of the Service" far into the future. Count de Marenches and David A. Andelman, *The Fourth World War* (New York: Morrow, 1992), 114–15.

10. Given its economic and technological strength, the United States has focused on protecting technology and trade secrets. Since 1995, the president has reported annually to Congress on foreign espionage targeted against U.S. industry. Those reports, and the Economic Espionage Act of 1996, can be found on the Website of the National Counterintelligence Center, www.nacic.gov.

Other sources include General Accounting Office, *Economic Espionage: Information on Threat from U.S. Allies* (GAO/T-NSIAD-96-114), available at www.nsi.org/Library/Espionage/allies.txt, and Peter Schweizer, "The Growth of Economic Espionage: America Is Target Number One," *Foreign Affairs* 75, no. 1 (January–February 1996): 9–14.

11. The restrictions the United States has imposed upon its own use of economic intelligence have not stopped the accusations of other states, as illustrated by the controversy surrounding the "Echelon" system for collecting data from international communications. "Echelon" refers to an automated system for sifting through the vast amount of data intercepted through various methods by the United States and its English-speaking allies. A somewhat sensationalistic report prepared for the European Parliament in February 2000 charged that the United States and its allies were using information obtained via this system to help their corporations gain commercial advantage. Duncan Campbell, *Interception Capabilities 2000,* Report to the Director General for Research of the European Parliament (Scientific and Technical Options Assessment Programme Office), available at www.iptvreports.mcmail.com/ic2kreport.htm#Report.

These charges were generally rebutted by former U.S. Director of Central Intelligence James Woolsey in a press briefing on March 7, 2000. Woolsey claimed that intelligence targeting of foreign corporations was limited to three areas: sanctions enforcement, sale of materiel and products used in the production of weapons of mass destruction, and detection of bribery attempts by non-U.S. corporations in competition with American ones. Woolsey noted that the specific cases mentioned by Campbell involved attempts by non-U.S. corporations to win export orders by bribing officials of the purchasing nation. Foreign Press Center Briefing, "Intelligence Gathering and Democracies: The Issue of Economic and Industrial Espionage," www.fpc.gov/wool0300.htm.

12. According to one study of this question, "The United States has an impressive array of technical systems for monitoring large areas of the earth, oceans, and atmosphere for national security purposes. These systems have collected sophisticated datasets that span decades, and constitute a unique historical record. These systems could be used for environmental monitoring as well." Scott Pace, Kevin M. O'Connell, and Beth E. Lachman, *Using Intelligence Data for Environmental Needs: Balancing National Interests,* MR-799-CMS (Santa Monica, Calif.: RAND, 1997), 2.

13. On the possible implications of the information age on intelligence and intelligence organizations, see Bruce D. Berkowitz and Allan E. Goodman, *Best Truth: Intelligence in the Information Age* (New Haven, Conn.: Yale University Press, 2000).

14. U.S. Commission on the Organization of the Government for the Conduct of Foreign Policy (Murphy Commission), *Report* (Washington, D.C.. Government Printing Office, 1975), 100.

15. See John Ranelagh, *The Agency: The Rise and Decline of the CIA* (New York: Simon and Schuster, 1986), 199–200, for a discussion of the conflicts in the late 1940s and early 1950s between the Office of Policy Coordination (the U.S. government's covert action agency) and the Office of Special Operations (the CIA's espionage arm). See Christopher Andrew, *Her Majesty's Secret Service: The Making of the British Intelligence Community* (New York: Viking, 1986), 476–77, for a discussion of the rivalry between Britain's Secret Intelligence Service and its Special Operations Executive, which had been established, in Prime Minister Winston Churchill's words, "to set Europe ablaze" (that is, conduct sabotage activities in Nazi-occupied Europe during World War II and support the partisan forces resisting the German occupation).

CHAPTER 2: SPIES. MACHINES. AND LIBRARIES: COLLECTING THE DATA

1. This categorization lists the most commonly used collection methods but is not meant to be complete. For example, intelligence information can also be collected by stealing documents or codes from an adversary's embassy. Such theft could be considered humint, but it differs from espionage as described in the text.

2. Unfortunately, the commonly used term "agent" is ambiguous: it usually refers to the source, although sometimes, as in the lexicon of the U.S. Federal Bureau of Investigation (FBI), it refers rather to the intelligence officer.

3. For the sake of simplicity, this discussion is in terms of intelligence officers tasked with spying on countries to which they are posted. This is not necessarily the case; officers may be posted to Freedonia to recruit Ruritanians (such as foreign service, intelligence, or military officers) who are also stationed there. In this case, the officers may be declared (their intelligence connection revealed) to the Freedonian authorities; the purpose of their cover would be to avoid arousing Ruritanian suspicions. Also, intelligence officers may work in their own country to recruit foreign diplomats stationed there.

4. In other intelligence lexicons (such as that of the former Soviet Union), a related distinction between "legal" and "illegal" officers takes the place of the official cover/nonofficial cover (NOC) one. The reference is not to whether the officer's presence in the host country is legal but to his means of communicating with his intelligence headquarters. An illegal officer is one who communicates directly with his intelligence headquarters, without maintaining contact with the "legal" establishments in the host country (the embassy, consulate, trade office, or so forth). In this way, an illegal is similar to an NOC.

5. Paradoxically, in some cases surveillance of foreign embassy personnel and foreigners generally by a country's secret service is so tight that the only safe way to communicate with a source in that country's government is for an intelligence officer working under diplomatic cover to contact him in a relatively "open" manner. For example, in the case of Oleg Penkovsky, a colonel in Soviet military intelligence (GRU) who worked for American and British intelligence in the early 1960s, a key operational

question was how to contact him in Moscow, where Soviet counterintelligence surveillance made it extremely risky to attempt to meet or communicate with him clandestinely. One solution was to make use of the fact that Penkovsky met various British and American diplomats in the normal course of his work with science and technology. An intelligence officer could pose as such a diplomat; he would use a predesignated signal (such as wearing a tie clip with red stones) to allow Penkovsky to recognize him. After identifying his contact at some routine diplomatic function, Penkovsky would be told he could

> go to the toilet, say, and [the diplomat/intelligence officer] could follow you five minutes later and pick up your message. There is no need for personal conversation or anything. [Such meets were] . . . safe because you know within two or three minutes that the material is in safe hands and the business is completed. There is no need to travel around. . . . [T]his is the method which gives . . . the greatest security.

Unfortunately, other less safe methods were more frequently used, and it has been suggested that this contributed to Penkovsky's being identified as a spy and his eventual arrest and execution. See Jerrold L. Schecter and Peter S. Deriabin, *The Spy Who Saved the World* (New York: Scribner, 1992), 98, 287–99, 314–15, 409–11.

6. For this "mailbox" function to work, it must be generally understood, even if not officially acknowledged, that an embassy or diplomatic establishment has on its staff officials capable of handling sensitive or secret information from unsolicited sources. An example of the quasi-public character of this kind of intelligence work is provided by Allen Dulles, the former director of central intelligence. According to Dulles, soon after he was sent as an intelligence officer to Switzerland during World War II, a leading Swiss journal published a story describing him as President Roosevelt's secret and special envoy. "Offhand," Dulles noted, "one might have thought this unsought advertisement would have hampered my work. Quite the contrary was the case. . . . As a result [of the story], to my network flocked a host of informants, some cranks, it is true, but also some exceedingly valuable individuals." Allen Dulles, *The Craft of Intelligence* (New York: Harper and Row, 1963), 7.

For an account of one of the more valuable agents for whom Dulles served as a "mailbox," see text to note 17 below.

7. The intelligence operation is designated by various terms, for instance, "station" (in U.S. parlance) and "residency" (*rezidentura,* in Soviet and Russian parlance.)

8. The problems arising from allowing host-country nationals to work in an embassy are long-standing ones. Writing about his tenure as the U.S. minister to St. Petersburg, Russia, in the early 1830s, James Buchanan remarked, "We are continually surrounded by spies both of high and low degree. You can scarcely hire a servant who is not a secret agent of the police." *Mission to Russia* (New York: Arno, 1970), 339.

For a more recent, journalistic account of the security problems posed by the extensive use of host-country nationals in an embassy, see Ronald Kessler, *Moscow Station: How the KGB Penetrated the American Embassy* (New York: Scribner, 1989).

9. For example, the occupation of the U.S. embassy in Teheran in November 1979 (and the taking hostage of its personnel) apparently shut down U.S. human intelligence collection in Iran completely. When planning began for the military operation to rescue the hostages, there were "no American agents on the ground," and the CIA was apparently forced to slip an agent back into Iran to help gather information required for planning the rescue attempt. Charlie A. Beckwith and Donald Knox,

Delta Force: The U.S. Counter-Terrorist Unit and the Iran Hostage Rescue Mission (New York: Harcourt Brace Jovanovich, 1983), 196–97, 220–21.

10. Cover may also be provided by a business established, owned, and run by the intelligence service itself; such an organization is known as a *proprietary*. A proprietary may be useful for covert action purposes as well as for providing cover for intelligence officers. For example, a shipping business could facilitate the clandestine transporting of arms and supplies to insurgents.

11. Earlier in 1941, Sorge had reported that Germany intended to break its nonaggression pact with the Soviet Union and attack it in June. His reports on Hitler's intent to break the accord and the specific date for the start of the German offensive were ignored by Stalin. The Soviet dictator was apparently convinced that this and similar intelligence about German perfidy had been fabricated by the British to provoke a rift between Germany and the Soviet Union and push Moscow into an alliance with London. It appears that Stalin gave Sorge's reports on Japanese intentions greater credence, in part because they were corroborated by Soviet intercepts of Japanese diplomatic messages. For an account of Sorge's life and activities as a Soviet intelligence officer, see Gordon W. Prange, with Donald Goldstein and Katherine V. Dillon, *Target Tokyo: The Story of the Sorge Spy Ring* (New York: McGraw-Hill, 1984).

12. For an account of Cohen's life as an Israeli agent, see Stanley A. Blumberg and Gwinn Owens, *The Survival Factor: Israeli Intelligence from World War I to the Present* (New York: Putnam, 1981), 208–24.

13. This account is based on John Barron, *KGB Today: The Hidden Hand* (New York: Reader's Digest, 1983; New York: Berkley, 1985), 247–314.

14. Of the members of the Soviet bloc, East Germany was particularly adept at placing NOCs (or, to use the Soviet term, "illegals") in the West, especially in West Germany, its principal target. In part, the use of illegals was forced on East Germany, since its failure during the first half of the Cold War to achieve wide diplomatic recognition meant that it lacked embassies and consulates in many noncommunist countries. It was also facilitated by the fact that West Germany actively encouraged immigration from the East. According to a former East German intelligence officer, there were two to three thousand agents in place by the late 1950s. The most famous was Guenther Guillaume, who was so successful in penetrating the West German political elite that he became personal secretary to Chancellor Willy Brandt. He served in this position from 1969 until his arrest in 1974. Christopher Andrew and Oleg Gordievsky, *KGB: The Inside Story* (New York: HarperCollins, 1990; HarperPerennial edition, 1991), 448–50. For an account of East Germany's use of illegals from the operational perspective of a former East German intelligence officer, see Werner Stiller, with Jefferson Adams, *Beyond the Wall: Memoirs of an East and West German Spy* (Washington, D.C.: Brassey's [U.S.], 1992), 41–118, passim.

15. For an overview of Chinese humint activities, see Nicholas Eftimiades, *Chinese Intelligence Operations* (Arlington, Va.: Newcomb, 1998), chap. 5, 28–44. On China's program to acquire U.S. high technology, see the "Cox Committee Report": *Report of the Select Committee on U.S. National Security and Military/Commercial Concerns with the People's Republic of China* (Washington, D.C.: Government Printing Office, 1999), chap. 1, available at www.house.gov/coxreport. See also "China's High-Tech Espionage," a two-part review of *Sources and Techniques of Obtaining National Defense Science and Technology Intelligence,* a Chinese "handbook" on spying in the

West, in National Counterintelligence Center [hereafter NACIC], *Counterintelligence News and Developments* (June and September 2000), vols. 2 and 3. The reviews can be found at www.nacic.gov, the NACIC Website.

16. Nevertheless, the possibility cannot be ruled out that the source, after being approached by a foreign intelligence officer, may report the recruitment attempt to his own government and be instructed to "play along."

17. See Joseph E. Persico, *Piercing the Reich: The Penetration of Nazi Germany by American Secret Agents during World War II* (New York: Viking, 1979), 62–72, 328.

18. Burgess and Maclean both served at the Foreign Office, while Philby joined the British foreign intelligence service (MI6) and rose to be head of its counterintelligence section and its Washington-based liaison officer with the CIA and FBI. See Andrew Boyle, *The Fourth Man* (New York: Dial, 1979), for an account of the Soviet spy ring that had its roots in Cambridge University in the 1930s. See also Robert Cecil, "The Cambridge Comintern," in *The Missing Dimension: Governments and Intelligence Communities in the Twentieth Century*, ed. Christopher Andrew and David Dilks (Urbana: University of Illinois Press, 1984).

19. Defense Security Service, Security Research Center, *Recent Espionage Cases, 1975–1999* (September 1999), available at www.dss.mil/training/pub.htm, contains an overview and summaries of recent cases. Various motives for engaging in espionage are analyzed in Theodore R. Sarbin, Ralph M. Carney, and Carson Eoyang, eds., *Citizen Espionage: Studies in Trust and Betrayal* (Westport, Conn.: Praeger, 1994).

20. David Wise, *The Spy Who Got Away: The Inside Story of Edward Lee Howard* (New York: Random House, 1988).

21. See Mary S. Lowell, *Cast No Shadow: The Life of the American Spy Who Changed the Course of World War II* (New York: Pantheon, 1992).

22. For an account of the Dejean affair, see John Barron, *KGB: The Secret Work of Soviet Secret Agents* (New York: Reader's Digest, 1974), 114–40.

23. Allan Dulles, *The Craft of Intelligence* (Boulder, Colo.: Westview, 1985), 216.

24. If the captured spy refuses to cooperate, it may be possible for the intelligence service that captured him to impersonate him by sending messages in his name. This could work in situations, such as wartime espionage on enemy territory, where the source would not be expected to have face-to-face meetings with his employers.

25. Christopher Andrew, *Her Majesty's Secret Service: The Making of the British Intelligence Community* (New York: Viking, 1986), 488. For a report on the "Double-Cross System" by the man who managed it, see J. C. Masterman, *The Double-Cross System in the War of 1939 to 1945* (New Haven, Conn.: Yale University Press, 1972).

26. A dated, but still interesting, training manual prepared by Soviet military intelligence provided lessons on how to communicate with and control intelligence sources in the United States. It was among the materials provided by Oleg Penkovsky, a Soviet military officer who spied for the United States and Britain in the late 1950s and early 1960s. "The Prikhodko Lecture," in *The Penkovsky Papers*, ed. Frank Gibney (New York: Doubleday, 1965), 102–62.

27. Wise, *The Spy Who Got Away*, 198–205. To complete the ruse, on her return home Howard's wife called Howard's doctor's office. At that hour, the doctor was predictably not in his office, and his answering machine came on; Howard's wife, assuming

that the phone was tapped, played into the phone a taped message for his doctor that Howard had recorded earlier. This would help the FBI confirm that Howard had returned home with his wife. As it turned out, the Howards' efforts were unnecessary; inexplicably, the FBI agent responsible for watching the house had missed the Howards' departure in the first place, and the Howards' car was in fact not being followed at all.

28. An example of this interaction between surveillance and countersurveillance is described by Peter Wright, an ex-MI5 (British counterintelligence) official, in his book *Spycatcher.* According to Wright, Soviet technicians operating in their London embassy were able to monitor the communications of the mobile surveillance teams (the "Watchers") used by MI5. By analyzing those communications and correlating them with their own operations, the Soviets could deduce whether a particular meeting between a Soviet intelligence officer and his source was likely to be surveilled. If it was, the officer would be alerted to scrub the meeting. British counterintelligence, according to Wright, was able to identify this weakness in its surveillance system when it detected from within the Russian embassy electronic emissions that were uniquely associated with the Soviets' radio intercept operations of the Watcher communications. In brief, as Wright tells it, MI5 was watching the Soviets watch the Watchers, who, in turn, were busy watching the Soviets. Wright, *Spycatcher: The Candid Autobiography of a Senior Intelligence Officer* (New York: Viking, 1987), 52–57, 91–93.

29. For an illustration of the particular tradecraft involved in making a "dead drop," see John Barron's account of the Soviet spy ring headed by John Walker, *Breaking the Ring* (Boston: Houghton Mifflin, 1987), 80–96.

30. The FBI's affidavit in support of the arrest and search warrants in the Hanssen case contains lengthy quotes from messages passed between Hanssen and the KGB and later its Russian successor agency, the Sluzhba Vneshney Razvedki (Foreign Intelligence Service, or SVR). In these messages Hanssen ruled out face-to-face meetings (even in foreign countries) on security grounds and insisted that dead drops be used almost exclusively. (The initial contact was made by mail to the residence of a Soviet intelligence officer; on a few occasions, there was some communication by telephone.) The affidavit is available at www.fas.org/irp/ops/ci/hanssen_affidavit.html; it is a veritable manual of tradecraft on dead drops.

31. Herbert Rommerstein and Stanislav Levchenko, *The KGB against the "Main Enemy": How the Soviet Intelligence Service Operates against the United States* (Lexington, Mass.: Lexington, 1989), 293. By keeping in the dark the Soviet intelligence officers stationed in Vienna, the KGB also reduced the risk that U.S. surveillance of Soviet intelligence officers there would compromise the Walker operation.

32. Nicholas Eftimiades, *Chinese Intelligence Operations* (Arlington, Va.: Newcomb, 1998), 33, 36–37.

33. In late 1953, the Soviet intelligence service, then called the MGB (Ministry of State Security), was part of the Ministry of the Interior (MVD); the consolidation of these two important bureaucracies was the result of a power play by former intelligence chief and key Kremlin intriguer Lavrenti Beria in the wake of Stalin's death in March 1953. After Beria's arrest and execution in December 1953, the Soviet intelligence service was again separated from the interior ministry and designated as the KGB (Committee of State Security). It was at the time of this unrest within the intelligence service that these defections took place. The five defectors (and the countries in which they defected) were: Yuri Rastvorov (Japan); Pyotr Deryabin (Austria); Vladimir and

Evdokia Petrova (Australia); and Nikolai Khokhlov (West Germany). See Gordon Brook-Shepherd, *The Storm Birds: Soviet Post-War Defectors* (London: Weidenfeld and Nicolson, 1988), 57–131.

34. According to Stockholm International Peace Research Institute, "Fact Sheet: Iraq: The UNSCOM Experience" (October 1998), 3 available at editors.sipri.se/pubs/Factsheet/UNSCOM.pdf, the significance of Iraq's largest research-and-development and production site for biological weapons, al-Hakam, was unrecognized until Hussein al-Kamal's defection, although UNSCOM inspectors had already visited it. Similarly, the 1994 defection of a leading scientist involved in the Iraqi nuclear weapon program provided the first detailed information about its history and inner workings. Judith Miller and James Risen, "Defector Describes Iraq's Atom Bomb Push," *New York Times,* August 15, 1998, A1.

35. The story is told in David C. Martin, *Wilderness of Mirrors* (New York: Harper and Row, 1980). More recent accounts of this debate within the American intelligence community include Tom Mangold, *Cold Warrior: James Jesus Angleton, the CIA's Master Spy Hunter* (New York: Simon and Schuster, 1991), and Edward J. Epstein, *Deception: The Invisible War between the KGB and the CIA* (New York: Simon and Schuster, 1989). The Mangold and Epstein books have decided but opposing points of view, reflecting the difficulty of reaching a definitive judgment about the bona fides of some defectors.

36. Even earlier, balloons were used as aerial observation posts—by the first French Republic in 1794, and by the Union army in the American Civil War. In neither case was great success achieved, and both armies later disbanded their fledgling "air forces." See William E. Burrows, *Deep Black: Space Espionage and National Security* (New York: Random House, 1987; New York: Berkley, 1988), 26–28.

37. Andrew, *Her Majesty's Secret Service,* 133.

38. William Mitchell, *Memoirs of World War I: "From Start to Finish of Our Greatest War"* (New York: Random House, 1960), 59, as cited in Russell F. Weigley, *The American Way of War* (Bloomington: Indiana University Press, 1977), 224.

39. For a masterful discussion of British scientific intelligence in World War II by one of its greatest practitioners, see R. V. Jones, *Most Secret War* (London: Hamish Hamilton, 1978), reprinted in the United States as *The Wizard War: British Scientific Intelligence, 1939–1945* (New York: Coward, McCann and Geoghegan, 1978).

40. John Prados, *The Soviet Estimate: U.S. Intelligence Analysis and Russian Military Strength* (New York: Dial, 1982), 38–50.

41. Prados, *The Soviet Estimate,* 29–30. For a more detailed account, see Curtis Peebles, *The Moby Dick Project: Reconnaissance Balloons over Russia* (Washington, D.C.: Smithsonian, 1991).

42. Stephen E. Ambrose, *Eisenhower: The President,* vol. 2 of *Eisenhower* (New York: Simon and Schuster, 1984), 264–65.

43. As early as 1946, the RAND Corporation, a think-tank under contract to what was then the Army Air Forces, was asked to look into the feasibility and utility of earth-orbiting satellites. In its study, RAND concluded that satellites could, among other things, provide "an observation aircraft which cannot be brought down by an enemy who has not mastered similar techniques." For a brief account of the RAND studies, see Walter A. McDougall, *The Heavens and the Earth: A Political History of the Space Age* (New York: Basic Books, 1985), 102–11. For a more detailed account, see

Merton E. Davies and William R. Harris, *RAND's Role in the Evolution of Balloon and Satellite Observation Systems and Related U.S. Space Technology*, R-3692-RC (Santa Monica, Calif.: RAND, September 1988).

44. Ambrose, *Eisenhower*, vol. 2, 228.

45. For the U.S. decision to build a reconnaissance satellite, and the program's early failures and successes, see McDougall, *The Heavens and the Earth*, 97–131, 190, and 224, and Dwayne A. Day, John M. Logsdon, and Brian Latell, *Eye in the Sky: The Story of the Corona Spy Satellites* (Washington, D.C.: Smithsonian, 1998).

46. See the testimony of Maj. Gen. B. L. Schriever, *Inquiry into Satellite and Missile Programs*, Hearings before the Preparedness Investigating Subcommittee of the Committee on Armed Services, U.S. Senate, 85th Cong., 2d sess., January 6–22, 1958, part 2, 1633–35.

47. Although it could be assumed that the Soviets understood that some such reconnaissance capability existed, it was not thought expedient to call public attention to the fact. At the time, the Soviet Union, consistent with its rejection of the "Open Skies" plan, took the position that space-based reconnaissance constituted espionage and was as contrary to international law as aerial reconnaissance. Given this position, the U.S. government worried that an open discussion of space-based reconnaissance would prompt Moscow to make an issue of it. Thus, despite public discussion of space reconnaissance at the end of the Eisenhower administration, the Kennedy administration, seeing no reason to goad Khrushchev by openly asserting the right of the United States to conduct such reconnaissance, took "steps . . . to turn the fledgling space reconnaissance program from medium gray to deep black." (Burrows, *Deep Black*, 107.) However, as Walter McDougall notes, "by 1963 the [U.S. government's] hand-wringing ended. . . . [T]he Soviets began launching their own spy satellites . . . [which, in effect] legitimized observation from space." *The Heavens and the Earth*, 348.

48. Eric Schmitt, "Spy-Satellite Unit Faces a New Life in Daylight," *New York Times*, November 3, 1992, A10.

49. Paradoxically, the distorting effects of the earth's atmosphere may be less of a problem for space-based than for aerial photography. Early in the development of space-based photography, the famous rocket expert Werner von Braun noted that "taking photos . . . from outer space, the disturbances and turbulence are far away. The atmosphere is much more transparent from without than from underneath." To illustrate the point, he suggested the following demonstration: "Pick up a piece of wax paper. Hold it close in front of your face and you see only a blur. Hold it on a piece of newsprint, and it is perfectly transparent. You have such the same situation here." Speech to the Second Annual Meeting of the Association of the U.S. Army, October 26, 1956, quoted in McDougall, *The Heaven and the Earth*, 224.

50. This explanation of a charge-coupled device is drawn from Harold Hough, *Satellite Surveillance* (Port Townsend, Wash.: Loompanics, 1991), 46–48.

51. Because it uses long wavelengths (as compared to light), radar produces a very fuzzy image—literally, a blip on the screen. The way to compensate for the longer wavelength is to increase the size of the antenna. For this reason, a technique known as synthetic-aperture radar (SAR) was developed, in which a small antenna moving in a straight line achieves the effect of a much bigger antenna. With powerful on-board

processors, SAR systems collect and in effect collate thousands of low-resolution "pictures" into a far more coherent image. For a more detailed account of how SAR systems work, see Charles Elachi, "Radar Images of the Earth from Space," *Scientific American* (December 1982), 54–61.

52. U.S. Department of Defense, *Conduct of the Persian Gulf War: Final Report to Congress* (Washington, D.C.: Government Printing Office, 1992), 138, discusses the tactic of "tank plinking," which was developed during the Gulf War to exploit this phenomenon. A satellite can also employ a multispectral scanner, which images the target using multiple frequencies, both within the visible light spectrum and outside it. A multispectral image can reveal information about the target that would be undetectable by unaided human vision. During the Gulf War, for example, multispectral imagery was used to identify shallow areas near coastlines, information necessary for planning amphibious operations. In addition, because most imagery is now digitally formatted, the data can be more easily manipulated to highlight small differences, resulting in greater contrast and, in turn, higher effective resolution. Thus, for example, subtle terrain differences that would not be detected in a traditional photo could be rendered more noticeable by means of advanced computer processing techniques.

53. According to the Federation of American Scientists' World Space Guide (www.fas.org/spp/guide/index.html), China has been conducting space-based photoreconnaissance since 1975, and France since 1995. Japanese plans call for the launching of four satellites (two optical and two synthetic-aperture radar), starting in 2002.

54. Vernon Loeb, "U.S. Is Relaxing Rules on Sale of Satellite Photos," *Washington Post,* December 16, 2000, A3.

55. The list is taken from a case study prepared for the John F. Kennedy School of Government at Harvard University. Rachel E. Billingslea, Matthew R. Domsalla, and Brian C. Payne, *The National Reconnaissance Office: A Strategy for Addressing the Commercialization of Space Imagery,* April 6, 1999, available at www.fas.org/eye/ADA366610.htm.

The widespread availability of commercial imagery presents both benefits and problems. On the one hand, a government might satisfy a portion of its imagery requirements by purchasing products of commercial vendors, thus allowing its intelligence services to focus on specialized needs not likely to be met by the commercial sector. On the other hand, the proliferation of commercial photoreconnaissance satellites makes it more difficult for a government to conceal sensitive military deployments and operations. (The United States has tried to deal with this problem by reserving "shutter control"—the authority, in times of crisis, to prevent operators from imaging certain areas—with respect to systems it licenses; this does not help in the case of foreign-operated systems.) For a brief overview of this topic, see the National Commission for the Review of the National Reconnaissance Office, *Report* (November 2000), at www.fas.org/irp/nro/commission.

56. The detection and analysis of electromagnetic radiations emanating from radioactive sources or nuclear detonations is not considered a part of elint. See, for example, the definition of "electronics intelligence" in U.S. Joint Chiefs of Staff, *Department of Defense Dictionary of Military and Associated Terms,* JCS Publication 1-02 (Washington, D.C.: Joint Staff, 12 April 2001), 144, available at www.dtic.mil/doctrine/jel/newspubs/jp1-02.pdf.

57. Thus, the electromagnetic waves given off by electric typewriters or computers can be intercepted and analyzed; in this manner, texts or data prepared on these machines might be recovered. One way to avoid this danger is to require that machines of this sort be shielded to reduce these emanations and impede attempts to intercept them.

A related phenomenon is the unintended emission of electromagnetic signals along a wire. In some cases, it has been found that devices intended to encrypt messages give off faint signals carrying the unencrypted text as well. According to a British counter-intelligence officer, the communications of the French embassy in London were vulnerable because the French had not properly shielded their information-processing machines to prevent such unintended electronic emissions. As a result, along with the properly enciphered text, the telex cable leading outside the embassy carried the faint, but still discernable, electronic "echo" of the diplomatic message as it had been initially typed into the machine. Surreptitiously tapping into the cable a short distance from the French embassy, the British were able to read their ally's unencrypted diplomatic messages. Peter Wright, *Spycatcher,* 109–11.

58. The practice of intercepting messages predates the use of radio as a means of communication; couriers were captured and letters opened long before radio existed. In addition, telegraph cables could be tapped. During World War I, the British gained an intelligence advantage from the fact that their companies owned and operated many of the major international cable lines.

59. Precisely because radio messages may easily be intercepted, important messages are likely to be sent in encrypted form. Thus comint and cryptanalysis, the breaking of codes and ciphers, are intimately related, although cryptanalysis should probably be viewed as an intelligence analysis (rather than collection) method—and is, for that reason, discussed in the next chapter.

60. Because of continuing secrecy concerns, a comprehensive account of the utility of comint during the Cold War is not likely to be written for some time to come. Nevertheless, historians of the National Security Agency (NSA, the U.S. sigint service) claim that American success in breaking Soviet cipher systems in the years following World War II "compared favorably to the successes of World War II" and that the loss of this capability in 1948 was "perhaps the most significant intelligence loss in U.S. history." The loss was eventually traced to the espionage of William Weisband, a Russian linguist of the Armed Forces Security Agency (the NSA's predecessor). David A. Hatch with Robert Louis Benson, *The Korean War: The Sigint Background* (2000), available at www.nsa.gov/korea/papers/sigint_background_korean_war.htm.

But without access to Soviet intelligence archives, it is not possible to determine precisely the damage done by American spy John Walker, who provided naval cryptographic materials to the Soviet Union from 1968 to 1985. On a worst-case basis, it can be argued that the material Walker and his fellow agents provided the KGB gave the Soviet Union an "advantage comparable to that which the Allies possessed over Nazi Germany through knowledge of Ultra. [In short, had war broken out between the two superpowers,] Walker might well have made the difference between a Soviet victory and an American one." Angelo Codevilla, *Informing Statecraft: Intelligence for a New Century* (New York: Free Press, 1992), 176–78.

61. For a full discussion of British naval comint during World War I, see Patrick Beesley, *Room 40: British Naval Intelligence 1914–18* (New York: Harcourt Brace Jovanovich, 1982).

62. The literature on American and British cryptography in World War II is voluminous. For a brief overview, see G. J. A. O'Toole, *Honorable Treachery: A History of U.S. Intelligence, Espionage, and Covert Action from the American Revolution to the CIA* (New York: Atlantic Monthly, 1991), 384–97.

63. In their messages, the Japanese referred to their intended target as *AF.* Intelligence officers in Hawaii believed *AF* was the code for Midway, but those in Washington believed that it might stand for some other location, such as Johnston Island, Oahu, or even the West Coast of the United States. To confirm that it was in fact Midway that the Japanese intended to attack, the Navy's Hawaiian communications intelligence station had the U.S. commander on Midway send a radio message to Hawaii reporting that the island was running out of fresh water. As anticipated, the Japanese intercepted the message, and two days later a Japanese radio communication (intercepted by the United States) reported to Tokyo that the water supply at *AF* was low, thus inadvertently confirming that *AF* was indeed Midway. Edwin T. Layton with Roger Pineau and John Costello, *"And I Was There": Pearl Harbor and Midway—Breaking the Secrets* (New York: Morrow, 1985), 421–22.

64. For an account of the battle and of the intelligence success that lay behind it, see Layton, *"And I Was There."*

65. See U.S. Senate, Select Committee on Intelligence, *Meeting the Espionage Challenge: A Review of United States Counterintelligence and Security Programs,* S. Rpt. 99-522 (Washington, D.C.: Government Printing Office, 1986), 33–34, 80–81. In addition, the Soviet Union maintained for many years (as Russia did until 2002) an extensive communications intercept facility at Lourdes, Cuba. Manned by more than 1,500 Russians, the facility monitored U.S. voice and data traffic. A description of the facility is contained in the "Findings" section of a bill passed by the U.S. House of Representatives on July 19, 2000, "Russian-American Trust and Cooperation Act of 2000," HR 4118, 106th Cong., 2d sess.

66. Peter Wright, the former MI5 official, writes in his memoirs that "traffic analysis" was used by Soviet intelligence to reduce the effectiveness of British surveillance efforts against Soviet intelligence operations in and around London. As previously noted, the Soviets monitored from inside their London embassy the radio communications of the British surveillance teams. The fact that the communications were enciphered made little difference; if anything, it made them "stand out even more" against the normal, unencoded radio traffic of the city. By analyzing those radio signals, especially the volume of radio activity, the Soviets could infer when British counterintelligence (MI5) surveillance operations were under way and whether one of their own operations, as a result, was in jeopardy of being compromised. By Wright's estimate, "the Russians were gathering most of the intelligence from the traffic itself, rather than from the content of the messages." *Spycatcher,* 52–53.

67. See David Kahn, *Seizing the Enigma: The Race to Break the German U-Boat Codes, 1939–1943* (Boston: Houghton Mifflin, 1991), 144–45, 215–16, and 244–51, and Patrick Beesly, *Very Special Intelligence: The Story of the Admiralty's Operational Intelligence Centre, 1939–45* (Garden City, N.Y.: Doubleday, 1978), 55–56, 97–98, 116, and 195.

68. For an account of this operation, see David E. Murphy, Sergei A. Kondrashev, and George Bailey, *Battleground Berlin: CIA vs. KGB in the Cold War* (New Haven, Conn.: Yale University Press, 1997), chap. 11. The existence of the tunnel was betrayed

to the Soviets by George Blake, a Soviet mole in the British Secret Intelligence Service (SIS); the book reprints an SIS/CIA planning-meeting report that Blake passed to the Soviets (449–53) and discusses whether the Soviets used their prior knowledge of the tap to deceive the United States and Britain (423–28).

69. This operation, code-named "Ivy Bells," is described in detail in Sherry Sontag and Christopher Drew, *Blind Man's Bluff: The Untold Story of American Submarine Espionage* (New York: Public Affairs, 1998), 158–83 and passim.

70. Wright, *Spycatcher,* 81–86. More recently, Soviet intelligence was enabled by poor U.S. security practice to get access to electric typewriters shipped to the American embassy in Moscow. (The U.S. State Department had shipped the typewriters to the Soviet Union by unaccompanied commercial transport.) By planting sophisticated bugs in the typewriters, the Soviets were able to "read" the material (classified or not) being typed. See U.S. Senate, Select Committee on Intelligence, *Meeting the Espionage Challenge,* 34–35; for an unofficial account of this episode, see Kessler, *Moscow Station,* 92–97.

71. For a discussion of the difficulties of surreptitiously tapping fiber-optic cables, particularly those running under the ocean, see Neil King Jr., "As Technology Evolves, Spy Agency Struggles to Preserve Its Hearing," *Wall Street Journal,* May 23, 2001, A1.

72. For example, in 2000 the Select Committee on Intelligence of the U.S. Senate reported as follows: "The Committee is increasingly troubled by the National Security Agency's (NSA) growing inability to meet technological challenges and to provide America's leaders with vital signals intelligence (SIGINT)." *Report of the Senate Select Committee on Intelligence Authorizing Appropriations for Fiscal Year 2001 for the Intelligence Activities of the United States Government and the Central Intelligence Agency Retirement and Disability System and for Other Purposes,* S. Rep. 106-279, May 4, 2000.

73. Jeffrey Richelson, *Sword and Shield: The Soviet Intelligence and Security Apparatus* (Cambridge, Mass.: Ballinger, 1986), 103–105. See also Curtis Peebles, *Guardians: Strategic Reconnaissance Satellites* (Novato, Calif.: Presidio, 1987), 279–89. Like photoreconnaissance satellites, elint satellites have specific collection tasks that determine their orbits and how many satellites are needed. In general, elint location and tracking of another country's military systems requires numerous, low-flying satellites. For elint collection to help determine the precise electronic characteristics of a military system, a satellite is likely to be put in a highly elliptical orbit. In such an orbit, the satellite, as it approaches apogee (the point at which it is farthest from earth), appears to fly relatively slowly over the targeted area. Thus, it has more time to capture and record the desired signals. It is possible, of course, to put a satellite in geosynchronous orbit. (A satellite in geosynchronous orbit circles the earth above the equator, making one complete circle per day; thus, from the earth, it appears to "hang" motionless above a given point on the equator.) This would allow a satellite's elint receivers "to stare" continuously into a country; the disadvantage would be its great distance from the transmitters. The utility of any geosynchronous system therefore would depend on the strength of the signal to be collected and the sensitivity of the receivers on board the satellite.

74. The calculation is made as follows: the radio wave emitted by a radar travels at the speed of light, or three hundred thousand kilometers per second. Hence, it can travel 300,000/500 = 600 kilometers between pulses. Therefore, if the wave is to reach the target and return to the radar before the next pulse is emitted, the target cannot be more than three hundred kilometers from the radar. Jones, *The Wizard War,* 198.

75. The account of this episode is drawn from *The Electronic Spies* (Alexandria, Va.: Time-Life, 1991), 106–107.

76. According to the official U.S. definition, masint sensors "include, but are not limited to, radar, laser, infrared, acoustic, nuclear, radiation detection, spectroradiometric, and seismic systems as well as gas, liquid and solid material sampling systems," whose data "when collected, processed and analyzed, results in intelligence that detects, tracks, identifies, or describes the signatures (distinctive characteristics) of fixed and dynamic target sources." Masint was classified formally as an intelligence discipline (an "int") in 1986, and in 1993 the DCI and the secretary of defense created the Central Masint Office (CMO) within the Defense Intelligence Agency to oversee national and defense masint activities. See section 7, "Masint: Measurement and Signals Intelligence," of U.S. House of Representatives, Permanent Select Committee on Intelligence, *IC21: Intelligence Community in the 21st Century* (Washington, D.C.: Government Printing Office, 1996), available at www.fas.org/irp/congress/1996_rpt/ic21/index.html.

77. For a generally sanguine description of the technology involved in seismic monitoring for underground nuclear testing, see U.S. Congress, Office of Technology Assessment, *Seismic Verification of Nuclear Testing Treaties,* OTAISC-361 (Washington, D.C.: U.S. Government Printing Office, May 1988). On remote detection of above-ground nuclear testing, see Peebles, *Guardians,* 331–42.

78. For a fictional account of intelligence collection using sonar, see Tom Clancy, *The Hunt for Red October* (Annapolis, Md.: Naval Institute, 1984). Nonfictional accounts are somewhat harder to come by in the open literature. However, see Joel S. Witt, "Advances in Antisubmarine Warfare," *Scientific American,* February 1981. On the possibility of detecting submarines by other means, see Tom Stefanick, "The Nonacoustic Detection of Submarines," *Scientific American,* March 1988.

79. Strictly speaking, there is no universal agreement that international law permits satellite reconnaissance. The Outer Space Treaty of 1967, for example, does not directly address the issue of space reconnaissance. Arms control treaties make reference to "national technical means of verification" but do not define those terms. Article IX of the 1991 Strategic Arms Reduction Treaty (between the U.S. and the former Soviet Union), for instance, only states that "national technical means of verification [be used] . . . in a manner consistent with generally recognized principles of international law."

The U.S. position has been that a nation's sovereignty does not extend into outer space (that is, beyond the earth's atmosphere) and that hence a nation is as free to conduct reconnaissance activities from outer space as it is on the high seas. At the start of the space age, the Soviet Union's view was that reconnaissance from space was just as illegal as aerial reconnaissance involving the unsanctioned overflight of another nation's territory. For all practical purposes, however, the actual use of space for reconnaissance by a number of states, including the former Soviet Union, has made the question of its legality under international law moot.

80. All countries keep the actual cost of space-based reconnaissance systems secret. For an unclassified estimate, see U.S. Congress, Congressional Budget Office, *U.S. Costs of Verification and Compliance under Pending Arms Treaties* (Washington, D.C.: Government Printing Office, 1990), 43–47. Because satellites are expensive to build and launch, the tendency has been to buy a few, highly capable satellites and design them for extended stays in space (perhaps seven or more years). This approach, while cost-

effective in one sense, has the downside that it may leave a country "blind" if something unexpected happens to one or more of its satellites or if something occurs in a part of the world not easily covered by the orbits of the existing reconnaissance systems.

An alternative strategy with more flexibility and surge capability would be to build more but cheaper satellites, with shorter space life-spans. In 1996, a staff study of the Permanent Select Committee on Intelligence of the U.S. House of Representatives noted that "continuing revolutions in processing capability . . . permit fielding of spacecraft that are not only lighter and cheaper, but also smarter. . . . For some applications, eventually 'micro-satellites' deployed in 'clouds' . . . might feature distributed collection and division of labor, thus allowing inexpensive reconstitution or selective parts replacement." *IC21: Intelligence Community in the 21st Century* (Washington, D.C.: Government Printing Office, 1996), 108, available at www.fas.org/irp/congress/1996_rpt/ic21/index.html.

However, cheaper satellites will in general be less capable and, in any case, a large part of the expense is driven by launch costs. The choice of strategy will be driven by the collection priorities set by a government and the technical sophistication of those building the satellites. For a brief discussion of this and related issues, see Codevilla, *Informing Statecraft,* 313–24.

81. See Victor Suvorov, *Inside the Soviet Army* (New York: Macmillan, 1982), 106. Minor but unpredictable changes in orbit can be accomplished by firing small rockets on the satellite; the number and magnitude of such maneuvers is limited by the fuel capacity of the satellite.

82. U.S. Department of Defense, *Conduct of the Persian Gulf War,* 338, 710.

83. Citations are from a joint statement by U.S. Secretary of Defense William Cohen and Gen. Henry H. Shelton, chairman of the Joint Chiefs of Staff, before the Armed Services Committee of the U.S. Senate, October 14, 1999, available at www.fas.org/man/dod-101/ops/docs99/b10141999_bt478-99.htm.

84. For a catalogue of what might be done under the guise of a common truck or van, see Desmond Ball, "Soviet Signals Intelligence: Vehicular Systems and Operations," *Intelligence and National Security* 4, no. 1 (January 1989): 5–27. On the more exotic front, see Alfred Price, *The History of U.S. Electronic Warfare: The Renaissance Years, 1946–1964* (Alexandria, Va.: Association of Old Crows, 1989), 89, 160–61, for an account of the U.S. Moonbounce project, which collected Soviet radar signals reflected off the moon.

85. In addition, miniaturization is allowing the U.S. Defense Department to develop palm-sized reconnaissance drones and toylike scouting robots for use on the battlefield. The tiny spy planes (called "micro aerial vehicles," or MAVs) and robots will give small combat units the ability to scout out their immediate environments. Michael A. Dornhein, "Tiny Drones May Be Soldier's New Tool," *Aviation Week and Space Technology,* June 8, 1998, 42–48, and Kevin Kaley, "Robot Scouts May Gather Info for U.S. Marine Corps," *Defense News,* July 24, 2000, 20.

86. Stansfield Turner, *Secrecy and Democracy: The CIA in Transition* (Boston: Houghton Mifflin, 1985; New York: Harper and Row, 1986), 92. After the Cold War, Turner argued that "Washington can easily construct a system that will detect any significant activity on the surface of the earth, day or night, under clouds or jungle cover, and with such frequency as to make deliberate evasion difficult. . . . [Costing] $5 billion

to purchase and $1 billion per year to operate[,] . . . it would be a bargain." According to the former DCI, there is a role for human collection in the post–Cold War era, but, in general, "the new world order will yield technical systems that will serve as a sword, the broad cutting edge of intelligence collection, and human spying operations will serve as the rapier, to be applied judiciously to very specific requirements." Turner, "Intelligence for a New World Order," *Foreign Affairs* 70, no. 4 (Fall 1991): 151, 159.

87. The Polish army officer, Col. Ryszard J. Kuklinski, also provided, during the decade he worked for U.S. intelligence, thousands of pages of secret documents, including Soviet battle plans for a war in Europe. For accounts of Colonel Kuklinski's espionage career, see Benjamin Weiser, "Polish Officer Was U.S.'s Window on Soviet War Plans," *Washington Post,* September 27, 1992, A1, and "A Question of Loyalty," *Washington Post Magazine,* December 13, 1992, 9–30.

88. Jozef Garlinski, *The Enigma War* (New York: Scribner, 1979), 16. The German agent, Hans-Thilo Schmidt, has been described by historian David Kahn as "the spy who most affected World War II." *Kahn on Codes: Secrets of the New Cryptology* (New York: Macmillan, 1983), 76–88.

89. Humint may play a role here as well. For example, according to news accounts, Colonel Kuklinski provided information on which "Soviet targets visible by satellite were actually deceptions—and which were real." In addition, Kuklinski's reporting enabled U.S. intelligence to keep track of a Soviet military program to build a network of hidden command-and-control bunkers that the Soviets and their allies intended to use if there was a war in Europe. Weiser, "Polish Officer Was U.S.'s Window on Soviet War Plans."

90. See R. Jeffrey Smith, "Iraq's Secret A-Arms Effort: Lessons for the World," *Washington Post,* August 11, 1991, C1; R. Jeffrey Smith, "Iraq's Nuclear Powers Underestimated by U.S.," *Washington Post,* November 13, 1991, A45; R. Jeffrey Smith and Glenn Frankel, "Saddam's Nuclear Weapons Dream: A Lingering Nightmare," *Washington Post,* November 13, 1991, A1.

91. Smith, "Iraq's Secret A-Arms."

92. For a discussion of the role of intelligence in the "revolution in military affairs," see James R. FitzSimonds, "Intelligence and the Revolution in Military Affairs," in *U.S. Intelligence at the Crossroads: Agendas for Reform,* ed. Roy Godson, Ernest R. May, and Gary Schmitt (Washington, D.C.: Brassey's [U.S.], 1995), 265–87. Among the tasks to be accomplished in order fully to exploit the techint for tactical purposes, FitzSimonds mentions the following: "Global coverage—broad-area, all-weather, day-night identification of both fixed and mobile targets ashore, at sea, in the air, and in space"; "Continuous targeting . . . in real time (or close to it)," including "battle damage assessment"; and "real-time linking of targeting information to warheads, including those in flight" (268).

93. Sherman Kent, *Strategic Intelligence for American World Policy* (Princeton, N.J.: Princeton University Press, 1949; reprint, 1966), 3–4. Kent, a veteran of the Office of Strategic Services (OSS), the U.S. intelligence service of the World War II era, provided a peculiarly American theory of intelligence right after World War II.

94. V. Zaykin, "'Secret' Classification Removed," *Izvestiya,* September 3, 1988, 2, reprinted and translated in Federal Broadcast Information Service (FBIS), *Soviet Report,* September 8, 1988 (FBIS-SOV-88-174), 53–54.

95. The strategic bombing campaign had mixed results. To their credit, OSS economists had designed a relatively sophisticated and useful system for selecting targets. But they lacked sufficient wartime data on the German economy to exploit their strategic analysis fully. On these points, see Stephen Peter Rosen, *Winning the Next War: Innovation and the Modern Military* (Ithaca, N.Y.: Cornell University Press, 1991), 148–70.

96. One might wonder why such an operation should be conducted by an intelligence agency at all, given the project's total reliance on open-source materials and on methodologies that, having been developed in the academic world, would be familiar to the country whose officialdom was being studied. Obviously, it need not be, but whether placing it in a nonclassified research center would be a good idea depends on a balance of several factors. On the one hand, it might be easier to recruit personnel for such an open center, and its product would be more easily shared with the academic community. On the other hand, special, potentially cumbersome procedures would be needed to integrate this open-source material with secret information or to use this information to support secret intelligence activities. For example, if information were needed to support the recruitment of an official for espionage purposes, the request would have to be camouflaged to conceal the reason for it.

97. Donald E. Queller, *The Office of Ambassador in the Middle Ages* (Princeton, N.J.: Princeton University Press, 1967), 90.

98. A classic example of diplomatic reporting of this type is George Kennan's 1946 "Long Telegram," written by Kennan while he was the U.S. chargé d'affaires in Moscow. Kennan's cable on the Soviet Union laid out the intellectual foundation for what became the U.S. "containment" policy toward the Soviet Union for most of the Cold War. For the text of the Kennan cable, see Kenneth M. Jensen, ed., *Origins of the Cold War: The Novikov, Kennan, and Roberts "Long Telegrams" of 1946* (Washington, D.C.: United States Institute of Peace, 1991).

99. What is described in the text is a military attaché's ordinary activity, which is essentially overt, although he may attempt to travel in or near restricted areas to observe objects the host country would prefer he did not. In addition, the position of military attaché (like any diplomatic position) can be used as cover by an intelligence officer.

CHAPTER 3: WHAT DOES IT ALL MEAN? INTELLIGENCE ANALYSIS AND PRODUCTION

1. This raises the intriguing question of whether an "unbreakable" cipher can be created. The answer (leaving aside some very abstruse considerations about the nature of randomness) is yes; it involves the use of what is referred to as a "one-time pad." For example, consider the following system involving a superenciphered code. Its first step is the conversion of the message being sent into code. (This code will differ from that discussed in the text in that the code groups will be four-digit numbers rather than four-letter groups.) Using a codebook, for example, "war starts tomorrow" might be encoded as "4251 1712 2844." The next step is to add to those number groups a series of randomly generated numbers (such as, "3648 5217 8150 . . .") taken in sequence

from a sheet of numbers, "a pad," of which only the sender and the recipient have copies. Adding, we get:

4251 1112 2844
<u>3648 5217 8150</u>
7899 6329 0994

(If a sum exceeds 9999, the first "1" is dropped.) This final series of number groups is then transmitted. Upon receipt, the process is reversed. Consulting his copy of the pad containing the random number groups, the recipient subtracts the additives from the ones he had received, revealing the first set of numbers, which is then decoded using the code book. What makes this system secure is that once a sheet's series of random numbers has been used, it is destroyed and never used again. Absent the "key" for a particular message, it is impossible for an adversary to decrypt the message even if the codebook falls into his hands, since the additives used are unrelated to any other. Accordingly, the numbers as transmitted will manifest no pattern that could be used by a cryptanalyst to help break the cipher.

Unfortunately, the "pad" (copies of which must be securely provided to both the sender and the recipient) must be at least as long as all the messages to be transmitted. Thus, this system is not very practicable in circumstances where secure communications between sender and recipient is difficult or where a large volume of message traffic is involved. See John Earl Haynes and Harvey Klehr, *Venona: Decoding Soviet Espionage in America* (New Haven, Conn.: Yale University Press, 1999), chap. 2, for an account of how U.S. cryptanalysts exploited Soviet misuse of the one-time pad system to read thousands of messages detailing Soviet espionage in the United States.

2. See David Kahn, *The Codebreakers: The Story of Secret Writing* (New York: Macmillan, 1967), for the most complete public treatment of the history of cryptography. Since his book was published, however, revelations about the British success in breaking German ciphers in World War II have added a new and most important chapter to that history. Kahn's own "update" can be found in *Kahn on Codes: Secrets of the New Cryptology* (New York: Macmillan, 1983); see, among other essays, "The Spy Who Most Affected World War II" and "Codebreaking in World War I and II: The Major Successes and Failures, Their Causes and Their Effects," 76–88 and 99–119. In addition, see his *Seizing the Enigma: The Race to Break the German U-Boat Codes, 1939–1943* (Boston: Houghton Mifflin, 1991).

3. See Patrick Beesly, *Room 40: British Naval Intelligence 1914–18* (New York: Harcourt Brace Jovanovich, 1982), 3–7, 22–33.

4. See Barbara Tuchman, *The Zimmermann Telegram* (New York: Macmillan, 1958, 1966), for a full account of this incident.

5. Herbert O. Yardley, *The American Black Chamber* (Indianapolis: Bobbs-Merrill, 1931; reprint, New York: Ballantine, 1981), 4.

6. Kahn, *The Codebreakers,* 348.

7. Such a mathematical theory was developed at the beginning of the 1930s by the Polish mathematician-cryptographers who laid the groundwork for the early Polish successes and the later Allied wartime successes against the German Enigma machine. See, for example, Jozef Garlinski, *The Enigma War* (New York: Scribner, 1979), 25, 196–204.

8. In addition to the books already cited, this literature includes such works as Peter Calvocoressi, *Top Secret Ultra* (New York: Ballantine, 1980); Jozef Garlinkski, *The Enigma War: The Inside Story of the German Enigma Codes and How the Allies Broke Them* (New York: Scribner, 1979); Ronald Lewin, *Ultra Goes to War* (London: Hutchinson, 1978; New York: McGraw-Hill, 1978); and F. W. Winterbotham, *The Ultra Secret* (New York: Harper and Row, 1974).

9. For example, there is now an academic journal called *Cryptologia* devoted to these topics.

10. Many possible mistakes in using a cipher can help the cryptanalyst. For example, the German procedure at the beginning of World War II of repeating, at the beginning of each message, a three-letter key was particularly damaging: Simply knowing that the first and fourth letters of the plaintext were the same (as were the second and fifth, and the third and sixth) was a tremendous help to British cryptanalysts. See Gordon Welchman, *The Hut Six Story: Breaking the Enigma Codes* (New York: McGraw-Hill, 1982), 59–73, for a discussion of how this German error was exploited by the British. Similarly, routine message formats, standard salutations, or other stock phrases may provide important clues for cryptanalysts. Welchman notes that he and other British cryptanalysts "developed a very friendly feeling for a German officer who sat in the Qattara Depression in North Africa for quite a long time reporting every day with the utmost regularity that he had nothing to report. In cases like this, we would have liked to ask the British commanders to be sure to leave our helper alone" (132).

11. For instance, it has been reported that the Walker espionage ring provided Soviet intelligence with a vast quantity of cipher material, thereby enabling it to decrypt a million U.S. secret messages. For a brief account of the Walker case, see Christopher Andrew and Oleg Gordievsky, *KGB: The Inside Story of Its Foreign Operations from Lenin to Gorbachev* (New York: HarperCollins, 1990), 524–31.

12. Kahn, *The Codebreakers,* 603; Ronald Lewin, *The American Magic: Codes, Ciphers and the Defeat of Japan* (New York: Farrar Straus Giroux, 1982), 113.

13. Kahn, *The Codebreakers,* 604.

14. Lewin, *The American Magic,* 116–17. See also Edwin T. Layton, *"And I Was There": Pearl Harbor and Midway—Breaking the Secrets* (New York: Morrow, 1985), 453–56, for a discussion of this incident.

15. Lewin, *The American Magic,* 117.

16. The difficulties involved in developing a new cryptographic system and distributing it to the fleet could easily explain why the Japanese reaction was limited merely to advancing the date of an already planned code change. More significantly, Japanese authorities sent a request to their embassy in neutral Lisbon for "newspapers, particularly the antigovernment *Chicago Tribune,* with as many back issues as possible." Although not conclusive, this suggests that they were aware of the *Tribune* article on Midway and were at least concerned enough about its possible significance to want to see it for themselves. Summary of Magic intelligence (derived from intercepted Japanese diplomatic cable traffic) dated September 11, 1942, cited in B. Nelson Macpherson, "The Compromise of U.S. Navy Cryptanalysis after the Battle of Midway," *Intelligence and National Security* 2, no. 2 (April 1987): 321. The summary does not indicate the date of the message from Tokyo to Lisbon.

17. Christopher Andrew, *Her Majesty's Secret Service: The Making of the British Intelligence Community* (New York: Viking, 1986), 331–32.

18. Bob Woodward and Patrick E. Tyler, "Libyan Cables Intercepted and Decoded," *Washington Post,* April 15, 1986, A1.

19. Stephen Engleberg, "U.S. Aides Worried over Libya Cables," *New York Times,* April 17, 1986, A24.

20. Lewin, *Ultra Goes to War,* 99–103. See also F. H. Hinsley, et al., *British Intelligence in the Second World War: Its Influence on Strategy and Operations* (New York: Cambridge University Press, 1979) 1, app. 9 ("Intelligence in Advance of the GAF Raid on Coventry, 14 November 1940"), 528–48.

21. For a rough analogy, one might imagine being confronted with a set of graphs, lacking both labels and scales for the *x* and *y* axes, and being told only the general nature of the phenomenon of which the graphs described various aspects. One would then be asked to figure out what each graph meant and to describe the phenomenon in detail. As Angelo Codevilla notes, "The intelligence service that intercepts the telemetry, unlike the engineers who designed it, does not know, and so must postulate the scale on which each channel is to be read." (Angelo Codevilla, *Informing Statecraft: Intelligence for a New Century* [New York: Free Press, 1992, 122.) The final check on these postulates and the process as a whole is whether a model of the missile can be deduced that is internally consistent and consistent with whatever other data has been obtained from other sources.

22. SALT II prohibited the use of telemetry encryption if it impeded verification of compliance with provisions of the treaty. Some have argued that U.S. insistence on including this anti-encryption clause in the treaty backfired by alerting the Soviet Union to U.S. success in intercepting and exploiting Soviet missile telemetry. Others argued that Soviet espionage success against a U.S. sigint-collecting satellite "may have contributed to the Soviet decision to encrypt telemetry." (Senator Gordon J. Humphrey, "Analysis and Compliance Enforcement," in *Verification and SALT: The Challenge of Strategic Deception,* ed. William C. Potter [Boulder, Colo.: Westview, 1980], 112.) For accounts of the espionage case involved, see Robert Lindsey, *The Falcon and the Snowman* (New York: Simon and Schuster, 1979), and Curtis Peebles, *Guardians: Strategic Reconnaissance Satellites* (Novato, Calif.: Presidio, 1987), 200–201.

23. Dino Brugioni, a former PI himself, emphasizes this point in his account of a key briefing during the Cuban missile crisis. He notes that the photo interpreter who first briefed Kennedy realized that the import of the photos of the missile sites was far from self-evident and took particular care to lead the president through the PI analysis—at the end of which Kennedy asked, "Are you sure?" Brugioni, *Eyeball to Eyeball: The Inside Story of the Cuban Missile Crisis* (New York: Random House, 1991), 230.

24. "Ground resolution" refers to the ability of a photograph to render barely distinguishable a standard pattern consisting of parallel black-and-white lines (that is, lines and spaces) of equal width. A ground resolution distance of, say, one foot would describe a photograph in which a pattern whose line-plus-space width was one foot would be barely recognizable as such. A finer pattern—one with a smaller line-plus-space width—would not be distinguishable at all. (This definition, and the citation in the text, are from Amrom Katz, "Observation Satellites: Problems and Prospects,"

Astronautics [April 1960]: 5–6, a discussion that is "essentially identical" to Amrom Katz, *Observation Satellites: Problems, Possibilities and Prospects,* RAND Paper P-1707 [Santa Monica, Calif.: RAND, May 25, 1959].)

25. For a sample listing of the required ground resolutions necessary to carry out different levels of photo analysis for different kinds of targets, see Amron Katz, "Technical Collection," in *Intelligence Requirements for the 1980s: Clandestine Collection,* ed. Roy Godson (Washington, D.C.: National Strategy Information Center, 1982), 109.

26. For a list of the basic elements that go into developing a signature, see Brugioni, *Eyeball to Eyeball,* 196.

27. For a discussion of crateology, see Robert S. Greenberger, "Can CIA Cratology Ultimately Outsmart Kremlin's Shellology?" *Wall Street Journal,* January 10, 1985, A1.

28. Brugioni, *Eyeball to Eyeball,* 104–105, 276–77.

29. Brugioni, *Eyeball to Eyeball,* 538–48.

30. Robin Wright, "U.S. Intelligence Failed to Warn of India's Atom Tests," *Los Angeles Times,* May 13, 1998, A1, and James Risen and Tim Weiner, "U.S. May Have Helped India Hide Its Nuclear Activity," *New York Times,* May 25, 1998, A3.

31. Sherman Kent, *Strategic Intelligence for American World Policy* (Princeton, N.J.: Princeton University Press, 1949; reprint, 1966), 12–13, gives the table of contents of one such book about a country of interest prepared in Germany for use during World War II:

> I. *General Background.* Location. Frontiers. Area. History. Governmental and Administrative Structure.
> II. *Character of the Country.* Surface Forms. Soils. Ground Cover. Climate. Water Supply.
> III. *People.* Nationalities. Language. Attitudes. Population Distribution. Settlement. Health. Structure of Society.
> IV. *Economic.* Agriculture. Industry. Trade and Commerce. Mining. Fisheries.
> V. *Transportation.* Railroads. Roads. Ports. Airfields. Inland Waterways.
> VI. *Military Geography.* [Detailed regional breakdown].
> VII. *Military Establishment in Being.* Army: Order of Battle, Fixed Defenses, Military Installations, Supply. Navy: Order of Battle, the Fleet, Naval Shore Installations, Naval Air, Supply. Air: Order of Battle, Military Aircraft, Air Installations, Lighter than Air, Supply.
> VIII. *Special Appendixes.* Biographical data on key figures of government. Local geographical terminology. Description of rivers, lakes, canals. List and specifications of electric power plants. Description of roads. List of airdromes and most important landing grounds. List of main telephone and telegraph lines. Money, weights, and measures. Beaches [as for amphibious military operations].

32. House of Representatives, Committee on the Armed Services, *Lessons Learned as a Result of the U.S. Military Operations in Grenada: Hearing,* 98th Cong., 2d sess., 1984, H. Rept. 98-43, 24. Given the Reagan administration's expressed concern with the Marxist-Leninist regime of Grenadian leader Maurice Bishop (whose arrest and execution by his colleagues set in motion the events that led to the invasion), this lack of maps and other basic data provides an illustration of a failure to anticipate U.S. policy.

33. For a full discussion of this task, described as the avoidance of technological surprise, see Michael I. Handel, "Technological Surprise in War," *Intelligence and*

National Security 2, no. 1 (January 1987): 1–53. Handel characterizes the importance of scientific and technical intelligence as follows:

> More than any other type of war in the past, modern warfare, based on the continuous development of new weapons systems at an ever-accelerating pace, depends on intelligence. . . . Victory or defeat [in the Battle of Britain] was often decided by the "battle of intelligence" before combat had even begun. The role played by scientific technological intelligence in war will increase in proportion to the technological advancement of the adversaries and the use they make of state-of-the-art weaponry [page 40].

34. R. V. Jones, *The Wizard War: British Scientific Intelligence, 1939–45* (New York: Coward, McCann and Geoghegan, 1978), 104. The *Knickebein* system involved two antennae transmitting unidirectional radio beams that intersected over the bombers' target; the German bombers would fly along one beam and drop their bombs when they crossed the other. Having ascertained the system's existence and characteristics, the British were able to design countermeasures—jamming and transmission of false beams—that significantly reduced its effectiveness, thereby frustrating German efforts to conduct precision bombing operations against Great Britain (127–28).

35. Eliot Cohen, "Analysis," in *Intelligence Requirements for the 1990s: Collection, Analysis, Counterintelligence and Covert Action,* ed. Roy Godson (Lexington, Mass.: Heath, Lexington, 1989), 82 [emphasis supplied].

36. Jan Karl Tanenbaum, "French Estimates of Germany's Operational War Plans," in *Knowing One's Enemies: Intelligence Assessment before the Two World Wars,* ed. Ernest May (Princeton, N.J.: Princeton University Press, 1984), 150–71.

37. Even in the case of Soviet economics, where the intelligence analysts' access to data that the Soviets had not publicly released might have given them an advantage over other experts, this was not necessarily the case. In 1977, for example, the CIA produced several studies of the Soviet oil industry that predicted that production would fall to eight million to ten million barrels per day (mb/d) by 1985 and that the Soviet Union would import between 3.5 and 4.5 mb/d. Academic and business experts were skeptical of these results, and indeed they turned out to be wide of the mark. Soviet oil production stayed at or near the 12 mb/d level through the 1980s. For a review of this issue generally sympathetic to the CIA, see U.S. Senate, Select Committee on Intelligence, *The Soviet Oil Situation: An Evaluation of CIA Analyses of Soviet Oil Production: Staff Report,* 95th Cong., 2d sess., 1978, Committee Print. For a critical review of American intelligence's performance over the years in analyzing the economy of the former Soviet Union in general, see U.S. Senate, Committee on Foreign Relations, *Estimating the Size and Growth of the Soviet Economy: Hearing,* 101st Cong., 2d sess., 1990, S. Hrg. 101-1112.

38. Kent, *Strategic Intelligence,* 7–8.

39. Intelligence agencies are sometimes regarded as competitors of the news media, often to the agencies' disadvantage. For example, news reports that U.S. officials followed the failed Panamanian coup d'état of October 1989 on the Cable News Network (CNN) insinuated that this was evidence of a failure of American intelligence. But it is an unfair comparison, since the CIA is not designed to provide up-to-the-minute reporting. Nevertheless, it is a criticism that seems to have had some impact. See George Lardner Jr., "On This Network, All the News Is Top Secret: Defense Intelligence Agency Acts to Win Back Audience from CNN," *Washington Post,* March 3, 1992, A1, and George Lardner Jr., and Walter Pincus, "Clearance Sought for New CIA Network:

Agency Would Transmit Latest Intelligence Only to Select Top Officials," *Washington Post,* February 5, 1992, A1.

40. Kent, *Strategic Intelligence,* 38.

41. CIA Directorate of Intelligence Website (accessed March 10, 2001) www.odci.gov/cia/di/work/daily.html.

42. Cord Meyer, *Facing Reality: From World Federalism to the CIA* (New York: Harper and Row, 1980), 352. According to former DCI Robert Gates, writing in 1989,

> the PDB has varied little from president to president: a few (three to six) DoS (Department of State) and CIA cables of special significance; occasionally a sensitive intelligence report from the CIA, the Defense Intelligence Agency, or the National Security Agency (NSA); selected wire service items; DoS or CIA situation reports (rarely both), if there is a crisis abroad; and often NSC and DoS morning cable summaries.

From Gates's point of view, the real revolution in current intelligence for the White House was the creation of the White House Situation Room by the Kennedy administration in the early 1960s. Before, "a president [had been] at the mercy of the bureaucracies for information." With the creation of the Situation Room, the State Department, the Defense Department, CIA, and NSA began to provide a president and his staff with "unevaluated or raw intelligence information electronically." "One result" of this innovation, Gates suggests, "was a significant diminution in the value to the White House of the CIA's and other agencies' current intelligence reporting." Robert Gates, "An Opportunity Unfulfilled: The Use and Perceptions of Intelligence at the White House," *The Washington Quarterly* 12, no. 1 (Winter 1989): 37.

43. CIA Directorate of Intelligence Website. Reflecting the Clinton administration's emphasis on the economic aspects of international issues, a third daily publication, the *Economic Executives' Intelligence Brief* (EEIB), is published to cover "the issues on economic officials' agendas, including foreign trade practices, illicit finance, and international energy developments."

44. U.S. Senate, Select Committee to Study Governmental Operations with Respect to Intelligence Activities [hereafter Church Committee], *Final Report,* book 1: *Foreign and Military Intelligence,* 94th Cong. 2d sess., 1976, S. Rept. 94-755, 272–73.

45. Consider the following reported remark of a high official of the U.S. State Department: "I had a friend of mine from the CIA come down yesterday to give me a briefing on East Germany. He told me that he revised his paper three times on the drive from the CIA to the State Department just because of things he was hearing on the radio." (Thomas L. Friedman, "In Quest of a Post–Cold War Plan," *New York Times,* November 17, 1989, A22.) The remark was meant to illustrate how quickly Eastern Europe was changing in November 1989; it also indicates that the analyst's briefing was concerned more with the latest events than with a deeper understanding of the political dynamics of East Germany.

46. See Timothy M. Laur, "Principles of Warning Intelligence," in *The Military Intelligence Community,* ed. Gerald W. Hopple and Bruce W. Watson (Boulder, Colo.: Westview, 1986), 149–68, for a fuller description of warning analysis.

47. Gordon Brook-Shepherd, *Storm Birds: Soviet Postwar Defectors* (New York: Weidenfeld and Nicolson, 1989), 330–31, and Christopher Andrew and Oleg Gordievsky, eds., *Instructions from the Centre: Top Secret Files on KGB Foreign Operations, 1975–1985* (London: Hodder and Stoughton, 1991), 67–90.

48. According to the most recent executive order on United States Intelligence Activities (EO 12333, December 4, 1981), the "intelligence community" is defined as the CIA, the National Security Agency, the Defense Intelligence Agency, "offices within the Department of Defense for the collection of specialized national foreign intelligence through reconnaissance programs," the State Department's Bureau of Intelligence and Research (INR), and the intelligence elements of the armed services, the FBI, and the Departments of the Treasury and of Energy (para. 3.4[f]). The text of the executive order is available on the National Archives Website at www.nara.gov/fedreg/codific/eos/e12333.html.

49. Avi Shlaim, "Failures in National Intelligence Estimates: The Case of the Yom Kippur War," *World Politics* 28, no. 3 (April 1976): 368–69.

50. Alexander Orlov, *Handbook of Intelligence and Guerrilla Warfare* (Ann Arbor: University of Michigan Press, 1965), 10. Stalin created a unified intelligence assessment office after World War II, apparently in intimation of the American system. However, as one might have expected, given his earlier instructions and behavior, this office was not given access to all information, and in any case, its analyses reflected what Stalin wanted to hear. (V. M. Zubok, "Soviet Intelligence and the Cold War: The 'Small' Committee of Information, 1952–1953," paper 4 of the Cold War History Project [Washington, D.C.: Woodrow Wilson Center, 1992]). The committee was disbanded in 1958.

In general, there is little publicly available material on estimative processes in countries other than the United States. However, for a broad overview of the British system and its organizational history, see Reginald Hibbert, "Intelligence and Policy," *Intelligence and National Security* 5, no. 1 (January 1990): 110–27, and Michael Herman, "Intelligence and Policy: A Comment," *Intelligence and National Security* 6, no. 1 (January 1991): 229–39.

51. Barton Whaley, *Codeword Barbarossa* (Cambridge: MIT, 1973); Shlaim, "Failures in National Intelligence Estimates," 348–80; Michael I. Handel, *Perception, Deception and Surprise: The Case of the Yom Kippur War* (Jerusalem: Leonard Davis Institute of International Relations, Jerusalem Paper 19, 1976); Eliot Cohen and John Gooch, *Military Misfortunes: The Anatomy of Failure in War* (New York: Free Press, 1990), chap. 5 ("Failure to Anticipate: Israeli Defense Forces on the Suez Front and the Golan Heights, 1973"), 95–131; Roberta Wohlstetter, *Pearl Harbor: Warning and Decision* (Stanford, Calif.: Stanford University Press, 1962); Edwin T. Layton, *"And I Was There": Pearl Harbor and Midway—Breaking the Secrets* (New York: Morrow, 1985); Gordon W. Prange et al., *At Dawn We Slept: The Untold Story of Pearl Harbor* (New York: McGraw-Hill, 1981); and, in general, Klaus Knorr and Patrick Morgan, eds., *Strategic Military Surprise: Incentives and Opportunities* (New Brunswick, N.J.: Transaction, 1983).

52. See Harvey de Weerd, "Strategic Surprise in the Korean War," *Orbis* 6, no. 3 (Fall 1962): 435–52, and Eliot Cohen, "'Only Half the Battle': American Intelligence and the Chinese Intervention in Korea, 1950," *Intelligence and National Security* 5, no. 1 (January 1990): 129–49. On the Battle of the Bulge, see Charles B. MacDonald, *A Time for Trumpets: The Untold Story of the Battle of the Bulge* (New York: Morrow, 1985), 17–92, and Hinsley et al., *British Intelligence in the Second World War*, vol. 3, pt. 2, 402–38. For the Tet offensive, see James J. Wirtz, *The Tet Offensive: Intelligence Failure in War* (Ithaca, N.Y.: Cornell University Press, 1991).

53. Lewin, *Ultra Goes to War,* 317–18.

54. The failure was considered sufficiently damaging at the time to prompt a handwritten note from President Carter to Cyrus Vance, Zbigniew Brzezinski, and Stansfield Turner (secretary of state, assistant to the president for national security affairs, and director of central intelligence, respectively) that stated, with a bluntness uncharacteristic of governmental bureaucracy, "I am not satisfied with the quality of our political reporting." Stansfield Turner, *Secrecy and Democracy: The CIA in Transition* (Boston: Houghton Mifflin, 1985; New York: Harper and Row, 1986), 113. See also, House of Representatives, Permanent Select Committee on Intelligence, Subcommittee on Evaluation, *Iran: Evaluation of U.S. Intelligence Performance prior to November 1978: Staff Report,* 96th Cong., 1st sess., 1979.

55. A report by the staff of the U.S. Senate Intelligence Committee contends that "the question of oil price levels was analyzed in the context of a narrow supply-and-demand framework, which tended to overlook both political influences and such economic factors as elasticities of supply and demand." It also claims that "political aspects of relationships among OPEC nations and the internal dynamics of the Saudi Government . . . were not consistently integrated into the community's economic analysis" (Select Committee on Intelligence, Subcommittee on Collection, Production, and Quality, *U.S. Intelligence Analysis and the Oil Issue, 1973–1974: Staff Report,* 95th Cong., 1st sess., 1977, Committee Print, 4, 5). This suggests that the intelligence analysts involved employed economic analysis that was too theoretical and hence apolitical.

56. Civil War general George McClellan's peninsula campaign in the spring and summer of 1862 provides a classic example of this kind of intelligence failure. McClellan had moved his Union army of eighty-five thousand by water from Washington to the peninsula formed by Virginia's James and York Rivers. His plan was to move up the peninsula and capture Richmond (the Confederate capital), thereby quickly putting an end to the war. However, at Yorktown, McClellan ran into Confederate resistance. Based on intelligence provided largely by the famous private detective Allan Pinkerton, McClellan believed he was facing a formidable enemy force; in fact, there were no more than seventeen thousand Confederate troops spread over an eight-mile front. Instead of attacking and breaking through the Confederate line, McClellan opted for a lengthy siege that gave the South time to reinforce its position.

Over the spring and summer, both Union and Confederate forces grew. However, again, based on faulty intelligence, McClellan was convinced he was facing a Southern army of two hundred thousand; in reality, it was only three-quarters the size of his own force of 112,000. In August, believing he was substantially outnumbered, General McClellan abandoned the campaign and with it the Union's best chance to deal the South an early, potentially decisive, defeat. See C. T. Schmidt, "G-2, Army of the Potomac," *Military Review* 28 (July 1948), 45–56, and Edwin C. Fishel, "Pinkerton and McClellan: Who Deceived Whom?" *Civil War History* 34, no. 2 (June 1988): 115–42.

More provocatively, Williamson Murray has argued that faulty assessments by France and Great Britain about the balance of power in Europe in 1938–39 resulted in those countries' not taking advantage of opportunities during that period to wage a successful and (compared with what resulted) less costly war against Nazi Germany. Williamson Murray, *The Change in the European Balance of Power, 1938–1939: The Path to Ruin* (Princeton, N.J.: Princeton University Press, 1984).

57. There were elements of tactical surprise, for example, in the Allied deployment of artificial harbors for use until major harbors such as Cherbourg could be captured. See Handel, "Technological Surprise in War," 14–15, for a discussion of the problem these artificial harbors posed for German intelligence.

58. See Cohen, "'Only Half the Battle.'" Cohen argues that although the political leadership in Washington may have been surprised by the Chinese attack, General MacArthur, the American and UN commander, was well aware of the massive infiltration of Chinese troops into Korea; the disaster was caused less by surprise than by the use of inappropriate tactics against the Chinese army. General MacArthur's command believed that U.S. supremacy in the air could be used as effectively against the Chinese People's Liberation Army (PLA) as it had been against the North Korean People's Army (NKPA). Ultimately, this mistaken judgment reflected a failure to assess the significance of the differences between the heavily mechanized and hence road-bound NKPA (formed on the Soviet model) and the unmechanized and non-road-bound PLA, whose more dispersed infantry hordes presented less lucrative targets for aerial attack.

59. Lewin, *Ultra Goes to War,* 347–51.

60. John Prados, *The Soviet Estimate: U.S. Intelligence Analysis and Russian Military Strength* (New York: Dial, 1982), 41–50, 76–95, 111–26.

61. Albert Wohlstetter, "Is There a Strategic Arms Race?" *Foreign Policy,* no. 15 (Summer 1974): 3–20, and "Rivals, but No Race," *Foreign Policy,* no. 16 (Fall 1974): 48–81.

62. For example, Donald Rumsfeld, then chairman of the 1998 Commission to Assess the Ballistic Missile Threat to the United States, has argued that an earlier NIE had understated that threat because, among other reasons, the analysts preparing it did not have access to information concerning the transfer of relevant technology among various states. As a result, their assessment of how long it would take certain states to develop ballistic missiles capable of reaching the United States was based on the time those states would need to develop the technology indigenously. Since it had access to information concerning technology transfer, the commission concluded that some of those states could pose a ballistic missile threat to the United States much more quickly. Eric Schmitt, "Panel Says U.S. Faces Risk of a Surprise Missile Attack," *New York Times,* July 16, 1998, A24, and *The News Hour with Jim Lehrer,* July 15, 1998, interview with Donald Rumsfeld

63. H. Norman Schwarzkopf, *It Doesn't Take a Hero: The Autobiography* (New York: Bantam, 1992), 293; Bob Woodward, *The Commanders* (New York: Simon and Schuster, 1991), 205–208, 215; and Bruce W. Jensen, *With Friends Like These: Reagan, Bush and Saddam, 1982–1990* (New York: Norton, 1994), 173–74.

64. Wesley K. Wark, *The Ultimate Enemy: British Intelligence and Nazi Germany, 1933–1939* (Ithaca, N.Y.: Cornell University Press, 1985), 228–29.

65. This is similar to the question of "paradigm shift" discussed in the philosophy of science—that is, the way in which one organizing framework, such as Newtonian physics, gives way to another (for example, relativity). However, two important differences, both of which suggest that paradigm shift can occur more easily with respect to scientific theory than to intelligence analysis, should be noted: (1) the pioneers of the new framework do not need even the tolerance, let alone the agreement, of the upholders of the old framework to publish their views, and (2) it is possible to conceive and

carry out experiments specifically designed to decide between the two frameworks. Even so, it has been claimed that shifts are due not so much to the conversion to the new framework of scientists already in the field as to its adoption by new entrants into the discipline.

66. This is sometimes referred to by the psychological term "projection," which means, more technically, the psychological mechanism by which one attributes to others feelings or characteristics (such as hostility or dishonesty) that one dislikes about oneself and wishes to disown. While this mechanism may be a psychological basis of mirror-imaging in some cases, the two concepts, which operate at different levels, are not identical; for example, projection could not be the cause of mistakenly attributing to an adversary a characteristic (such as peacefulness or satisfaction with the status quo) that one possesses and with which one is comfortable.

67. The failure of Israeli intelligence in this case is discussed in Shlaim, "Failures in National Intelligence Estimates." Shlaim suggests that a key cause of the failure was the continued adherence by Israeli intelligence, in the face of accumulating evidence of a possible attack, to the "conception," or view, that Egypt would not attack until it was able to stage deep air strikes to destroy the Israeli air force and that Syria would not attack without Egypt. The first and crucial part of the conception reflects, on the military level, the same mirror-imaging that existed on the political level—the belief that Egypt would not start a war it did not stand a good chance of winning. However, Cohen and Gooch in their analysis of the 1973 war (*Military Misfortunes,* chap. 5) argue that this "conception" was based on more than just mirror-imaging; Israel had relatively up-to-date and direct evidence concerning Egypt's assessment of what was required to wage war successfully with Israel (116). The analytic failure in this instance, then, was not so much one of mirror-imaging on the military level as a failure to anticipate that Egypt's notion of strategic success (success with respect to a war's overall political goal) might change (123–24). This failure seems to indicate some mirror-imaging on the political level.

68. *Al-Hamishmar,* September 14, 1975, as cited in Shlaim, "Failures in National Intelligence Estimates," 362.

69. This passage was deleted from the final version of the NIE but survived as a dissenting footnote expressing the separate views of the director of the State Department's INR. Church Committee, *Final Report,* book 1, 78. The complete text of the NIE is available in Donald Steury, ed., *Intentions and Capabilities: Estimates on Soviet Strategic Forces, 1950–1983* (Washington, D.C.: Center for Study of Intelligence, CIA, 1996), 253–61. The footnote appears on 261.

70. Jones, *The Wizard War,* 457.

71. Jones, *The Wizard War,* 458. Developments in radar before World War II offer an interesting pair of examples of the failure to appreciate that an adversary's approach to a technical problem might differ from one's own. In the mid-1930s, both Great Britain and Germany had demonstrated that long-range detection of airplanes was possible by the use of radio transmissions (radar). However, neither knew that the other understood the "secret" of radar, although both had developed and fielded systems by 1939. The British technical and intelligence community, in the absence of a detected German radar transmission, dismissed all other evidence (photographic or human) that Germany had developed radar. Yet the reason that no signal was detected was that Germany had developed radars that differed significantly from the British ones. In many respects German radars were superior, but they had one drawback: limited range. As a

result, the radar signals were not detected in Great Britain simply because they were too weak to be detectable that far away.

The German technical community was less inclined than the British to believe that radar was its "breakthrough" alone. As a result, the Germans made efforts to collect British signals. But they mistakenly identified the radar signals they collected as coming from England's electrical power grid, since they were looking for a signal similar to their own; in fact, however, the British had been unable to produce such a high-performance signal and had designed a radar along different but still effective lines. Because of this analytic mistake, the Luftwaffe did not develop the equipment needed to counter British radar in time for the Battle of Britain, giving the Royal Air Force a decided edge in the skies over England. Jack Nissen, with A. W. Cockerill, *Winning the Radar War* (London: Robert Hale, 1989), 17–39, and Jones, *The Wizard War,* 189–202.

72. In principle, one could speak of failures of intelligence collection; however, one rarely hears of them. Part of the reason may be that the most interesting cases of intelligence failure are those for which relevant information was in fact available.

73. To the extent that intelligence shifts its focus from political and military matters to economic and social ones (as suggested by, for example, former director of central intelligence William Colby, and discussed in chapter 7), this assertion becomes less convincing. An intelligence service concerned primarily with forecasting socioeconomic trends might find that its adversaries were unconcerned about its progress and not interested in impeding it. (But not necessarily: A major Soviet deception effort of the 1920s tried to convince Western intelligence services that communism in the Soviet Union was fading and that its leaders were moving toward an unthreatening nationalism. John J. Dziak, *Chekisty: A History of the KGB* [Lexington, Mass.: Heath, Lexington, 1988], 48.)

Similarly, sometimes one *wants* an adversary to understand the situation correctly. For example, a strategy of nuclear deterrence (assuming one possesses adequate forces to carry it out and is not bluffing) depends on the other government's correctly assessing that one's forces, even after an initial attack, would still be capable of wreaking unacceptable damage on its country. Such was the case in the fall and winter of 1961, when senior officials in the Kennedy administration purposely set out, through a series of speeches and newspaper articles, to make clear to the Soviets that the United States no longer had any doubts about its superiority in the area of nuclear weapons. Based on its ability to "penetrate" the secrecy surrounding Soviet military forces, the U.S. government now knew that there was no "missile gap" and that it had more than enough weapons to carry out a devastating second strike against the USSR should a war start. See Prados, *The Soviet Estimate*, 172.

74. U.S. Senate, Select Committee on Intelligence, Subcommittee on Collection, Production and Quality, *The National Intelligence Estimates A-B Team Episode Concerning Soviet Strategic Capability and Objectives,* 95th Cong., 2d sess., 1978, Committee Print. (That part of the A-B Team report concerned with Soviet strategic intentions was released to the public in a sanitized form by the CIA in 1992.)

75. The congressional mandate to create the bipartisan commission followed two earlier reviews of the NIE, both of which found its analysis flawed. U.S. Senate, Select Committee on Intelligence, *Hearing on Intelligence Analysis on the Long-Range Missile Threat to the United States,* December 4, 1996, available at www.fas.org/

irp/congress/1996_hr/index.html; "Foreign Missile Threats: Analytic Soundness of Certain National Intelligence Estimates," GAO Letter Report (GAO/NSAID-96-225), August 30, 1996, available at www.fas.org/irp/gao/nsi96225.htm; and the *Report of the Commission to Assess the Ballistic Missile Threat of the United States,* July 15, 1998, available at www.fas.org/irp/threat/bm-threat.htm.

76. According to Shlomo Gazit, Israeli military intelligence routinely employs a devil's advocate as part of its efforts to promote open-mindedness in the analytic process. Shlomo Gazit, "Estimates and Fortune-Telling in Intelligence Work," *International Security* 4, no. 4 (Spring 1980): 40, n. 3.

In 1985, the United States used a devil's-advocate approach to reexamine the question of Soviet complicity in the attempted assassination of Pope John Paul II in 1981. In the aftermath of the shooting, the dominant opinion within CIA was that the assassination attempt had been the work of a lone gunman. In 1985, after new intelligence became available that suggested possible Bulgarian and Soviet complicity, Robert Gates, then deputy DCI, ordered the preparation of a devil's-advocate estimate to argue the case for Soviet involvement. This estimate was used during the hearings by opponents of Gates's nomination as an example of his supposed willingness to tailor analysis to fit an administration's general views. As this dispute (and the A-B Team exercise before it) suggests, an attempt to employ a devil's-advocate approach on an ad hoc basis is easily criticized as an effort to politicize intelligence analysis. U.S. Senate, Select Committee on Intelligence, *Nomination of Robert Gates to be Director of Central Intelligence: Hearings,* 102d Cong., 1st sess., 1991, S. Hrg. 102-799: vol. 1, 637; vol. 2, 347 ff. and 619; vol. 3, 62–118. Benjamin Weiser, "Papal-Shooting Analysis: Case Study in Slanting?" *Washington Post,* October 1, 1991, A8.

Despite the fact that the Rumsfeld Commission had its roots in a partisan dispute over whether the United States should deploy national ballistic missile defenses, it largely escaped the charge of politicization, because its final report was unanimously agreed to by its members, which included experts associated with both parties. It also helped that shortly after it issued its report in July 1998, North Korea launched a missile assessed as being capable of hitting Alaska or Hawaii.

77. Richard K. Betts, "Analysis, War, and Decision: Why Intelligence Failures Are Inevitable," *World Politics* 31, no. 1 (October 1978): 61–89.

CHAPTER 4: WORKING BEHIND THE SCENES: COVERT ACTION

1. Intelligence Authorization Act, Fiscal Year 1991, L. 102-88, August 14, 1991 [50 USC 413b].

2. Covert action was first "defined" in 1974 by legislation known as the Hughes-Ryan Amendment (Section 662 of the Foreign Assistance Act of 1961, as amended [22 USC 2242]). Strictly speaking, the act did not provide a definition; rather, it required presidents to authorize explicitly, and then report to Congress, all "operations [involving the expenditure of funds by or on behalf of the CIA] in foreign countries, other than activities intended solely for obtaining necessary intelligence." Until 1991, specific definitions of covert action (or, as it is sometimes referred to, "special activities") were left to later interpretation by presidential orders and guidelines issued by the congressional oversight committees. For an overview of the evolution of the definition of covert action prior to 1991, see Americo R. Cinquegrana, "Dancing in the Dark:

Accepting the Invitation to Struggle in the Context of 'Covert Action,' the Iran-Contra Affair and the Intelligence Oversight Process," *Houston Journal of International Law* 11, no. 1 (Fall 1988): 177–209.

3. John Bruce Lockhart, a former officer of Britain's Foreign Office with practical experience in intelligence, uses the term "special political action" as a synonym for covert action; this presumably reflects British usage. John Bruce Lockhart, "Intelligence: A British View," in *Approaches to Intelligence,* ed. K. G. Robertson (London: Macmillan, 1987), 37, 46.

4. This definition of active measures is taken from Richard H. Shultz and Roy Godson, *Dezinformatsia: Active Measures in Soviet Strategy* (McLean, Va.: Pergamon-Brassey's, 1984), 193.

5. The United States has invented a term, "public diplomacy," that would cover some of the overt active measures techniques, but it has not created the organizational structures to implement it. National Security Decision Directive 77 (NSDD-77), January 14, 1983, defines public diplomacy very broadly as "those actions of the U.S. Government designed to generate support for our national security objectives."

6. In their exposé of the CIA, Victor Marchetti and John D. Marks mention critically a police-training program in South Vietnam; however, their main complaint is directed against the involvement of an academic institution (Michigan State University, in this case) in a covert program. Victor Marchetti and John D. Marks, *The CIA and the Cult of Intelligence* (New York: Knopf, 1974), 234.

7. Section 660 of the Foreign Assistance Act of 1961, as amended in 1974 by L. 93-559 [22 USC 2420]. This provision was modified in 1985 by the enactment of exemptions for Costa Rica, El Salvador, and Honduras.

8. An example of a dispute about whether intelligence sharing should be considered covert action arose when Robert Gates was nominated to be DCI in 1991. It concerned the early 1980s decision of the Reagan administration to pass selected items of intelligence to Iraq to assist it in its war with Iran. Gates argued that the activity fell within the parameters of a traditional intelligence-liaison relationship. Senator Bill Bradley (D-N.J.), however, suggested that since the activity was not principally intended to affect a mutual exchange of information but rather was designed to influence Iraqi military behavior, it fell within the definition of covert action and, as such, should have been reported to Congress. See U.S. Senate, Select Committee on Intelligence, *Nomination of Robert Gates to Be Director of Central Intelligence: Hearings,* 102d Cong., 1st sess., 1991, S. Hrg. 102-799 I, 578–79, 945–50.

9. For an overview of Soviet penetration of the U.S. government in the 1930s and 1940s, see John Earl Haynes and Harvey Klehr, *Venona: Decoding Soviet Espionage in America* (New Haven, Conn.: Yale University Press, 1999), chaps. 5–7, and Herbert Romerstein and Eric Breindel, *The Venona Secrets: Exposing Soviet Espionage and America's Traitors* (Washington, D.C.: Regnery, 2000).

10. Christopher Andrew and Oleg Gordievsky, *KGB: The Inside Story of Its Foreign Operations from Lenin to Gorbachev* (New York: HarperCollins, 1990; Harper-Perennial edition, 1991), 280–82, 334–37. Romerstein and Breindel, *The Venona Secrets,* 41–44, claim that White was following Soviet instructions when in the period prior to Pearl Harbor he recommended a tough policy toward Japan. (The Soviet Union at the time regarded U.S.-Japanese tension as a guarantee against a Japanese

attack on the Soviet Far East.) According to news sources cited by Haynes and Klehr, Henry Wallace, Franklin Roosevelt's vice president from 1941 to 1945, remarked that had he succeeded to the presidency, he would have nominated White to be secretary of the treasury and Laurence Duggan, also a Soviet agent, to be secretary of state. Haynes and Klehr, *Venona,* 139 and 411, n. 49, and Christopher Andrew and Vasili Mitrokhin, *The Sword and the Shield: The Mitrokhin Archive and the Secret History of the KGB* (New York: Basic Books, 1999), 105, 109.

11. Andrew and Gordievsky, *KGB: The Inside Story,* 568–71.

12. Shultz and Godson, *Dezinformatsia,* 133–49, contains a discussion of the case and a detailed analysis of the contents of the newsletter.

13. Shultz and Godson, *Dezinformatsia,* 38. Andrew and Gordievsky have argued that Harry Hopkins, a close and trusted advisor to President Franklin Roosevelt, falls into the category of an unwitting agent of influence who assisted in keeping Roosevelt "neutral" between America's principal allies in the war, Great Britain and the Soviet Union. Gordievsky claims to have attended a lecture by Hopkins's ostensible controller in which Hopkins's role as an agent was described in detail. Gordievsky's description of the case suggests that Hopkins was unwittingly manipulated by Stalin through personal flattery, as well as by a Soviet intelligence officer claiming to be the Soviet leader's personal envoy. Andrew and Gordievsky, *KGB: The Inside Story,* 287, 334, 349–50. Romerstein and Breindel (*The Venona Secrets,* 214–15), on the other hand, argue that decrypted Soviet communications reporting Hopkins's meetings with the Soviet illegal *rezident* in the United States indicate that Hopkins was in fact a controlled Soviet agent.

14. The quoted material is from Bob Woodward, "CIA Curried Favor with Khomeini, Exiles," *Washington Post,* November 19, 1986, A1, 28. The defection was reported in "Soviet Diplomat in Iran Defects and Flees to Britain," *New York Times,* October 24, 1982, A14.

15. Churchill relates the story of this attempt in his history of World War II. He tried to get around Stalin's suspicions by sending a "short and cryptic" message that did not warn of the German attack but merely discussed German troop movements that pointed in that direction; he hoped that such a message "would arrest [Stalin's] attention and make him ponder," thereby leading him to draw the desired conclusion on his own. Unfortunately, the implementation of Churchill's tactic was somewhat botched by the British ambassador in Moscow (*The Grand Alliance,* vol. 3 of *The Second World War* [Boston: Houghton Mifflin, 1951], 357–61). Gabriel Gorodetsky, *Grand Delusion: Stalin and the German Invasion of Russia* (New Haven, Conn.: Yale University Press, 1999), 155–78, has argued that the full story is much more complicated than Churchill's account would indicate.

16. Richard H. Schultz Jr., *The Secret War against Hanoi: Kennedy's and Johnson's Use of Spies, Saboteurs, and Covert Warriors in North Vietnam* (New York: HarperCollins, 1999), 130–48, 162–63. Schultz reports that those running the program eventually realized that it was not undermining North Vietnamese confidence; in the absence of a real resistance movement, the North Vietnamese were able to determine over time that the league was a hoax.

17. Ladislav Bittman, *The KGB and Soviet Disinformation: An Insider's View* (McLean, Va.: Pergamon-Brassey's, 1985), 112–13.

18. Andrew and Mitrokhin, *The Sword and the Shield,* 461–74.

19. See John Barron, *KGB Today: The Hidden Hand* (New York: Reader's Digest, 1983; New York: Berkley, 1985), 32–159, for Levchenko's account, as told to Barron, of his intelligence career and eventual defection.

20. Barron, *KGB Today,* 76–81, 85–90, and 93–94. The article, by suggesting that the double-agent operation was an American provocation, sought to reduce public support for a tough stand by the Japanese government against Soviet diplomatic pressure; the GRU agent was in fact released. The letter, on the other hand, which sought to create public pressure on the Japanese government to accede to the Soviet demand that the pilot be returned, did not achieve its purpose.

21. Total concealment may not be possible, depending on the case. Thus, a foreign intelligence service can determine the location from which a "black" radio station is broadcasting by using direction-finding equipment. This information, however, will not typically be available to the average listener.

22. G. J. A. O'Toole, *Honorable Treachery: A History of U.S. Intelligence, Espionage, and Covert Action from the American Revolution to the CIA* (New York: Atlantic Monthly, 1991), 236–39. Typically, the stories run by the *Providence Journal* were slightly skewed or exaggerated versions of the original intelligence information. This had the useful effect of not alerting the Germans to the fact that their operations had been penetrated. In a similar vein, British intelligence made an extensive covert effort to bolster opinion in America in favor of Great Britain and against isolationism before the United States entered World War II. According to accounts taken from a still-secret British official history, British intelligence activities in the United States included planting stories with friendly journalists and newspapers, using a New York radio station as an unwitting propaganda vehicle, establishing front groups, and harassing opposition figures in Congress and in the American labor movement. See David Ignatius, "How Churchill's Agents Secretly Manipulated the U.S. before Pearl Harbor," *Washington Post,* September 17, 1989, Outlook section, 1. It remains unclear to what extent the British program was kept secret from the U.S. government and from President Roosevelt in particular. According to Ignatius's account, when the "secret" British history was completed toward the war's end, copies were given not only to Churchill and British intelligence officials but to Roosevelt as well. For an account of this activity, see Thomas E. Mahl, *Desperate Deception: British Covert Action Operations in the United States, 1939–44* (Washington, D.C.: Brassey's, 1998). British activities included propaganda and "dirty tricks" aimed at defeating Congressman Hamilton Fish, a prominent isolationist (chap. 6).

23. The National Voice of Iran (NVOI) and its inflammatory anti-American rhetoric are discussed in a CIA study, "Soviet Covert Action and Propaganda," presented to the Oversight Subcommittee, Permanent Select Committee on Intelligence, House of Representatives, February 6, 1980, by the deputy director for operations, Central Intelligence Agency. The study is reproduced in U.S. House of Representatives, Permanent Select Committee on Intelligence, Subcommittee on Oversight, *Soviet Covert Action (The Forgery Offensive): Hearings,* 96th Cong., 2d sess., 1980. The discussion of the NVOI appears on pages 78–79.

24. Ray S. Cline, *The CIA: Reality vs. Myth,* rev. ed. (Washington, D.C.: Acropolis, 1982), 151.

25. Following the public confirmation by Senator Clifford Case that they had enjoyed covert CIA funding, Congress decided in 1973 to support the radio operations

openly via the Board for International Broadcasting, which was established as an independent federal agency. Cord Meyer, *Facing Reality: From World Federalism to the CIA* (New York: Harper and Row, 1980), 110–13.

26. The speech was also published in the *New York Times,* which received it from the Department of State. However, the version provided to foreign media included thirty-four paragraphs on Soviet foreign policy that were absent from the *New York Times* version. From the fact that the Soviets never disputed their authenticity, John Ranelagh concludes that the additional paragraphs were genuine (*The Agency: The Rise and Decline of the CIA* [New York: Simon and Schuster, 1986], 287 n). According to Ranelagh, the CIA received two copies of the text, a complete version (presumably from a source in the Soviet Union) as well as an expurgated version from an East European source. The explanation of the difference between the two versions would then be that to help protect the (Soviet) source, the complete version was made available only to non-U.S. newspapers, in order to obscure the link between it and American intelligence. However it seems equally plausible that the thirty-four extra paragraphs made available to the foreign media were written by CIA experts in Khrushchev's style and were designed to cause confusion in the Soviet bloc countries. If true, the reason the U.S. government gave the *New York Times* only the genuine version of the speech was presumably to reduce the possibility that American public opinion would be misled by the fictional segments.

27. Jerrold L. Schecter and Peter S. Deriabin, *The Spy Who Saved the World* (New York: Scribner, 1992), 380–88.

28. Ignatius, "How Churchill's Agents Secretly Manipulated the U.S. before Pearl Harbor." See also Mahl, *Desperate Deception,* 34.

29. For examples and discussion of this technique as used by the former Soviet Union, see U.S. House of Representatives, Permanent Select Committee on Intelligence, *Soviet Covert Action (The Forgery Offensive),* and U.S. Department of State, *Soviet Influence Activities: A Report on Active Measures and Propaganda, 1986–87,* August 1987, 29–32 and 79–80. A question relating to a possible U.S. use of this technique has arisen with respect to the CIA's dissemination of Khrushchev's "secret speech" on Stalin. See note 26 above.

30. The term is derived from the Russian word *dezinformatsia,* which refers to the active-measures technique of misleading an audience to induce it to act in one's own interest. See Shultz and Godson, *Dezinformatsia,* 194–95.

31. Edwin Meese III, *With Reagan: The Inside Story* (Washington, D.C.: Regnery Gateway, 1992), 170–71.

32. Defending its 1991 ban of the Communist Party before the Russian Constitutional Court, the Russian government released documents from the party archives showing that its International Department had covertly supported over the years nearly a hundred parties and friendly political groups in some eighty countries. As late as 1988, three million dollars was secretly transferred to the Communist Party of the United States, and over twenty million during the 1980s. These funds were typically passed to the foreign recipients through KGB channels; in the 1920s and 1930s, the Comintern was used for this purpose. See Michael Dobbs, "Panhandling the Kremlin: How Gus Hall Got Millions," *Washington Post,* March 1, 1992, A1, and Harvey Klehr, John Earl Haynes, and Kiril Mikhailovich Anderson, *The Soviet World of American Communism* (New Haven, Conn.: Yale University Press, 1998), chap. 2.

33. For an overview of this effort, see Sallie Pisani, *The CIA and the Marshall Plan* (Lawrence: University Press of Kansas, 1991).

34. Cline, *The CIA,* 123–24.

35. NSC Directive 10/2 (June 1948), as cited in Cline, *The CIA,* 126.

36. U.S. Senate, Church Committee, *Final Report,* book 1: *Foreign and Military Intelligence,* 94th Cong., 2d sess., 1976, S. Rept. 94–755, 145.

37. Cline, *The CIA,* 150–51.

38. Church Committee, *Staff Report: Covert Action in Chile: 1963–1973,* 94th Cong., 1st sess., 1975, Committee Print, 29, 45.

39. Church Committee, *Staff Report,* 49 [emphasis in original].

40. Gregory F. Treverton, *Covert Action: The Limits of Intervention in the Postwar World* (New York: Basic Books, 1987), 142.

41. Treverton, *Covert Action,* 143.

42. Early in the Cold War, the CIA organized coups in Iran (1953) and Guatemala (1954). Kermit Roosevelt, *Countercoup: The Struggle for Control of Iran* (New York: McGraw-Hill, 1979); James Risen, "How a Plot Convulsed Iran in '53 (and in '79): A Secret CIA History," *New York Times,* April 16, 2000; Nick Cullather, *Secret History: The CIA's Classified Account of Its Operations in Guatemala, 1952–54* (Stanford, Calif.: Stanford University Press, 2000); and Richard H. Immerman, *The CIA in Guatemala* (Austin: University of Texas Press, 1982).

43. See Church Committee, *Alleged Assassination Plots Involving Foreign Leaders: Interim Report,* 94th Cong., 1st sess., 1975, S. Rept. 94-465, for the committee's investigation of these issues.

44. Executive Order 11905, "United States Foreign Intelligence Activities," February 18, 1976, sect. 5(g) [41 Fed. Reg. 7733 (1976)].

45. Executive Order 12036, January 24, 1978, sect. 2-305 [43 Fed. Reg. 3687 (1978)] and Executive Order 12333, December 4, 1981, sect. 2.11 [48 Fed. Reg. 59947 (1981)]. Both provisions drop the adjective "political," but the meaning is presumably unchanged.

46. Broadly speaking, the issue is whether the executive order banning assassination also prohibits operations that might, inadvertently, result in the death of a political leader or (more restrictively) might reasonably be thought to expose a political figure to a significant risk of being killed.

47. Jules Witcover, *Sabotage at Black Tom: Imperial Germany's Secret War in America, 1914–1917* (Chapel Hill, N.C.: Algonquin, 1989).

48. Testimony of Stansfield Turner, in U.S. House of Representatives, Permanent Select Committee on Intelligence, Subcommittee on Legislation, *HR 1013, HR 1371, and Other Proposals Which Address the Issue of Affording Prior Notice of Covert Actions to the Congress: Hearings,* 100th Cong., 1st sess., 1987, 44–49.

49. For a recent account of the covert program to assist the mujahedeen by someone involved in its management, see Mohammad Yousaf and Mark Adkin, *The Bear Trap: Afghanistan's Untold Story* (London: Leo Cooper, 1992). Yousaf was the head of the Afghan section of Pakistan's intelligence service in the mid-1980s.

50. Sefton Delmer, *Black Boomerang* (New York: Viking, 1962), 120.

51. Note that the 1991 law (PL 102-88) which defines covert action refers to activities "where it is intended that the role of the United States Government will not be apparent or *acknowledged publicly*" [emphasis supplied]. This would appear to envisage cases where the government's role, though apparent to an observer of international affairs, or even reported in the press, is not publicly acknowledged.

52. See the discussion of this incident in chapter 3.

53. For a more favorable view of the status of covert activities under international law, see W. Michael Reisman and James E. Baker, *Regulating Covert Action: Practices, Contexts, and Policies of Covert Coercion Abroad in International and American Law* (New Haven, Conn.: Yale University Press, 1992). In general, Riesman and Baker argue that the actual practice of states and the reaction of states and the international community to that practice imply that many covert actions are not necessarily illegal under international law. However, in making this argument, they interpret rather narrowly the nonintervention provisions of the UN Charter and rather broadly such key notions as "covert action," "law," and "accepted practice."

54. Nikita S. Khrushchev, *Khrushchev Remembers: The Last Testament* (Boston: Little, Brown, 1974), 447–48.

55. See John Dyson, *Sink the Rainbow! An Enquiry into the "Greenpeace Affair"* (London: Gollancz, 1986), 157–86, for an account of the French government's handling of the episode.

56. Section 662(a) of the Foreign Assistance Act of 1961, as amended. Hughes-Ryan was formally repealed with passage of the Intelligence Authorization Act for fiscal year 1991. The new law retained the presidential finding requirement and broadened it to include covert actions carried out not only by the CIA but by all U.S. government agencies. In addition, it mandated that all findings be "in writing." If there is a need to take immediate action and no time to produce a written finding, the president is still obligated to produce a written finding "no . . . more than 48 hours after the decision is made" to authorize the activity.

57. In its *Final Report,* the Church Committee ignored the issue of plausible denial in discussing the amendment's effects. Instead, it describes the two results of the amendment as (1) the statutory responsibility of the executive branch to inform Congress about covert actions, and (2) the inclusion of the Senate and House foreign affairs committees among the committees to be informed. Book 1: *Foreign and Military Intelligence,* 151.

58. *Report of the Congressional Committees Investigating the Iran-Contra Affair,* 100th Cong., 1st sess., 1987, H. Rept. 100-433, S. Rept. 100-216, 271.

59. "Iraq Liberation Act of 1998," L. 105-338, October 31, 1998. The measure was enacted into law following reports of failed covert efforts to remove Saddam Hussein from power. Don Oberdorfer, "A Covert Plan to Oust Hussein," *Washington Post Weekly Edition,* January 25–31, 1993, 19, and Jim Hoagland, "How CIA's Secret War on Saddam Collapsed," *Washington Post,* June 26, 1997, A21. Also see Marie Colvin, "Revealed: CIA's Bungled Iraqi Coup," *The Sunday Times (London),* April 2, 2000.

60. David Lowe, "Idea to Reality: A Brief History of the National Endowment for Democracy," provides an account of the legislative history of NED's creation. Available at www.ned.org/about/about.html.

61. For example, the Konrad Adenauer Foundation (Stiftung), associated with the Christian Democratic Party, has, according to its own self-description,

> for more than thirty years . . . been cooperating with partners everywhere in the world. . . . [The] budget for these international activities . . . is funded by the [German] Federal Ministry for Economic Cooperation and Development as well as by the Foreign Office. . . . [P]artners abroad include political parties, parliaments and governments; education and research institutes; universities; industry confederations and trade unions; cooperative societies; women's, environmental, and self-help organisations; and the media. Basically, all . . . projects serve the goal of promoting democracy and development, improving understanding across national and cultural borders, providing help towards self-help, and combatting the root causes of poverty and environmental destruction. [Quoted at www.kas.de/stiftung/englisch/international.html.]

62. Christopher Andrew, *Her Majesty's Secret Service: The Making of the British Intelligence Community* (New York: Viking, 1986), 476–77. It has been suggested that the creation of SOE as an agency separate from the MI6 was due in part to domestic political considerations. By placing SOE under the minister of economic warfare, a member of the Labour party, Churchill met the demands of his coalition partners for a share of control of the intelligence services. M. R. D. Foot, *SOE: An Outline History of the Special Operations Executive, 1940–46,* rev. ed. (n.p.: University Publications of America, 1986), 19–20.

63. Church Committee, *Final Report,* book 1, 106. See also Arthur B. Darling, *The Central Intelligence Agency: An Instrument of Government, to 1950* (University Park: Pennsylvania State University Press, 1990), 245–81. (Darling was CIA historian from 1952 to 1954; originally classified, Darling's history was released in 1989 under the agency's Historical Review Program.)

64. The name was later changed to the Directorate of Operations (DDO).

65. Church Committee, *Final Report,* book 1, 107–108.

66. For a critique of the concept of the elements of intelligence, see Kenneth G. Robertson, "The Study of Intelligence in the United States," in *Comparing Foreign Intelligence: The U.S., the USSR, the UK and the Third World,* ed. Roy Godson (McLean, Va.: Pergamon-Brassey's, 1988), 26–28.

67. Accordingly, George Kennan, the senior State Department official involved in establishing OPC's initial operational guidelines, argued that covert action was an instrument of foreign policy. It was therefore the particular concern of the Department of State and the national military establishment. Certain attributes placed it in the Central Intelligence Agency, but its "policy direction and guidance" properly belonged to the Department and the Establishment. Hence, during peacetime, it was the secretary of state's prerogative to name the head of OPC and direct its activities. Darling, *The Central Intelligence Agency,* 277.

CHAPTER 5: SPY VERSUS SPY: COUNTERINTELLIGENCE

1. The term *counterintelligence* is sometimes defined to include protection against "sabotage, or assassinations conducted for or on behalf of foreign powers, organizations or persons, or international terrorist activities." (The quoted words are from the definition of counterintelligence in President Reagan's Executive Order 12333 of December 4, 1981, "United States Intelligence Activities," para. 3.4[a].) This is a rea-

sonable development, since these activities are identical with or similar to the kinds of covert action a hostile intelligence service might carry out; protecting against them, therefore, is likely to involve many of the same skills and methods as protecting against hostile intelligence activities.

2. The executive order definition of counterintelligence referred to in note 1, above, specifically excludes "personnel, physical, document or communications security programs." This reflects the bureaucratic fact that, in general, U.S. departments and agencies dealing with secret information are responsible for the security programs to protect that information, while the FBI and CIA have primary responsibility for counterintelligence (as defined in the executive order) at home and abroad, respectively. For our (theoretical) purposes, however, security should be considered as a part of counterintelligence, since it serves the same function.

3. Harold C. Relyea, "The Presidency and the People's Right to Know," in *The Presidency and Information Policy,* ed. Harold C. Relyea (New York: Center for the Study of the Presidency, 1981), 11–19.

4. "Regulations Establishing Minimum Standards for the Classification, Transmission, and Handling, by Departments and Agencies of the Executive Branch, of Official Information Which Requires Safeguarding in the Interest of the Security of the United States," Executive Order 10290, September 24,1951.

5. Executive Order 12958, "Classified National Security Information," April 17, 1995. The Information Security Oversight Office (ISOO) is the entity responsible for overseeing the government's security classification program. The ISOO's annual report provides an overview of the classification and declassification program. According to the most recent report, 3,846 government officials had initial classification authority. and more than eight million decisions to classify documents were made during the year: Of these, CIA accounted for 44 percent; the Defense Department, 27 percent; the National Reconnaissance Office, 24 percent; the Justice Department, 2 percent; the State Department, 2 percent; and all other agencies, 1 percent. (Nearly 127 million pages of previous classified materials were declassified.) ISOO, *FY1999 Report to the President,* August 15, 2000. ISOO annual reports can be found at www.fas.org/sgp/isoo/index.html.

6. Executive Order [hereafter EO] 12958, sect. 1.3.

7. National Security Act of 1947, sect. 102(d) (3) [50 USC 403 (d) (3)]. The authority of the DCI and of the secretaries of state, defense, and energy to establish special access programs is contained in EO 12958, sect. 4.4.

8. EO 12958, sect. 4.4(a) and (b)(3). The oversight is conducted by the director of the Information Security Oversight Office, who has an overall responsibility for the operation of the national security information classification system.

9. EO 12958 defines "need-to-know" as "a determination . . . by a . . . holder of classified information that a prospective recipient requires access . . . in order to perform or assist in a lawful and authorized governmental function" (sect. 4.1[c]).

10. *Keeping the Nation's Secrets: A Report to the Secretary of Defense by the Commission to Review DoD Security Policies and Practices,* November 1985, 23, cited in U.S. Senate, Select Committee on Intelligence, *Meeting the Espionage Challenge: A Review of United States Counterintelligence and Security Programs,* 99th Cong., 2d sess., 1986, S. Rept. 99-522, 66.

11. Until 1989, the Soviet Union published only a single number, which it described as its defense budget. However, the number was patently too small to include all Soviet military expenditures. In 1989, disclosing a much higher total defense expenditure, the Soviets explained that the previously published budget figure had included only the salaries and upkeep of the members of the armed forces. Similarly, the People's Republic of China publishes a figure that purports to represent its defense spending; again, it is much too low, but it is not known what part of China's defense spending is included in it, if indeed the figure is meaningful at all.

12. *Keeping the Nation's Secrets,* 49.

13. For an analysis of the system of official secrecy in Great Britain, broadly compared with those of Sweden and the United States, see K. G. Robertson, *Public Secrets: A Study in the Development of Government Secrecy* (New York: St. Martin's, 1982). Since the publication of Robertson's study, Great Britain has enacted two significant pieces of legislation affecting government secrecy: an amendment (in 1989) to the Official Secrets Act, and a Freedom of Information Act (in 2000.) For a discussion of the Official Secrets Act and the 1989 amendment, see Rosamund Thomas, *Espionage and Secrecy: The Official Secrets Acts 1911–1989 of the United Kingdom* (New York: Routledge, 1991). The text of the Freedom of Information Act can be found at www.legislation.hmso.gov.uk/acts/acts2000/20000036.htm.

14. In 1997, a commission set up to review government classification programs claimed that "the classification system . . . is used too often to deny the public an understanding of the policymaking process" and that "the best way to ensure that secrecy is respected, and that the most important secrets *remain* secret, is for secrecy to be returned to its limited but necessary role. Secrets can be protected more effectively if secrecy is reduced overall." *Secrecy: Report of the Commission on Protecting and Reducing Government Secrecy* (Washington, D.C.: Government Printing Office, 1997), xxi [emphasis in original], available at www.access.gpo.gov/int.

15. EO 12958 states that "in no case shall information be classified in order to . . . prevent embarrassment to a person, organization, or agency" (sect. 1.8[a][2]). This would seem to leave open the possibility of classifying information in order to prevent embarrassment to the government itself. This implication is strengthened by the fact that "information that would seriously and demonstrably impair relations between the United States and a foreign government" is exempted from automatic declassification (sect. 3.4[b][6]).

16. Bob Woodward, "CIA Paid Millions to Jordan's King Hussein," *Washington Post,* February 18, 1977, A1.

17. Atomic Energy Act of 1954, sect. 11y [42 USC 2014y].

18. Sect. 148 [42 USC 2168].

19. Adm. B. R. Inman, "National Security and Technical Information," paper presented to the annual meeting of the American Association for the Advancement of Science, January 1982, Washington, D.C. mimeo.

20. U.S. Senate, Committee on Commerce, Science, and Transportation, *Statement of Louis J. Freeh, Director, FBI on July 25, 1996, Regarding "Impact of Encryption on Law Enforcement and Public Safety"* [Hereafter Freeh statement]. Available at www.fas.org/irp/congress/1996_hr/s960725f.htm.

21. Additionally, it was proposed that all encryption software manufacturers be required to provide an "escrow key"—that is, information that would allow the

rapid breaking of the resulting cipher. A law enforcement agency could then use this key to read intercepted materials or seized computer data, provided that it had obtained a search warrant. As FBI Director Freeh argued, strong commercially available "encryption has the effect of upsetting the delicate legal balance of the Fourth Amendment, since when a judge issues a search warrant it will be of no practical value when this type of encryption is encountered" (Freeh statement). According to Freeh, key escrow encryption would restore that balance. This argument failed to gain much support.

22. On January 12, 2000, the U.S. Department of Commerce (DOC) announced streamlined regulations that substantially allowed the unfettered export of quite powerful encryption software. DOC Press release, available at www.fas.org/irp/news/2000/01/000113-crypto-bxa.htm.

23. In the United States, at least theoretically, lack of loyalty to the government disqualified a person from any federal civil service position; however, this criterion has been in effect dropped with respect to jobs that do not require access to classified information. See Guenter Lewy, "The Federal Loyalty-Security Program," in *Intelligence Requirements for the 1980's: Domestic Intelligence,* ed. Roy Godson (Lexington, Mass.: Lexington, 1986), 147 and passim, for a discussion of this development. The loyalty requirement is contained in President Truman's Executive Order 10450, "Security Requirements for Government Employment," April 27, 1953.

24. Provided that no violent, criminal action had been taken based on this belief. Even then, it would not be permissible to compile a complete membership list of the organization, unless it could be shown that the membership at large was involved in the organization's violent activities. These issues are discussed further in the next chapter.

25. U.S. Senate, Subcommittee on Criminal Laws and Procedures Committee on the Judiciary, *Hearings on the Erosion of Law Enforcement Intelligence and Its Impact on the Public Security,* part 8, 95th Cong., 2d sess., 1978, as cited in Guenter Lewy, "The Federal Loyalty-Security Program," 152.

26. In 1983, the Office of Technology Assessment (OTA) of the U.S. Congress produced a study generally critical of the claims made on behalf of the polygraph. *Scientific Validity of Polygraph Testing: A Research Review and Evaluation-Technical Memorandum,* OTA-TM-H-15 (Washington, D.C.: Government Printing Office, 1983). The following year, the Defense Department, whose National Security Agency makes widespread use of the polygraph, published a rebuttal. U.S. Department of Defense, *The Accuracy and Utility of Polygraph Testing* (Washington, D.C.: Government Printing Office, 1984).

27. See the discussion, later in this chapter, of the Cuban double-cross operation run against the United States. Presumably, at least some of these double agents, whom the intelligence community accepted as genuine, had been subjected to polygraph tests.

28. These polygraph sessions are discussed in U.S. Senate, Select Committee on Intelligence, *An Assessment of the Aldrich H. Ames Espionage Case and Its Implications for U.S. Intelligence,* November 1, 1994, 32–34, 71–74. According to the FBI, a June 1993 review of the 1986 polygraph results by its experts indicated deception on Ames's part; however, by the time this reexamination occurred, Ames was already under "intensive investigation" (82). Thus, it is difficult to know to what extent the subsequent review of the polygraph results was affected by the knowledge that there were other strong grounds for suspicion.

29. See U.S. Senate, Select Committee on Intelligence, *Meeting the Espionage Challenge,* 12–15, for a summary of the major cases between 1980 and 1986. For a useful listing of some later cases, see Defense Security Service, *Recent Espionage Cases, 1975–1999: Summaries and Sources,* Security Research Center (September 1999), available at www.dss.mil/training/pub.htm.

30. For example, an army warrant officer who sold top secret communications intelligence to the Soviet Union and Warsaw Pact nations for six years told an undercover FBI agent, "I wasn't terribly short of money. I just decided I didn't ever want to worry where my next dollar was coming from. I'm not anti-American. I wave the flag as much as anybody else." Defense Security Service, *Recent Espionage Cases,* 22.

31. On the other hand, Hanssen did not appear to have been motivated by greed, either. In one message, he suggests that his attraction to Soviet intelligence began when he read Kim Philby's memoirs at the age of fourteen; this, however, is nonsense, since Hanssen was born in 1944, and Philby's book was not published until the late 1960s. This message is cited in the U.S. government's affidavit in support of arrest and search warrants against Hanssen, filed in the U.S. District Court for the Eastern District of Virginia. (Other messages cited in the affidavit show Hanssen as relatively unconcerned about money, although he does ask for an initial payment of a hundred thousand dollars.) As noted in chapter 2, the affidavit may be found at www.fas.org/irp/ops/ci/hanssen_affidavit.html.

32. As noted in a Senate Intelligence Committee report, "The hostile intelligence threat to U.S. computer systems is magnified by the enormous growth in the number and power of computers and the vast amount of data contained in them. . . . Computers multiply enormously the information to which a single individual may obtain access." (*Meeting the Espionage Challenge,* 35–36.) For a lively account of lax computer security and the computer-related espionage that resulted, see Clifford Stoll, *The Cuckoo's Egg: Tracking a Spy through the Maze of Computer Espionage* (New York: Doubleday, 1989).

33. For an example, see text to note 70 in chap. 2.

34. U.S. Senate, Select Committee on Intelligence, *Meeting the Espionage Challenge,* 34–35.

35. As former Defense Secretary James Schlesinger testified in 1987,

> In past years, the Soviets were sufficiently behind us that we were able to detect penetrations, and neutralize them. . . . We now face a rising curve of Soviet technology, with no gap between what the Soviets can do and what we can do; indeed, in some areas they have been ahead of us. . . . With respect to both embassy construction and operations, we have a lot to learn from the Soviets. The Soviets have thought long and hard about how to design embassies for security, and they have thought long and hard about the construction process.

Testimony of James Schlesinger before the Senate Budget Committee, as cited in "For the Record," *Washington Post,* July 1, 1987, A18.

36. Christopher Andrew and Oleg Gordievsky, *KGB: The Inside Story of Its Foreign Operations from Lenin to Gorbachev* (New York: HarperCollins, 1990; HarperPerennial edition, 1991), 296–98, 389–90, and 598–99.

37. As already noted, Howard evaded FBI surveillance and turned up several months later in Moscow. Yurchenko redefected to the Soviet Union, which suggests that

his original defection might have been bogus and that he might have been dispatched by the Soviets to mislead U.S. intelligence or for some other reason. If so, giving up Pelton and Howard—no longer employed by the United States, they were presumably of no further use to the Soviets in any case—was intended to bolster Yurchenko's authenticity or bona fides. See David Wise, *The Spy Who Got Away: The Inside Story of Edward Lee Howard* (New York: Random House, 1988), 17–21 and passim.

38. For a discussion of "Tricycle" (a Yugoslav named Dusko Popov) and the questionnaire's handling, see B. Bruce Briggs, "Another Ride on Tricycle," *Intelligence and National Security* 7, no. 2 (April 1992): 77–100. Interestingly, the questionnaire was in American hands at the same time as the famous Japanese "bomb plot" message of September 1941. In this intercepted message, the Japanese consulate in Honolulu was instructed to provide the precise berths of the U.S. Navy ships at Pearl Harbor. The message was decoded, but apparently no one took the next step of asking why Japan wanted such detailed information. See Gordon W. Prange, *At Dawn We Slept: The Untold Story of Pearl Harbor* (New York: McGraw-Hill, 1981), 248–52.

39. For an account of what was apparently the longest-running U.S. double-agent case of the Cold War, see David Wise, *Cassidy's Run: The Secret Spy War over Nerve Gas* (New York: Random House, 2000), the story of a U.S. Army master sergeant, Joseph Cassidy, who was "dangled" in front of Soviet intelligence and run as a double agent for more than two decades. According to Wise, the case exposed nearly a dozen Soviet case officers, surfaced three "illegals" and an "Armageddon code" employed by Soviet intelligence, and provided insights into Soviet tradecraft. Over that period, Cassidy provided more than 4,500 pages of classified documents to the Soviets, including "information" designed to mislead Soviet analysts about U.S. successes in developing chemical weapons. One goal was to induce the Soviet Union to spend time and resources on trying to duplicate, and counter, a supposed chemical weapon whose formula U.S. scientists had already determined was a dead end (45–51). Wise speculates that the deception backfired when Soviet scientists were able to overcome the problems that had stymied the United States and actually produced a deadly new chemical; however, his evidence for this is circumstantial and not particularly persuasive (63–69).

40. John C. Masterman, *The Double-Cross System in the War of 1939 to 1945* (New Haven, Conn.: Yale University Press, 1972), 3 [emphasis original]. This work, by the man who managed the system, is the source of the account in the text; further citations are from 30–31, 38–40, 41, 49, and 58.

41. The original agent had worked for the German Abwehr (military intelligence) in the late 1930s; the British, aware of his existence, allowed him to continue operating in part because he had also had some dealings with British MI6, which would have complicated any attempt to prosecute him.

42. Even after the Allied landings at Normandy on June 6, British double agents continued to carry out the deception. For instance, on June 9, "Garbo" (codename for Juan Pujol, one of MI5's more successful double agents) radioed Berlin that the invasion at Normandy was "diversionary," designed to draw in German reserves and weaken the forces protecting Calais, where the real assault was to take place. After receiving the message, the German high command countermanded a previously given order for a German counterattack on the Allied beachhead at Normandy. In gratitude for the "intelligence" Pujol had provided, Hitler awarded him the Iron Cross. Christopher Andrew,

Her Majesty's Secret Service: The Making of the British Intelligence Community (New York: Viking, 1986), 488. For an account of Pujol's life as a British double agent, see Juan Pujol with Nigel West, *Garbo* (London: Weidenfeld and Nicolson, 1985).

43. Michael Wines and Ronald J. Ostrow, "Cuban Defector Claims Double Agents Duped U.S.," *Washington Post,* August 12, 1987, A8.

44. According to the former ranking minority member of the Permanent Select Committee on Intelligence of the U.S. House of Representatives, "almost all" U.S.-recruited "East German 'agents' were found to be 'doubles'" as well. Bud Shuster, "HiTech vs. Human Spying," *Washington Times,* February 11, 1992, F3.

45. NSA Director Lt. Gen. Michael V. Hayden, USAF, described his agency's major challenges as follows: "Our adversary communications are now based upon the developmental cycle of a global industry that is literally moving at the speed of light[—] . . . cell phones, encryption, *fiber-optic communications,* digital communications." Dan Verton, "NSA Warns It Can't Keep Up with Rapid Changes in IT," Infoworld.com, February 19, 2001 [emphasis supplied].

46. Two general treatments of the issue of military deception are Donald Daniel and Katherine Herbig, eds., *Strategic Military Deception* (New York: Pergamon, 1982) and John Gooch and Amos Perlmutter, *Military Deception and Strategic Surprise* (London: Frank Cass, 1982).

47. On deception before and during World War II, see: Michael Howard, *British Intelligence in the Second World War: Strategic Deception* (London: Her Majesty's Stationery Office, 1990); Michael Mihalka, *German Strategic Deception in the 1930s,* RandNote N-1557-NA (Santa Monica, Calif.: RAND, 1980); Barton Whaley, "Covert Rearmament in Germany 1919–1939: Deception and Misperception," *Journal of Strategic Studies,* no. 5 (March 1982): 3–39; Barton Whaley, *Codeword Barbarossa* (Cambridge, Mass.: MIT, 1973); David M. Glantz, *Soviet Military Deception in the Second World War* (London: Frank Cass, 1989); Charles Cruickshank, *Deception in World War II* (Oxford: Oxford University Press, 1979); Michael Handel, ed., *Strategic and Operational Deception in the Second World War* (London: Frank Cass, 1987); and a special issue of *Intelligence and National Security* 2, no. 3 (July 1987).

48. "Cheka" is an acronym based on the second and third words in Russian of the formal name "All-Russian Extraordinary Commission to Combat Counterrevolution and Sabotage."

49. For a discussion of the Trust, see John J. Dziak, *Chekisty: A History of the KGB* (Lexington, Mass.: Heath, Lexington, 1988), 47–50, and Andrew and Gordievsky, *KGB: The Inside Story,* 97–106.

In a similar fashion, Soviet and Polish intelligence in the years following World War II were able, using a Polish double agent, to convince the British and the Americans that a Polish resistance group (Wolnosc i Niepodleglosc, WiN) was still viable within Poland and was worth providing with covert assistance; in fact, WiN was under the control of the KGB and the Polish security service. Until 1952, when the Poles and the Soviets publicly revealed their deception, the Polish service was able to use WiN to surface the remaining active anticommunists within Poland and to pass along misleading intelligence on Poland's internal situation to the West. Dziak, *Chekisty,* 123–24.

50. John Prados, *The Soviet Estimate: U.S. Intelligence Analysis and Russian Military Strength* (New York: Dial, 1982), 42–43.

51. See Arnold L. Horelick and Myron Rush, *Strategic Power and Soviet Foreign Policy* (Chicago: University of Chicago Press, 1966), 42–116, for a full discussion of these exaggerated claims and the purposes they served.

52. Horelick and Rush, *Strategic Power,* 117–40.

53. Prange, *At Dawn We Slept,* 338, 353.

54. One must also take into consideration how the adversary processes the information. If, for instance, because of the time pressure of combat, he will not have the opportunity to analyze the photographs fully before having to take action, it may be possible to fool him with an inferior imitation. By the time detailed analysis reveals to him that the object was a dummy, he will have already acted on the basis of his mistaken first impression. This is another reason why successful deception operations are more to be expected in wartime than in peacetime.

55. Howard, *British Intelligence in the Second World War: Strategic Deception,* 224.

56. H. J. Giskes, *London Calling North Pole* (London: William Kimber, 1953) and M. R. D. Foot, *SOE: An Outline History of the Special Operations Executive, 1940–46,* rev. ed. (Frederick, Md.: University Publications of America, 1986), 130–34. Giskes was the German counterintelligence officer who ran the operation. It does not appear that the Germans used this channel to deceive the British on matters other than the operations of their supposed SOE agents in the Netherlands.

57. This incident is recounted in H. M. G. Lauwers, "Epilogue," in Giskes, *London Calling North Pole,* 194. Lauwers, a Dutch SOE agent captured by the Germans, tried unsuccessfully to alert London to the deception operation by transmitting messages without the proper security checks. Unfortunately, headquarters ignored their absence and treated the messages as genuine.

Leo Marks, the officer in charge of devising SOE's codes, suggests that suspicions concerning the agents in Holland were downplayed in part because the SOE leadership feared that a failure of this magnitude, if confirmed, would have resulted in the organization's being closed down or subordinated to its bureaucratic rival, the Secret Intelligence Service, MI6. *Between Silk and Cyanide: The Story of the S.O.E.'s Code War* (London: HarperCollins, 1998), 112–25, 146–48.

58. Stansfield Turner, *Secrecy and Democracy: The CIA in Transition* (Boston: Houghton Mifflin, 1985; Harper and Row, 1986), 65.

59. As with everything else, a trade-off is involved here. Varying the orbit means that some satellites follow orbits that are less than optimal in coverage; what is required is a balance between the ordinary measures of cost-effectiveness and the more subtle (and less measurable) requirement to counter the adversary's concealment and deception operations.

60. David Kahn, an expert on cryptology, makes these points in "Discussion," in *Intelligence Requirements for the 1980s: Clandestine Collection,* ed. Roy Godson (Washington, D.C.: National Strategy Information Center, 1982), 119.

61. Andrew and Gordievsky, *KGB: The Inside Story,* 529–30, 610.

62. The minutes of the planning meeting are reproduced in David E. Murphy, Sergei A. Kondrashev, and George Bailey, *Battleground Berlin: CIA vs. KGB in the Cold War* (New Haven, Conn.: Yale University Press, 1997), 449–53.

63. The CIA had noticed that one type of U.S. electric cipher machine transmitted an electrical signal representing the plaintext character (the machine's input) along with the enciphered character (its intended output); the former signal, although faint compared to the enciphered character, could be picked up from the transmission wire, far away from the cipher machine. It turned out that Soviet cipher machines suffered from the same defect, enabling the United States to recover the plaintext messages along with their encrypted versions. John Ranelagh. *The Agency: The Rise and Decline of the CIA* (New York: Simon and Schuster, 1986), 140.

Murphy et al., *Battleground Berlin,* denies that this "echo effect" existed (206–207). It is impossible to settle this dispute here; the account in the text nevertheless serves to illustrate the types of considerations to which an operation of this sort could give rise.

64. Murphy et al., *Battleground Berlin,* 289.

65. Murphy et al., *Battleground Berlin,* 295.

66. Why would the Soviets want to close down the operation if they were using it to pass deceptive information? They might have done so to harm CIA and MI6 morale, believing the Western powers would soon discover that the Soviets knew about the operation in any case. Or, the Soviets might have shut the operation down simply because the cost in "chicken feed" (legitimate information deliberately given away to bolster confidence in the operation) was higher than they wished to pay. Possibly the discovery was accidental, in the sense that the repair party was not in the know and stumbled across the tunnel because no one who *was* in the know had thought to prevent it from working in the tunnel area (if the Soviets were running a deception operation, knowledge of it would be kept within a small circle). Once the United States and Britain became aware of the discovery, they would have become suspicious had the Soviets continued to use the cable without removing the taps.

67. Cruickshank, *Deception in World War II,* 182.

68. This entire controversy has been called the "wilderness of mirrors" and is the subject of a book with that title by David Martin (New York: Harper and Row, 1980). For more recent accounts of the controversy, see David Wise, *Molehunt: The Secret Search for the Traitors That Shattered the CIA* (New York: Random House, 1992) and works cited in note 35, chapter 2.

69. John Barron, *Breaking the Ring* (Boston: Houghton Mifflin, 1987), 23–25.

70. This discussion draws on the U.S. Senate, Select Committee on Intelligence, *An Assessment of the Aldrich H. Ames Espionage Case,* 24–28.

71. Ironically, the KGB behavior in "rolling up" all the cases at once seemed to indicate that the KGB had *not* found out about them from a single, highly placed source; otherwise, it was believed, they would never behave in such a blatant manner, since that would put the source at risk. According to Ames, his KGB handlers recognized that the KGB's behavior was endangering him; they told him that "they regretted putting him in such a position but believed their political leadership felt they had little choice but to take those steps." U.S. Senate, Select Committee on Intelligence, *An Assessment,* 25.

72. U.S. Senate, Select Committee on Intelligence, *An Assessment,* 46–53. Clayton Lonetree, a marine security guard at the U.S. embassy in Moscow, had had a relationship with a Russian woman who was a KGB-controlled asset. A fellow marine initially stated (and later denied) that Lonetree had let the KGB into the U.S. embassy. This

incident obviously had the effect of confusing the investigation and diverting attention away from the possibility—which the CIA was in any case loathe to credit—that a CIA officer was the source of the problem.

73. U.S. Senate, Select Committee on Intelligence, *An Assessment,* 64–66. For various reasons, this initial tip, in November 1989, was not exploited in an efficient manner; Ames was not arrested until February 1994.

CHAPTER 6: GUARDING THE GUARDIANS: THE MANAGEMENT OF INTELLIGENCE

1. Although Senator Church, chairman of the Senate committee formed in 1975 to investigate the intelligence agencies, used the term "rogue elephant" early in the investigation to describe the CIA, that characterization had been generally abandoned by the time the investigation was completed. In the view of Loch Johnson, a Church Committee staffer sympathetic to Senator Church, the chairman's use of the term "derived from a sense that the evidence needed to be dramatized to have an effect upon the public," whereas the final report of the committee "carefully steered clear of the 'rogue elephant' theory." Loch Johnson, *A Season of Inquiry: The Senate Intelligence Investigation* (Lexington: University Press of Kentucky, 1985), 224, 268.

2. U.S. Senate, Select Committee to Study Governmental Operations with Respect to Intelligence Activities, *Alleged Assassination Plots Involving Foreign Leaders: Interim Report,* 94th Cong., 1st sess., 1975, S. Rept 94-495, 263.c.

3. On May 7, 1962, Attorney General Robert F. Kennedy was officially informed of actions taken during 1960 and 1961 in connection with attempts to assassinate Castro, specifically the CIA's involvement in this connection with two Mafia figures, John Roselli and Sam Giancana. The formal necessity for the briefing arose from the fact that the FBI wanted to prosecute Robert Maheu, the CIA's go-between with the Mafia figures, for installing an illegal wiretap, and the CIA wanted to forestall this prosecution to prevent the revelation of the entire story. Kennedy is reported to have been very angry about the Mafia involvement, which would have complicated prosecution of Roselli or Giancana for any involvement they may have had in organized crime; he is not reported as being angry about the assassination attempt itself. Select Committee, *Alleged Assassination Plots,* 131–34.

4. The best evidence for this latter proposition is the lack of outrage exhibited by administration figures when the operations against Castro finally did become public. Admittedly, this point is of the "dog that didn't bark" variety; nevertheless, one would have expected major Kennedy administration members, such as former Defense Secretary Robert McNamara, to express some degree of exasperation had they believed that the CIA had undertaken such an action without approval by higher authority. Instead, McNamara emphasized, in testifying before the Church Committee, his belief that "the CIA was a highly disciplined organization, fully under the control of senior officials of the government" (Select Committee, *Alleged Assassination Plots,* 158, citing McNamara's testimony of July 11, 1975). Robert Kennedy's reaction in 1962 is reported to have been similar; see the preceding note.

5. Christopher Andrew, *Her Majesty's Secret Service: The Making of the British Intelligence Community* (New York: Viking, 1986), 1.

6. Winston S. Churchill, *Marlborough: His Life and Times* (New York: Scribner, 1938), vol. 6, 482–84 and 526–29. Marlborough's opponents claimed that these monies were public funds and should have been accounted for as such; since he had spent the funds to pay his secret agents for information, this would have been impossible. Churchill makes a strong case that his illustrious ancestor behaved properly in using traditional sources of money to finance intelligence operations, which were not otherwise funded by the government.

7. An approximation of the older system seems to have been attempted in the early years of the American republic, when Congress established a contingency fund for the president to use at his discretion to pay persons "serv[ing] the United States in foreign parts." The president was obligated to inform Congress only that money had been spent; neither the purpose for the expenditures nor the persons receiving money had to be disclosed. Closely connected to this practice was the custom adopted by early presidents of using private persons to conduct executive branch business abroad; these "executive agents" were appointed without the advice and consent of the Senate. On the creation of the fund and the early use of these agents, see Stephen F. Knott, *Secret and Sanctioned: Covert Operations and the American Presidency* (New York: Oxford University Press, 1996), 49–60.

8. These provisions originally appeared in the resolutions that established the Senate and House intelligence committees and were enacted into law in 1980; with minor changes, they were retained by the Intelligence Authorization Act, fiscal year 1991. The relevant provisions are sections 501 and 502 of the National Security Act of 1947, as amended.

9. Robert M. Gates, "The CIA and American Foreign Policy," *Foreign Affairs* 66, no. 2 (Winter 1987–88): 225. According to one account, "the Congress received more than 1,000 CIA briefings and 7,000 intelligence reports in 1991." Loch K. Johnson, "Smart Intelligence," *Foreign Policy*, no. 89 (Winter 1992–93): 67. In the 1990s, this trend continued: In the 1990 Intelligence Authorization Act (PL101-193, November 30, 1989), Congress mandated that the appointment of the CIA's inspector general (IG) require Senate confirmation. In addition, the law required the director of central intelligence to send to the congressional oversight committees copies of the IG's semiannual reports to the director on his office's activities and investigations. Subsequently, in the 1999 Intelligence Authorization Act (PL105-272, October 20, 1998), Congress enacted provisions to protect so-called "whistle blowers" within the intelligence community. The act sets out procedures by which intelligence agency employees can provide information on an urgent basis to the oversight committees through their agency's IG and director. Speaking on behalf of the measure, the chairman of the House intelligence committee claimed, "We have created a front door for rank and file information-sharing with Congress." *Congressional Record*, October 7, 1998, H9729.

10. This consciousness of respective "turf" has been reinforced by theories of public administration that, reflecting a variation of the "fact-value" distinction, attempt to draw a clear line between persons who determine policy (politics) and the bureaucracy (administration) whose task it is to implement a chosen policy in the most efficient and rational manner possible. For the classic American statement of this theory, see Woodrow Wilson, "The Study of Administration," *Political Science Quarterly* 2 (June 1887): 197–222. Few serious scholars of public administration accept this dichotomy today, but it remains (in the absence of a coherent alternative view) the prevailing orthodoxy among

bureaucrats themselves and among most reformers intent on improving government administration.

11. To a more limited degree, this organizational theory is reflected in Britain's decision in 1983 to have the chairman of the Joint Intelligence Committee (JIC, the British government body charged with coordinating intelligence collection requirements and producing national-level assessments) be a prime-ministerial appointee and a member of the cabinet office staff; previously, the chairman had been selected from within the ranks of the Foreign Office. The change, recommended by a panel (the Franks Committee) charged with reviewing the performance of British intelligence during the Falklands crisis, was designed to give the chairman of the JIC "a more critical and independent role." For an account of the Franks Committee review, see Robert Cecil, "The Assessment and Acceptance of Intelligence: A Case-Study, " in *British and American Approaches to Intelligence,* ed. K. G. Robertson (London: Macmillan, RUSI Defense Studies Series, 1987), 166–83.

Similarly, the initial impetus for the creation of the U.S. Defense Intelligence Agency (DIA) was, at least in part, attributable to the desire to establish (within the Department of Defense) a centralized assessment organization that would be independent of the more parochial views and interests of the military services and their respective intelligence organizations. For an account of the less-than-successful effort to establish the DIA along these lines, see Patrick Mescall, "The Birth of the Defense Intelligence Agency," in *North American Spies: New Revisionist Essays,* Rhodri Jeffreys-Jones and Andrew Lownie, eds. (Lawrence: University Press of Kansas, 1991), 158–201.

12. Graham E. Fuller, "Intelligence, Immaculately Conceived," *The National Interest,* no. 26 (Winter 1991–92): 98.

13. *Antony and Cleopatra,* 2.5.85–88.

14. The famous military theorist Carl von Clausewitz, who took a very skeptical view of the accuracy and value of most intelligence reporting, believed that constancy of purpose in the face of confusing and contradictory intelligence was a crucial quality for the military commander: "The commander must trust his judgment and stand like a rock on which the waves [of false intelligence] break in vain." Carl von Clausewitz, *On War,* ed. and trans. Michael Howard and Peter Paret (Princeton N.J.: Princeton University Press, 1976), 117.

15. Henry Brandon, *The Retreat of American Power* (New York: Doubleday, 1973), 103. President Johnson is said to have made this remark at a White House dinner in the presence of the DCI, Richard Helms.

16. "Managing/Teaching New Analysts," *Studies in Intelligence* 30, no. 3 (Fall 1986): 3–4. The name of the author (apparently a manager in the Directorate of Intelligence, CIA) was deleted when the article was released in response to a Freedom of Information Act request. I am grateful to Eliot Cohen for calling my attention to this article. He discusses it in "Analysis," in *Intelligence Requirements for the 1990s: Collection, Analysis, Counterintelligence and Covert Action,* ed. Roy Godson (Lexington, Mass.: Heath, Lexington, 1989), 71–96.

17. Cohen, "Analysis," 76.

18. Charles H. Fairbanks Jr., "Where Is the Secret?" *Washington Post,* February 25, 1987, A23 [emphasis in original].

19. Fairbanks, "Where Is the Secret?"

20. Fuller, "Intelligence, Immaculately Conceived," 96–97. However, Fuller does not appear to draw from the inherently ideological character of strategic intelligence analysis any implications for the intelligence-policy relationship. In particular, it does not seem to make him more sympathetic to a policy maker's concern that intelligence views will tread on or undermine an administration's policy positions (see text to note 12 on previous page). As an intelligence analyst, Fuller wants his independence (the ability to tell a policy maker "to shove off"), but he leaves unaddressed the grounds that might justify it.

21. Bob Woodward and Dan Morgan, "Soviet Threat toward Iran Overstated, Casey Concluded," *Washington Post,* January 13, 1987, A1.

22. Loch K. Johnson, *Secret Agencies: U.S. Intelligence in a Hostile World* (New Haven, Conn.: Yale University Press, 1996), 129.

23. Robert M. Gates, "The CIA and Foreign Policy," *Foreign Affairs* 66, no. 2 (Winter 1987–88): 221.

24. This section draws heavily on Abram N. Shulsky and Gary Schmitt, *The Future of Intelligence: Report Prepared for the Working Group on Intelligence Reform* (Washington, D.C.: Consortium for the Study of Intelligence, 1996), 14–16.

25. The National Security Act of 1947, sect. 501(a)(1), as amended [50 USC 413].

26. Gates, "The CIA and Foreign Policy," 225.

27. Intelligence oversight legislation in 1980 explicitly provided that "the foregoing [notification] provision shall not require approval of the intelligence committees as a condition precedent to the initiation of any such anticipated intelligence activity [i.e., covert action]." The Intelligence Authorization Act, fiscal year (FY) 1991, which revised the covert action reporting requirements to Congress, retained a similar provision. The National Security Act of 1947, as amended, section 501(a)(3) [50 USC 413(a)(3)]. An example of one of the committees exercising its advisory "veto" power apparently arose in connection with a Bush administration proposal in 1989 to provide covert assistance to anti-Noriega forces in Panama. See Stephen Engleberg, "U.S. Officials Say Senators Balked at Noriega Ouster," *New York Times,* April 24, 1989, A1.

28. Another example of the open use of the power of the purse over covert action concerned assistance to the noncommunist resistance in Cambodia. In the Conference Report accompanying the Intelligence Authorization Act for FY 1991, submitted in October 1990, the two intelligence committees stated in general terms what assistance could be provided (nonlethal) and for what purpose (to promote a peace settlement). U.S. House, Permanent Select Committee on Intelligence, *Conference Report: Intelligence Authorization Act for Fiscal Year 1991,* 101st Cong., 2d sess., H. Rept. 101-928, 34. The Congress thus denied a Bush administration request for funds for lethal military aid to the noncommunist forces of Cambodia. Peter Rodman, "Supping with Devils," *The National Interest,* no. 25 (Fall 1991): 47.

29. Not only is information on leaks rare, but such information as exists may be misleading. A reference in a news report to a "congressional source" or an "administration official" may not indicate who first tipped off the journalist; the original source may have spoken on "deep background," precluding any reference to him or her at all. Thus, the reference in the article could refer to a source who commented on some

aspect of a story the journalist already had, not the source who first leaked it. Leon V. Sigal, *Reporters and Officials: The Organization and Politics of Newsmaking* (Lexington, Mass.: Heath, 1973), 113–14, discusses the use of deep background to help an official "establish an alibi."

30. U.S. Senate, Select Committee to Study Governmental Operations with Respect to Intelligence Activities [hereafter Church Committee], *Final Report,* book 1: *Foreign and Military Intelligence,* 94th Cong. 2d sess., 1976, S. Rept. 94-755, 522. Halperin was arguing at this point for the abolition of the capacity for carrying out covert operations.

31. As Samuel Huntington has pointedly noted:

> In a different atmosphere . . . congressional committees investigating the CIA might have been curious as to why the Agency failed so miserably in its efforts to assassinate Lumumba and Castro. . . . [At the time, however] no one was interested in the ability of the Agency to do what it was told to do, but only in the immorality of what it was told to do.

Huntington, *American Politics: The Promise of Disharmony* (Cambridge, Mass.: Harvard University Press, 1981), 191.

32. For overviews of the Canadian system, see Geoffrey R. Weller, "Accountability in Canadian Intelligence Services," *International Journal of Intelligence and Counterintelligence* 2, no. 3 (Fall 1988): 415–41, and Reg Whitaker, "The Politics of Security Intelligence Policy-making in Canada: II, 1984–91," *Intelligence and National Security* 7, no. 2 (April 1992): 53–76.

33. See Frank Cain, "Accountability and the Australian Security Intelligence Organization: A Brief History," in *Security and Intelligence in a Changing World: New Perspectives for the 1990s,* ed. A. Stuart Farson, David Stafford, and Wesley K. Wark (London: Frank Cass, 1991), 10–24, 104–25.

34. On the whole, there is little publicly available information on intelligence oversight in countries other than those already noted. While new oversight arrangements have been established in various countries, there has not been a great deal published that describes and compares the various oversight systems. Alfred B. Prados and Richard A. Best, "Intelligence Oversight in Selected Democracies," CRS Rept. 90-483, Congressional Research Service, Library of Congress, September 21, 1990, although somewhat dated, remains a valuable source on this issue.

35. Intelligence Services Act 1994, sect. 10(3), cited by the House of Commons, Select Committee on Home Affairs, *Third Report: Accountability of the Security Service,* June 14, 1999. Report is available at www.fas.org/irp/world/uk/docs/291/29102.htm.

36. House of Commons, *Third Report.* New Zealand's oversight system also gives the prime minister a great deal of power. The Intelligence and Security Committee Act of 1996 created an intelligence oversight committee with the following membership: the prime minister, the opposition leader, two members of the parliament nominated by the prime minister, and a member of the opposition nominated by the leader of the opposition. Although the committee has the broad mandate "to examine the policy, administration, and expenditure of each intelligence and security agency," its oversight authority is effectively limited by the facts that the prime minister and his appointees make up a majority of the committee and that the prime minister has sole authority to call committee hearings. In addition, the committee is excluded from looking into "any

matter that is operationally sensitive, including any matter that relates to intelligence collection and production methods or sources of information." The law can be found on the World Wide Web at rangi.knowledge-basket.co.nz/gpacts/public/text/1996/se/046sel.html.

37. Parliament of Australia Website, www.aph.gov.au/house/committe/pjcasio/ppgrole.htm.

38. "The right of the people to be secure . . . against unreasonable searches and seizures, shall not be violated, and no warrants shall issue, but upon probable cause." U.S. Constitution, Fourth Amendment.

39. P.L. 95-511 [50 USC 1801-11]. For an overview of the act and its creation, see Americo R. Cinquegrana, "The Walls (and Wires) Have Ears: The Background and First Ten Years of the Foreign Intelligence Surveillance Act of 1978," *University of Pennsylvania Law Review* 137 (January 1989): 793–828, and Elizabeth B. Bazan, "The Foreign Intelligence Surveillance Act: An Overview of the Statutory Framework for Electronic Surveillance," Congressional Research Service, Library of Congress, May 17, 2000.

40. Intelligence Authorization Act for FY 1995 (P.L. 103-359, October 14, 1994), sec. 807. "Physical search" is defined as "any physical intrusion . . . into premises or property . . . that is intended to result in a seizure . . . or alteration of information, material, or property, under circumstances in which a person has a reasonable expectation of privacy and a warrant would be required for law enforcement purposes, but does not include [signals intelligence]."

41. In a thorough survey entitled "The Study of Intelligence in the United States," Kenneth G. Robertson notes: "So far there has been little work on the nature of internal threats and how these can be linked to intelligence requirements for domestic intelligence." In *Comparing Foreign Intelligence: The U.S., the USSR, the UK and the Third World,* ed. Roy Godson (McLean, Va.: Pergamon-Brassey's, 1988), 19. The situation has not changed appreciably since Robertson's survey was published.

42. Of course, not all illegal actions are of interest from the point of view of domestic intelligence; the criminal standard does not indicate what domestic intelligence should do, only what it may not do. In general, domestic intelligence collection related directly to law enforcement is concerned with organized criminal activity—Mafia and other gangsters, large-scale narcotics trafficking, etc.—rather than with sporadic crime.

43. According to that act, electronic surveillance of "U.S. persons" (citizens and permanent resident aliens) is permitted only if there is "probable cause" to believe that the individual knowingly engages, for or on behalf of a foreign power, in sabotage, international terrorism, or other clandestine intelligence activities that involve or are about to involve a violation of criminal law.

44. A sanitized version of these guidelines was released in connection with a Freedom of Information Act request and appears in U.S. Senate, Select Committee on Intelligence, *National Intelligence Reorganization and Reform Act of 1978: Hearings,* 95th Cong., 2d sess., 1978, Committee Print, 774–90.

45. U.S. Senate, Select Committee on Intelligence, *Hearings,* para. II.A., 775 [emphasis supplied].

46. The Foreign Agents Registration Act of 1938, as amended, requires

> public disclosure by persons engaging in propaganda activities and other activities for or on behalf of . . . foreign principals so that the government and people of the

> United States may be informed of the identity of such persons and may appraise their statements and actions in the light of their associations and activities.

The citation is from the act's statement of "Policy and Purpose." The act itself, less this statement, is codified at 22 USC 611-21.

47. On February 7, 1989, Alan Thomson, director of the National Council of American-Soviet Friendship, was arrested in connection with a bank deposit of seventeen thousand dollars in cash. The money was allegedly provided by the Soviet Society for Friendship and Cultural Relations with Foreign Countries, which, according to an FBI report, was directed by the International Department of the Central Committee of the Communist Party of the Soviet Union. While this may have been the first arrest in the United States connected with a Soviet active measures or covert action operation, the actual charge involved the failure to report large cash transactions (as required by anti–money laundering statutes) rather than failure to register as a foreign agent. (Associated Press, February 8, 1989; *Washington Post,* February 8, 1989, A4.) In May 1992, Thomson pleaded guilty to the charge of having failed to declare the money upon entering the United States as required by customs regulations. Dan Herbeck, "Man Fined $1,000 for Not Declaring Cash," *Buffalo News,* July 31, 1992 (local section).

48. U.S. Senate, Select Committee on Intelligence, *The FBI and CISPES: Report,* 101st Cong., 1st sess., 1989, S. Rept. 101-46, 21. A longer investigation of CISPES was subsequently undertaken by the FBI on other grounds.

49. In 1983, the Levi Domestic Security Guidelines were superseded by new "Guidelines on General Crimes, Racketeering Enterprise and Domestic Security/Terrorism Investigations," promulgated by Attorney General William French Smith. The text of both guidelines may be found in Roy Godson, ed., *Intelligence Requirements for the 1980s: Domestic Intelligence* (Lexington, Mass.: Heath, 1986), 225–64. For an overview of the Smith guidelines and the continuity between them and the Levi guidelines, see John T. Elliff, "The Attorney General's Guidelines for FBI Investigations," *Cornell Law Review* 69, no. 4 (April 1984): 785–815.

50. Levi, Domestic Security Guidelines, para. I.A., in *Domestic Intelligence,* ed. Godson, 225.

51. The Levi guidelines do not say precisely this; rather, they state that "all investigations undertaken through these guidelines shall be designed and conducted so as not to limit the full exercise of rights protected by the Constitution and laws of the United States" (para. II.B). This leaves open whether the mere act of investigation is regarded as limiting free speech by chilling it; if so, an investigation based only on the individual's or group's protected speech would violate this provision.

In this connection, one of the more controversial aspects of the Smith guidelines was a provision allowing the FBI to open an investigation based on statements that "advocate criminal activity or indicate an apparent intent to engage in crime." By comparison, the Levi guidelines made no mention of investigations based on advocacy alone. However, as the above quotation makes clear, the type of statement that would be of possible investigative interest is still tied to a criminal standard under the Smith regulations.

52. *Laird v. Tatum,* 408 U.S. 1 at 10 (1972), 13–14.

53. Robertson, "The Study of Intelligence in the United States," 18–21.

54. *Brandenburg v. Ohio,* 395 U.S. 444 at 447 (1969) [emphasis supplied].

55. *Scales v. United States,* 367 U.S. 203 at 220 (1961). The Supreme Court is paraphrasing and (with respect to the material inside the quotation marks) citing the trial judge's instructions to the jury; the Supreme Court later goes on to uphold these instructions (224).

56. John T. Elliff, *The Reform of FBI Intelligence Operations* (Princeton, N.J.: Princeton University Press, 1979), 57.

57. Of course, the group would have to be capable of sufficient self-control to refrain from violence or other major violations of law during the period in which it was trying to penetrate the government. It would appear that the right-wing extremist groups that currently exist in the United States and in other democracies lack such sophistication.

58. Shlomo Gazit and Michael Handel, "Insurgency, Terrorism and Intelligence," in *Domestic Intelligence,* ed. Godson, 134.

59. The precise standard (the "threshold") varies in the different guidelines. Under the Levi domestic security guidelines, the FBI could not use an informer unless it already possessed "specific articulable facts giving reasons to believe that . . . a group is or may be engaged in activities which involve the use of force or violence and which involve or will involve the violation of federal law" (sec. II[I], 227–28). Under the Smith guidelines, an informant may be used in a "preliminary" investigation with the approval of a supervisory agent when circumstances dictate its use and other, less intrusive investigative means are not likely to be successful. A "preliminary inquiry" may be started when the FBI receives an allegation of possible criminal activity that, while "not warranting a full investigation," nevertheless requires more than a limited effort to check out initial leads (sec. II[B](1)(6), 248–51).

60. This, and the two subsequent, citations are from John M. Walker Jr., "Discussion," in *Domestic Intelligence,* ed. Godson, 194–96.

61. Attorney General (Smith) Guidelines on Domestic Security, III.B.1(a), in *Domestic Intelligence,* ed. Godson, 258.

62. David M. Park, "Re-examining the Attorney General's Guidelines for FBI Investigations of Domestic Groups," *Arizona Law Review* (Summer 1997): 774, citing Freeh's testimony before U.S. House of Representatives, International Relations Committee, Crime Subcommittee, *Terrorism Hearings,* 104th Congress, 1st sess., 1995, 12.

63. Smith Guidelines, III.B.1(a), in *Domestic Intelligence,* ed. Godson, 258.

64. Testimony of Laurence H. Silberman, July 18, 1978, in U.S. Senate, Select Committee on Intelligence, *Hearings,* 616.

65. Church Committee, *Final Report,* book 2: *Intelligence Activities and the Rights of Americans,* 94th Cong., 2d sess., 1976, S. Rept. 94-755, 166. With issuance of the Levi guidelines, the number of domestic security investigations dropped significantly. In April 1976, 4,868 investigations were, to one degree or another, under way; by the end of September, there were only 626. In August 1982, there were only thirty-eight domestic security investigations under way. U.S. Senate, Subcommittee on Security and Terrorism, Committee on the Judiciary, *Impact of Attorney General's Guidelines for Domestic Security Investigations (The Levi Guidelines): Hearing,* 98th Cong., 1st sess., 1983, S. Prt. 98-134, 5.

66. Church Committee, *Final Report,* book 2, 225–40, lists cases in which purely political information was collected and disseminated to administration political operatives.

67. Canadian Security Intelligence Act, 1984, sects. 2, 12. Under Canadian law, the functions of collecting and analyzing intelligence on security threats and conducting personnel security assessments are carried out by the Canadian Security Intelligence Service, while the Royal Canadian Mounted Police is responsible for the enforcement of criminal laws related to national security and for providing protective security for government figures and property. The act can be found at www.csis-scrs.gc.ca/end/act/csisact_e.html.

CHAPTER 7: TWO VIEWS OF INTELLIGENCE

1. Sun Tzu, *The Art of War,* trans. Samuel B. Griffith (Oxford: Oxford University Press, 1963), 144–45 (chap. 13, paras. 3–4). "Tzu" is the older but familiar romanization (transliteration into the Latin alphabet) of a Chinese character that would now be rendered "Zi."

2. Sun Tzu, *The Art of War,* 146 (chap. 13, paras. 9–10).

3. Sun Tzu, *The Art of War,* 77–78 (chap. 3, paras. 4–6). This view may be contrasted with that of Carl von Clausewitz, for whom the destruction of the enemy's fighting forces is crucial. Carl von Clausewitz, *On War,* ed. and trans. Michael Howard and Peter Paret (Princeton, N.J.: Princeton University Press, 1976), 90 (book 1, chap. 2). As already noted, Clausewitz has a much more skeptical view about the possibility that intelligence will enable a commander to engage in complicated maneuvers that will yield victory at low cost. He goes so far as to claim that "in short, most intelligence is false" (117, book 1, chap. 7).

4. William E. Colby, "Intelligence in the 1980s," *The Information Society* 1, no. 1 (1981): 53–54.

5. Colby, "Intelligence in the 1980s," 65.

6. On July 11, 1941, President Roosevelt ordered the establishment of "the position of Coordinator of Intelligence, with authority to collect and analyze all information and data, which may bear upon national security; to correlate such information and data, and to make [it] available to the President and to such departments and officials . . . as the President may determine" (Presidential Order, "Designating a Coordinator of Information," para. 1). The order is reprinted in Thomas F. Troy, *Donovan and the CIA: A History of the Establishment of the Central Intelligence Agency* (Frederick, Md.: University Publications of America, 1981), 423.

7. Colby, "Intelligence in the 1980s," 54.

8. See Ray S. Cline, *The CIA: Reality vs. Myth,* rev. ed. (Washington, D.C.: Acropolis, 1982), 78, 80–81, for a discussion of the inability of the research and analysis branch of the OSS to fulfill the analytic function of a central intelligence operation. Cline states that "[no] component of the OSS ever used signals intelligence in its reporting" (78). Thus, it lacked access to the major intelligence sources (Ultra and Magic) available to the U.S. government.

9. Sherman Kent, *Strategic Intelligence for American World Policy* (Princeton, N.J.: Princeton University Press, 1949; reprint with a new preface, 1966), 155. Kent's

ideas about intelligence were authoritative in two respects. As Berkowitz and Goodman point out, "*Strategic Intelligence* was probably the most influential book on intelligence analysis ever written. Not only did it become a standard text for American students of intelligence, it was also widely read abroad, eventually being translated in French, Russian, German, and other languages." In addition, after the intelligence community's failure to predict the invasion of South Korea by the North in 1950, Walter ("Beedle") Smith, the DCI, ordered the creation of "a new unit responsible for comprehensive, forward-looking intelligence assessments. These assessments became known as National Intelligence Estimates (NIEs), and the organization . . . established became the Office of National Estimates (ONE)." Kent was chosen ONE's first deputy director and in 1952 became its head, holding the community's senior analytic post for some sixteen years. "Needless to say," according to Berkowitz and Goodman, "ONE and the process of developing NIEs bore a strong resemblance to the principles for analysis Kent described in *Strategic Intelligence.*" Bruce D. Berkowitz and Allan E. Goodman, *Strategic Intelligence for American National Security* (Princeton, N.J.: Princeton University Press, 1989), 4–5.

10. Kent, *Strategic Intelligence,* 3–4 [emphasis supplied].

11. Colby, "Intelligence in the 1980s," 59. The "Club of Rome" produced a series of studies in the late 1970s that projected demographic, economic, and environmental trends into the twenty-first century. Its predictions have turned out to be unduly pessimistic.

12. According to Alexander Orlov, a defector from the Soviet NKVD (a predecessor organization of the current KGB), analysis, or evaluation, in the Soviet context "concerns itself more with establishing the authenticity of the stolen documents rather than with the significance of the information. The political significance of the information is evaluated principally by the policy-making members of the government and the Party Presidium [Politburo]." Alexander Orlov, *Handbook of Intelligence and Guerrilla Warfare* (Ann Arbor: University of Michigan Press, 1965), 187.

An interesting dispute over the appropriate role of analysis arose in connection with the early warning system (DISTANT) given to Oleg Penkovsky by MI6 (the British foreign intelligence service) and CIA to use in case he had information about an impending Soviet attack on the West. According to a comprehensive account of the Penkovsky case, MI6 "was concerned that a DISTANT early warning signal, unless carefully controlled and evaluated, could lead to misinterpretation and an outbreak of hostilities." The British were adamant that any warning should first be reviewed by the Joint Intelligence Committee, Britain's senior assessment body, before being passed to policy makers. According to the MI6 representative in Washington, "A DISTANT report will not be treated by the U.K. as an indicator unless the JIC accept it as such." In contrast, reflecting perhaps the experience of Pearl Harbor, the CIA view was that the message should be relayed to policy makers at once; the only (albeit critical) analysis involved in this instance would be first to confirm the source. Jerrold L. Schecter and Peter S. Deriabin, *The Spy Who Saved the World* (New York: Scribner, 1992), 284–86.

13. Eliot A. Cohen, "Analysis," in *Intelligence Requirements for the 1990s: Collection, Analysis, Counterintelligence and Covert Action,* ed. Roy Godson (Lexington, Mass.: Heath, Lexington, 1989), 83.

14. Kent, "Preface to the 1966 Edition," *Strategic Intelligence,* xxiv.

15. Kent, "Preface," 58-59 [emphasis in original].

16. In part, this expansion of the intelligence analytic function in the United States was the result of the historical anomaly of having an adversary in the postwar period like the Soviet Union. Information that other countries would publish as a matter of course was regarded by the Soviets as a state secret. As a consequence, all manner of information that might otherwise have been considered routine and outside a traditionalist's view of what should fall within the intelligence community's purview became subjects for intelligence collection and, in turn, analysis. While distinct from Kent's theoretical arguments about the nature of strategic intelligence, the closed nature of the Soviet state reinforced on a practical level the idea that intelligence deals with all policy-relevant information.

17. As noted above, chap. 6, section on "Imperial Intelligence."

18. This particular view of the policy-intelligence analysis nexus, and the foundation on which it rested, was first articulated by Kent and others during their service in the Research and Analysis Branch of the OSS during World War II. According to historian Barry Katz, in the face of entrenched bureaucratic hostility, and

> without the secure patronage of some entrenched constituency, the only protection available to the [newly formed] Branch was the invisible mantle of social science objectivity. . . . Remarkably, a theoretically explicit inquiry into the nature of objectivity, resting on "some basic analysis of the whole process of scientific thought in the social field" was sustained throughout the entire wartime history of the Branch. [According to Kent], the "official" position derived precisely from the fields in which the senior American scholars of R&A were such eminent practitioners, namely, "that area of knowledge usually referred to as social science." Across these disciplines the antinomies of fact and value, scholarship and partisanship with which Max Weber had struggled so heroically had been largely resolved . . . the age of sociologists, economists, and calculators had succeeded. . . . Just as the political credibility of the R&A Branch rested upon its image of disinterested professionalism, the epistemological credibility of the disciplines represented in it was held to rest on a positivist standard of objectivity that could be defined in theory even if only approximated in practice.

Barry M. Katz, *Foreign Intelligence: Research and Analysis in the Office of Strategic Services, 1942–1945* (Cambridge, Mass.: Harvard University Press, 1989), 14–15.

19. In February 1992, the two intelligence committees of the U.S. Congress introduced legislation that would have substantially reorganized the American intelligence community. One of the key proposals in the legislation was to create a centralized analytical unit into which the analytical assets of the intelligence community would be pooled. In addition, the new analysis center, imitating an academic setting, would be fully separated from any operational elements within the community or policy-making departments of the government. According to the chairman of the House Intelligence Committee, Rep. Dave McCurdy, the reorganization was designed to "create in one place, a world-class 'think tank.'" "Intelligence Committee Chairmen Introduce Sweeping Reorganization Plan," Press Release, U.S. Senate Select Committee on Intelligence, February 5, 1992. See also, David L. Boren, "The Intelligence Community: How Crucial," *Foreign Affairs* 71, no. 3 (Summer 1992): 61. Senator Boren was at the time chairman of the Senate Intelligence Committee and sponsor of that committee's version of the reorganization legislation.

20. See, for example, Stansfield Turner's suggestions in his intelligence memoir, *Secrecy and Democracy: The CIA in Transition* (Boston: Houghton Mifflin, 1985; New York: Harper and Row, 1986). After proposing the creation of an Open Skies

Agency that would release satellite reconnaissance information to the world at large, he concludes:

> Our intelligence capabilities are suited to this special role on behalf of our own security and the welfare of all mankind, because we have our own reconciled the necessary secrecy of intelligence to the democratic processes on which our government is founded. . . . [W]e have opened vast new opportunities to demonstrate the superiority of our democratic system through the employment of our intelligence capabilities to serve not only our nation, but the rest of the world and all mankind (285).

21. Colby, "Intelligence in the 1980s," 69.

22. For a statement supporting the primacy of techint in this new era, see chapter 2, note 86, above. Regardless of the question of whether techint or humint will gain pride of place with respect to high-level, strategic intelligence, there is no doubt that, as discussed in chapter 2, above, technical intelligence collection systems—which previously had concentrated on fulfilling the requirements of national-level decision-makers—will play an increasing role in supplying tactical intelligence to commanders on the battlefield.

23. Kent, *Strategic Intelligence,* viii [emphasis supplied].

24 On this and related points, see Thomas F. Troy, "The 'Correct' Definition of Intelligence," *International Journal of Intelligence and Counterintelligence* 5, no. 4 (Winter 1991–92): 433–54.

25. Turner, *Secrecy and Democracy,* 279–85. Turner does not state clearly how far he would go in making U.S. technical collection capabilities, or the information obtained by means of them, available to the entire world. While he notes that we *"might"* (emphasis supplied) begin by providing only "intelligence collected by systems so old that they were no longer a mystery to" an adversary (282), he also believes that "it will not be long before we reach a point where all satellite photography will be so good that the differences between vario s models of satellites will be insignificant" (280).

26. This and the subsequent citation are from Colby, "Intelligence in the 1980s," 69.

27. Of course, committing treason against a tyrannical or aggressive regime is defensible in moral terms. In the case of a Ryszard Kuklinski, the Polish army officer who spied for the United States against the Soviet oppressors of his homeland, the motivation was of this kind of ideological character, and Western intelligence officers did not have to manipulate or suborn him in any manner. In other cases, however, where the motivation is money or excitement, the intelligence officer often must play on these weaknesses to help the potential spy succumb more fully to them. For a fuller discussion of these issues, see E. Drexel Godfrey Jr., "Ethics and Intelligence," *Foreign Affairs* 56, no. 3 (April 1978): 624–42, and response to it by Arthur L. Jacobs in "Comments and Correspondence," *Foreign Affairs* 56, no. 4 (July 1978): 867–75.

28. Sun Tzu, *The Art of War,* 63–64 (chap. 1, paras. 2–4).

29. Sun Tzu, *The Art of War,* 144 (chap. 13, para. 2).

30. Henry L. Stimson and McGeorge Bundy, *On Active Service in Peace and War* (New York: Harper, 1948), 188. Stimson probably did not make this famous and oft-quoted remark at the time; he expressed the thought later on, in the course of defending his decision both as appropriate to 1929, when "the world was striving with good will for lasting peace, and in this effort all the nations were parties," and as not inconsistent with his later support (as secretary of war) for cryptanalytic efforts. However, it is

unlikely that the World War II successes could have been achieved without the prewar efforts to build on. For example, the successful U.S. attack on the Japanese Purple enciphering machine, first used in 1939, depended critically on the fact that the previous Red machine, dating from 1931, had already been mastered. See Ronald Lewin, *American Magic: Codes, Ciphers and the Defeat of Japan* (New York: Farrar Strauss Giroux, 1982), 42–43. For an overview of intelligence in the interwar period, see Robert G. Angevine, "Gentleman Do Read Each Other's Mail: American Intelligence in the Interwar Era," *Intelligence and National Security* 7, no. 2 (April 1992): 1–29.

31. Consider, for example, David Kahn's discussion of this issue: "Immanuel Kant, in his book, *Perpetual Peace,* stated that spying is a kind of crime against the international order because if discovered, it causes international difficulties. But this doesn't seem to happen with SIGINT." *Intelligence Requirements for the 1980s: Clandestine Collection,* ed. Roy Godson (Washington, D.C.: National Strategy Information Center, 1982), 120.

In fact, however, the revelation in 1931 by Herbert Yardley, the head of the Black Chamber, that the United States had read the encrypted messages between Tokyo and its delegation to the Washington Naval Arms Limitation talks (1921–22) caused quite a sensation in Japan. *The American Black Chamber* (Indianapolis: Bobbs-Merrill, 1931; reprint, New York: Ballantine, 1981), 187–211.

Similarly, E. Drexel Godfrey Jr., a former CIA officer, argues that "photographic and audio satellites and other interception devices are immensely expensive, but they have the advantage of doing only minimal damage to the ethical standards of the operators and processors." "Ethics and Intelligence," 637.

CHAPTER 8: TOWARD A THEORY OF INTELLIGENCE

1. As noted in chapter 1, this threefold description of intelligence as knowledge, activity, and organization is taken from Sherman Kent, *Strategic Intelligence for American World Policy* (Princeton, N.J.: Princeton University Press, 1949; reprint 1966). Kent, however, does not regard the denial of information to others as a major component of intelligence.

2. Kent, *Strategic Intelligence,* 3–4.

3. If during time of war it is necessary to use clandestine or technical means (such as agents' reports or communications intercepts) to learn about weather conditions over enemy territory, the term "meteorological intelligence" might be used to describe the resulting information. However, the "intelligence" part of the term clearly refers to the methods by which the raw data are obtained, not the meteorological knowledge that allows it to be evaluated or that permits forecasts to be made on the basis of it.

4. As Willmoore Kendall wrote in 1949, in an important review of Kent's book: "The course of events is conceived [by the 'state of mind' reflected in Kent's book] not as something you try to influence but as a tape all printed up inside a machine; and the job of intelligence is to tell the planners how it reads." "The Function of Intelligence," *World Politics* 1, no. 6 (July 1949): 549.

5. Kent, *Strategic Intelligence,* viii [emphasis supplied].

6. William E. Colby, "Intelligence for the 1980s," *The Information Society* 1, no. 1 (1981): 59.

7. For this formulation of the relationship between intelligence and open-source information, I am indebted to Michael Herman of Nuffield College, Oxford, who proposed it at a panel of the 1989 Convention of the International Studies Association.

In addition, open-source information might be collected by an intelligence agency in anticipation that the information will at some point become secret. For example, during wartime, data (such as information pertaining to a country's transportation systems or its reserve stocks of strategic materials) that during peacetime are openly available will be protected by a government as a state secret. In this instance, the collection of open-source information is an effort to avoid the potential security barriers that might obstruct access to the information at some time in the future.

8. Avi Shlaim, "Failures in National Intelligence Estimates: The Case of the Yom Kippur War," *World Politics* 28, no. 3 (April 1976): 355.

9. Intelligence analysts sometimes distinguish between "secrets" and "mysteries." Secrets are bits of information that exist somewhere but to which one does not have direct access; therefore, one must use intelligence methods of some sort to find them out. An example would be the thickness of the armor of the adversary's new tank; the adversary obviously knows the information, but he takes steps to keep others from discovering it. Mysteries, on the other hand, are things that nobody can know for certain. For example, will the adversary use those tanks to attack its neighbor in the next ten years? Even if the adversary has decided to attack three years hence, he cannot know that he will not change his mind sometime between now and then. Kent implies that the type of strategic intelligence he advocates will be able to unravel mysteries or, at least, will be clearly better at doing so than any other process.

10. Kent, *Strategic Intelligence,* 206–207.

11. According to Kent, this is known as "spot intelligence," or less respectfully, "Information Please" (Kent, *Strategic Intelligence,* 28–29). An intelligence service like the CIA thus serves as a reference service, similar to the function performed for the U.S. Congress by the Congressional Research Service of the Library of Congress.

12. William E. Colby, *Honorable Men: My Life in the CIA* (New York: Simon and Schuster, 1978), 245.

13. Ray S. Cline, *The CIA: Reality vs. Myth,* rev. ed. (Washington, D.C.: Acropolis, 1982), 175.

Index